D1074948

50 Moments That Defined Major League Baseball

50 Moments That Defined Major League Baseball

Rocco Constantino

ROWMAN & LITTLEFIELD
Lanham • Boulder • New York • London

Published by Rowman & Littlefield
A wholly owned subsidiary of The Rowman & Littlefield Publishing Group, Inc.
4501 Forbes Boulevard, Suite 200, Lanham, Maryland 20706
www.rowman.com

Unit A, Whitacre Mews, 26-34 Stannary Street, London SE11 4AB

British Library Cataloguing in Publication Information Available

Library of Congress Cataloging-in-Publication Data

Names: Constantino, Rocco, 1974– author.
Title: 50 moments that defined major league baseball / Rocco Constantino.
Other titles: Fifty moments that defined major league baseball
Description: Lanham : ROWMAN & LITTLEFIELD, [2016] | Includes bibliographical
references and index.
Identifiers: LCCN 2015043571 (print) | LCCN 2015046206 (ebook) | ISBN
9781442260542 (hardcover : alk. paper) | ISBN 9781442260559 (electronic)
Subjects: LCSH: Baseball—United States—History. | Major League Baseball
(Organization)—History.
Classification: LCC GV863.A1 C598 2016 (print) | LCC GV863.A1 (ebook) | DDC
796.357/64—dc23
LC record available at http://lccn.loc.gov/2015043571

∞™ The paper used in this publication meets the minimum requirements of
American National Standard for Information Sciences—Permanence of Paper
for Printed Library Materials, ANSI/NISO Z39.48-1992.

Printed in the United States of America

Contents

Acknowledgments

This book would not be possible without the people who introduced me to baseball and who passed on an appreciation for the game's history. My earliest memories of the sport date back to 1981, when I was seven years old. I was introduced to the sport through Yankees games on New York's Channel 11, Phil Rizzuto's commentary, and Mets games on Channel 9 with *Kiner's Korner*. More importantly, however, my father Rocco and his twin brother Canio provided their own commentary as they ran their family video business while watching the games on a nightly basis. Their input was equally entertaining, provided stories about the game's history, and contained significantly more cursing than the Yankees telecasts. Through the years, other people, like Ken Constantino, Ray Monahan, Jimmy Miele, Pat Barbone, Dan Constantino, Pop Roberto, Brian Sheridan, Paul Marcantuono, and Irene Constantino, have enhanced that love of the sport by being great baseball fans, always ready for a conversation about the game's history.

In addition, I would like to thank Curtis Russell, P.S. Literary Agency, and Rowman & Littlefield for believing in this book and shaping the final project into a fantastic representation of baseball history. A great baseball fan himself, Curtis and his staff are the reason these stories are able to be shared with the fans who read this book. Thank you as well to Keith Allison and Arturo Pardavila, who took the brilliant action color photos and were generous enough to share them. The historic black-and-white photos were taken by famed Boston photographer Leslie Jones and provided by the Boston Public Library. Thank you to the Boston Public Library, Bob Cullum, and the Jones family for sharing these amazing photos with baseball fans worldwide.

This book would also not be possible without the incredible accomplishments and personal insight of former major leaguers. These athletes generously took the time to provide their own personal insight on life in the majors, giving vivid accounts of their own accomplishments, teammates, mentors, and places in the history of Major League Baseball. Thank you to the following players who shared their own personal reflections as major leaguers:

Rod Carew	Jason Bergmann
Fred Lynn	Aaron Small
Jim Wohlford	Paul Bako
Rod Gaspar	Jeff Ballard
Don August	Brendan Harris
Tim Leary	Juan Padilla
Brian Holman	Don Slaught
Gregg Zaun	Barry Bonnell
Eric Valent	Scott Pose
Jeff Montgomery	Matt Walbeck
Kelly Paris	Barry Foote
Mark Dewey	Fred Valentine
Shawn Estes	Stanley Jefferson
Dave Borkowski	Matt Galante
Don DeMola	Adam Melhuse
Ted Power	Matt LaPorta
John Stuper	Ron Oester
Benny Ayala	Tim Crabtree
Dave Schuler	Kevin Mench
Lary Sorensen	Mark Grant
Jack Perconte	Andy McGaffigan
Rudy May	Ted Barrett

Foreword

MLB All-Star Jeff Montgomery

Almost every great baseball fan can tell vivid stories from their younger years as they grew up watching and listening to their favorite team. For some, their dream of growing up to play for their favorite team eventually becomes reality. I consider myself one of the fortunate ones, as I had the unique opportunity to have that dream come true.

As a kid growing up in southern Ohio during the era of the Big Red Machine, it was easy to fall in love with the Cincinnati Reds and every player on the team. Even though there were not many televised games back then, it was easy to listen to every game on the radio. The voices of Marty Brennaman and Joe Nuxhall were heard more frequently on my family's radios than anything else as they called Reds games throughout the baseball season. Although it has been roughly 40 years since listening to those games during the era of the Machine, I can still name almost every player on those teams and remember numerous heroic game-winning home runs or diving catches that helped the Reds win championships. I can also remember their uniform numbers and where they normally played, as well as where they hit in the batting order.

In grade school I always told people that I was going to grow up and play for the Cincinnati Reds. After being drafted in the ninth round of the 1983 draft by the Reds out of Marshall University and playing five seasons in the Reds farm system, I eventually made my major-league debut in Riverfront Stadium in August 1987. As a kid, our family would take summer vacation trips to Cincinnati for weekend games at Riverfront, so it had very special meaning to me. Not only was I making my debut in the uniform of my favorite team, in the only stadium in which I had ever witnessed a major-league game, but my manager was also Pete Rose, who was my all-time favorite player as a kid. For all these reasons I still consider my first day in the major leagues my favorite memory.

As you read through the various chapters of *50 Moments That Defined Major League Baseball*, you will be reminded of some of the greatest moments in the history of the great game of baseball. Some of the quotes and stories from former players like me will shed some new light on the game as well. It doesn't matter if you grew up a Yankees fan or an Expos fan, partial to the American League or the National League, hearing stories that you likely have never heard will almost make you feel like you were in the clubhouse with the players as they are telling the stories. And even though the game is about wins and losses, batting averages, and ERAs, as a former player I still think back, and some of the greatest memories were not always between the white lines, they were the stories being told on the team bus, in the bullpen, in the clubhouse, or really anywhere a group of players would be hanging out together.

I was very happy to have the chance to contribute to this book. When Rocco asked me about the possibility of writing the foreword I was even more honored to have a chance to add more to a book that will provide great enjoyment to all those who read it and provide unique insight that is not always provided just by watching the game.

Introduction

On September 23, 1845, Alexander Cartwright recorded the "Rules and Regulations of the Knickerbocker Base Ball Club." By documenting and ratifying these 20 rules, most of which still have direct descendants in today's baseball rule book, Cartwright set forth a sport that has captured the imagination of generations, bridged socioeconomic groups, survived world wars, and created tradition in families throughout the world.

When Cartwright penned what is now known as the "Knickerbocker Rules," there were only 27 states in the United States, Abraham Lincoln was 16 years away from starting his presidency, and Babe Ruth wouldn't be born for 50 years. America was 79 years old when the rules were written. Phil Rizzuto was the same age when he called Derek Jeter's first career home run in 1996.

In the 170 years since the Knickerbocker Rules were ratified, the game has been in a perpetual state of transformation. Teams originally had to score 21 runs to win a game; foul balls were not strikes; and on the rare occasion that a ball was hit over the outfield fence, it was deemed a foul ball instead of a home run. For the first 20 years after the rules were approved, if a ball was caught on one bounce it was still considered an out. Cap Anson, who is seventh in major-league history with 3,435 hits, had 1,290 of those hits before pitchers were allowed to throw overhand.

So, how did the game transcend from Al Spalding lobbing pitches to Anson to Matt Harvey, Jacob deGrom, and Noah Syndergaard carrying the Mets to an improbable World Series run in 2015 on the strength of high-90s fastballs? The answer is too complex to cover in general terms and there are too many people who've shaped the game throughout time, but there are some who stand out from the others. Players like Babe Ruth, Ty Cobb, Jackie Robinson, Hank Aaron, and Willie Mays surely have their places cemented

1

among the game's trailblazers, but what about players like Candy Cummings, Pete Reiser, Smoky Joe Wood, and Pumpsie Green? They are pioneers in their own right, even if their on-field accomplishments pale in comparison to those of Ruth, Aaron, and Mays.

The fairest way to track the game's progression is by acknowledging that every player who has suited up in the bigs has had some impact on the sport. One example is the color barrier that existed in baseball during the first 70 years of professional status: When the American Association and National League settled a racial dispute between Anson and Moses Fleetwood Walker—a black catcher for the Toledo Blue Stockings—by siding with Anson, the color lines that segregated the sport until 1947 were drawn.

Years before the American civil rights movement took place, Robinson took the field for the Brooklyn Dodgers on April 15, 1947, as the first black player since Walker. It was clearly a game-changing event in the grand scope of baseball, but the game continued to change racially as more black pioneers helped establish integration as the norm. Larry Doby faced many of the same obstacles when he debuted as the first black player in the American League three months later. It took 12 years before every team integrated, with players like Monte Irvin, Ernie Banks, and Elston Howard bridging the gap to 1959, when the Red Sox became the last team to integrate with Pumpsie Green.

Integration was a major movement that helped shape what today's game looks like, and those are the stories at the heart of this book. This book takes a look at 50 players, games, personalities, and achievements that shaped the history of Major League Baseball. From historic moments like Hank Aaron's 715th home run to Smoky Joe Wood's fateful thumb injury in 1913, this is not a typical "Top 50 Moments" project. This is not a comprehensive list of mammoth home runs and historic feats on the mound. Instead, this is a look at players who shaped the game through fine performances, impactful milestones, and overcoming tremendous odds to play the game they love.

Additionally, *50 Moments That Defined Major League Baseball* uses input from former major-league players from the past seven decades to elaborate on these accomplishments and describe what it's like to fight through the minors and play in the major leagues.

"I was under the illusion [growing up] that I was an elite talent. Turns out I wasn't," said Gregg Zaun, a veteran of 16 major-league seasons from 1995 to 2010. "I had an elite passion and work ethic, but that was due to my love of the game. I wouldn't let anyone stop me or tell me I couldn't do it. I loved to practice because I wanted to be great and was never satisfied."

When you read about that kind of passion, desire, and the hard work it takes to get to the highest level of sport, the game sounds so intense, but the game can be looked at through a different lens as well.

"I always said that every day is a Saturday in the major leagues," said Andy McGaffigan, who pitched in 363 games in 11 seasons. "Think about it. As a kid, you didn't have school, you don't have work, maybe you had a couple of chores, but Saturday is just a day to play. That's what the majors was like."

Mark Grant, the popular and eccentric Padres announcer, is expectedly enthusiastic when discussing the sport's history.

Grant said, "What's great about baseball is that when you ask any fan, 'What's the greatest era of baseball?' a majority of fans will say the time period from when they were eight to 18 years old. Mine was 1970–1980. That's why it's such a great game. It grabs us and molds us into the fans we are today. That's why every era is great!"

The final aspect of this book examines the sacred nature of the game's history and how players influence and mentor one another. As the game was being shaped throughout the past 150 years, players have leaned on one another to learn the nuances of being professional. Players often speak of the camaraderie and brotherhood that the sport encourages. They influence one another more than the common fan realizes, and this support allows them to excel.

Jeff Montgomery, a member of the Royals Hall of Fame, recognized the importance and responsibility of perpetuating the game throughout the generations. "When I came up [with the Reds in 1987], Buddy Bell and Terry Francona were veteran players who helped the young guys out a lot," said Montgomery. "I learned a lot of things from veterans. They pass the game down to you, and then when I became a veteran, I felt like I had a responsibility to pass what I learned down to younger players too. I have heard a lot of younger players credit me with helping them out, and that's great to hear."

Sometimes mentoring can go even further than just passing the game along. Shawn Estes, an All-Star pitcher for the Giants, points to the impact of two people who turned his baseball career around while he was in the minor leagues and two more who helped him once he reached the majors: "I was drafted in the first round out of high school and sent right to the minors. I was totally overmatched and not ready for the minors at all at 18 years old though," said Estes. "I spun my wheels for three years and just wasn't polished at all. I went to the Instructional League in 1994, and worked with pitching coach Ron Romanick and sports psychologist Gary Mack. Their help turned my whole career around."

With their assistance, Estes felt stronger psychologically and was ready to get his career going again. The only problem was that the Major League Baseball players' strike prevented anyone from playing ball at the time. Once the sport picked back up in 1995, Estes found himself in low A ball and about to skyrocket through the Giants' system. By the end of the minor-league season, he was a key pitcher on the Texas League champion Shreveport Captains in AA. When the season ended, Estes was content with his progression and was excited to continue that progress the next season; however, his season would continue unexpectedly from there.

"The night before I was going to leave for the winter, I got a call that I was going up to the majors," said Estes, who was 22 at the time.

> I was chomping at the bit [at the start of the season] to get out to the mound. I worked my way up from low A to the Texas League championship then to the majors in one season. Dusty Baker and Dick Pole, my pitching coach, were great influences when I first got to the majors. I might not have been quite ready for the majors when I first got there, but having those two in my corner really helped a lot.

Estes went on to win 101 games in the majors in 13 seasons and was an All-Star at the age of 24, when he went 19–5 in 1997. That type of veteran guidance paid off, as a young player who was mentored in the early part of the season could, in turn, help those veterans earn the title they've been working for.

John Stuper was a 25-year-old rookie when he was called up by the Cardinals in the midst of their 1982 championship season: "To be honest, I was happy just to be in the big leagues," started Stuper. "As the season wore on, I was even happier to be a contributing member of the starting rotation. I learned so much from guys like Jim Kaat, Bruce Sutter, Bob Forsch, Doug Bair, Gene Tenace, and others. They taught me how to be a big leaguer." Veteran leadership was incredibly helpful, as Stuper was asked to pitch Game 6 of the 1982 World Series as a rookie, down three games to two, against future Hall of Famer Don Sutton and a powerful Brewers lineup. Stuper responded with a complete game four-hitter in a 13–1 win. The Cardinals went on to win Game 7 and the World Series. This was the only World Series title Kaat won in his 25-year career and the only championship Hall of Famer Sutter won.

Whether a player has a legendary career or just plays a handful of games in the majors, they all have a story to tell. It's those stories that help bridge six months of summer every year. It's those stories, shared among the people who live them and the fans who enjoy them, that bring the game to life. Baseball is a developing drama, told during seven months every year and 170 years of the sport's existence, and it allows these stories the time to flourish and become part of American culture.

"Baseball is the one sport in which every other sport uses its vernacular," said Grant. "That's why it's America's favorite pastime. You can't go through a day in life without dropping a baseball term."

The game has been shaped by owners, commissioners, and managers. It's been shaped by presidents, world events, and social movements; however, it is the players on the field who most effectively shape the game through their abilities and accomplishments. The following 50 stories celebrate the players who took us from Cap Anson to Bryce Harper, through world wars, the Great Depression, global expansion, and everything in between.

・ *1* ・

Noteworthy Debuts, Pioneers, and Baseball Firsts

HANK AARON: NUMBER 1 OF 755

April 23, 1954

The exploits of Hank Aaron and his remarkable career are well known. The lasting image of Aaron is of the 40-year-old circling the bases after hitting his 715th home run, running into a swarm of teammates and family at home plate.

He had come a long way since his first home run on April 23, 1954.

It had been seven years since Jackie Robinson had broken the color barrier, and only nine teams had integrated by the time Aaron reached the majors. When he made his debut on April 13, 1954, Aaron was the first black ballplayer to play for the Milwaukee Braves. At that time, the only National League teams that were integrated were the Dodgers, Giants, and Cubs.

In 1952, Aaron was a 17-year-old high school student from Mobile, Alabama, who cared more for playing semipro baseball with the Mobile Black Bears than he did his schoolwork. His path to the majors came when the Black Bears scrimmaged against the Indianapolis Clowns of the Negro Leagues. The Clowns were one of the staple franchises of the Negro Leagues and were so impressed by Aaron that they offered him a spot on their team. Aaron quit school to make $200 a month playing ball.

Aaron played a year as a shortstop in the Negro American League and led the league with a .467 batting average. Amazingly, he grew up hitting cross-handed because, as he said, he hit so well that nobody ever corrected him. Scouting the Negro Leagues became more of a common practice in the early '50s, and Aaron was noticed quickly. Multiple teams inquired about his services, with the Milwaukee Braves finally purchasing his contract for $10,000, just outbidding the New York Giants. Aaron later said that the only thing that

7

kept the Giants from getting him and Willie Mays in the same outfield was that the Braves offered him $50 more per month.

After a quick trip to the minors, where he played for Eau Claire and Jacksonville, Aaron was impressive in spring training of 1954, but not on track to make the big-league ball club; however, an injury to Bobby Thomson left the Braves short an outfielder. Aaron changed position to outfield and was in the starting lineup on Opening Day.

Aaron started the season as the Braves' left fielder and batted fifth behind Eddie Mathews and Andy Pafko. Through the first six games of the season, Aaron was still trying to find his footing as a 20-year-old big leaguer. On the morning of April 23, he was hitting just .217 with no homers, but three of his five hits had gone for doubles. He was also making good contact, as he struck out just once in his first 23 at-bats.

The Braves went to St. Louis to start a three-game weekend series at Busch Stadium against the Cardinals. Both teams were considered middle-of-the-road teams, slightly behind the Giants and Dodgers in the National League in 1954. The Cardinals' starter that night was Vic Raschi, whom the Cardinals had purchased from the Yankees in the offseason for $85,000. Raschi had been a four-time All-Star for the Yankees between 1948 and 1952, but his 10-year career was now winding down. He was making his third start of the season for the Cardinals. Hall of Fame umpire Al Barlick was behind the plate for the game. The Braves were 3–3 on the young season, having just defeated the Cubs.

Aaron found himself as sixth batter that night, as Joe Adcock had been moved to cleanup. His first at-bat came in the first inning, as Raschi got himself into early trouble. Danny O'Connell, Mathews, and Pafko singled to load the bases with two outs. Aaron stepped up to the plate and singled to drive in O'Connell for a 1–0 lead.

With the Cardinals leading 4–1 behind RBIs from Stan Musial and Ray Jablonski, Aaron grounded out in his second at-bat in the fourth inning. Johnny Logan homered after the Aaron groundout, and the score would stay 4–2 until Aaron came up again in the sixth.

It was then, the third at-bat of the game and the 26th of his career, that Hank Aaron would homer for the first time. The blast made the score 4–3, but the game was far from over.

With two outs in the ninth, Jack Dittmer drove home pinch-runner Sibby Sisti to tie the game at four. Charlie White hit a solo homer in the 13th to give the Braves a 5–4 lead, but Hall of Famer Red Schoendienst tied the game in the bottom of the inning with a sacrifice fly, scoring Wally Moon.

Aaron came to bat in the 14th inning for the seventh time in the game with the score still tied at five. With Pafko on first, Aaron singled to continue what would ultimately be the game-winning rally. Both Pafko and Aaron scored on a hit by pinch-hitter Jim Pendleton to give the Braves the 7–5 win.

Aaron hit just one more homer in the month of April (off All-Star Stu Miller on April 25) and ended his rookie campaign with 13 round-trippers. He went on to finish fourth in the Rookie of the Year voting in 1954, behind winner Wally Moon, former Negro League star and Hall of Famer Ernie Banks, and teammate Gene Conley.

Aaron's power came soon after, as he hit 27 and 26 home runs in 1955 and 1956, respectively; however, his first real outburst came in 1957, when he hit a league-leading 44 home runs in his only MVP season. By that point, Aaron was on his way to the remarkable numbers that would become part of baseball lore: 3,771 hits, 2,297 RBIs, and 755 home runs.

KEN GRIFFEY JR.: THE KID DEBUTS

April 3, 1989

Opening Day is beloved by fans and players for many reasons. The baseball world is filled with optimism as a new calendar begins. Opening Day is also a big day for young players. Some who were role players or September call-ups in previous years are anxious to prove themselves in new starting roles, and true rookies are eager to make an impression. In the Mariners' opener against the A's on April 3, 1989, one much-heralded rookie not only showed he belonged, but also gave a glimpse of what most consider one of the greatest pure talents to ever play the game.

In 1977, the Seattle Mariners and Toronto Blue Jays joined the American League in another expansion move by Major League Baseball. In 1969, the Expos, Royals, Padres, and Seattle Pilots had been added, as baseball's popularity was growing around the country. Those franchises had moderate to excellent success throughout the next 20 years, except the Mariners. To put it bluntly, the Mariners were consistently awful.

They rarely had young talent and didn't have the financial bearings to attract top free agents. In their first 20 years of existence, the best season the Mariners could muster was a 78–84 record in 1987; however, on April 3, 1989, there was reason for optimism. The Mariners finally showed the ability to develop young players. Alvin Davis and Mark Langston finished first and second, respectively, in the 1984 Rookie of the Year balloting and went on to good careers, and Harold Reynolds and Jim Presley were solid everyday players.

The Mariners also had high hopes as they started four rookies on Opening Day 1989. Omar Vizquel and Edgar Martinez started on the left side of the infield, and highly touted Greg Briley started in left. They had such young stars in the rotation as Brian Holman, Erik Hanson, and Randy Johnson, all 25 or younger.

However, the real reason for optimism was the 19-year-old who started in center field that day: Ken Griffey Jr.

Griffey was clearly the top pick in the 1987 MLB Draft and put up great numbers in his two-year minor-league stint. Griffey batted .318 with 27 homers and 49 steals in just 140 games, while displaying eye-popping athleticism in center field in the minors. The son of popular veteran Ken Griffey Sr. was destined to be a star, and everyone knew it.

Barry Foote, who played with Griffey Sr. as a member of the Yankees, knew Griffey Jr. as a kid and as a big leaguer: "When he was a little kid, he was always around the team," said Foote. "We played under the stands, and he used to hit little plastic balls in the cages. He was just a great player. God gifted him and he took advantage of it."

Stanley Jefferson, an outfielder who played against Griffey throughout his career, recalled seeing Griffey as a rookie during spring training:

> They told us he was a teenager. Well he was the biggest damn teenager I'd ever seen! He was just knocking the ball a zillion miles in batting practice and then went out to the outfield and throwing cannons in from center field. We were all like, "He's 19? I wanna see a birth certificate!"

Holman, who would come over later in the 1989 season with Randy Johnson in exchange for Langston, knew Griffey would be special right from the start: "I saw him do things on the field that you'd never seen before. It was just special to see such pure God-given ability in a 19-year-old."

While rookie manager Jim Lefebvre protected Briley, Martinez, and Vizquel by batting them at the bottom of the order that Opening Day, he saw that Griffey was too valuable to hide. He placed the 19-year-old in the second spot as the starting center fielder, and he became the youngest rookie to play in a game since Dwight Gooden for the Mets in 1984.

The Mariners had the unenviable task of facing Dave Stewart, possibly the most feared pitcher in baseball at the time, and the powerful Oakland A's. The Mariners countered with Langston, their All-Star lefty, who'd accumulated 70 wins in his five-year career.

While the Mariners featured four rookies in their lineup, the A's trotted out some of the biggest names of the '80s on Opening Day. Mark McGwire was in his third full season in the big leagues but had already established his reputation as a feared power hitter. Veterans Carney Lansford and Dave Parker anchored the rest of the lineup, which also featured talented youngsters like

Terry Steinbach and Tony Phillips. José Canseco was usually right in the middle of them all, but he missed much of the '89 season with a broken wrist.

The Monday night game began with Stewart on the mound in the first, and he retired Reynolds to start the game on a fly ball to center. Griffey then came up to the plate for his first major-league at-bat. He took the first pitch for a strike as Stewart looked to get ahead. Griffey had a classic lefty swing and loved the ball low, and Stewart's forkball played right into Griffey's strength. He got the forkball on the second pitch and drilled it to the center-field wall for a double.

As Griffey stood on second with his trademark smile, his manager looked on in awe. It took just that one at-bat for him to recognize that Griffey belonged and would be the key to leading the Mariners out of their doldrums. Davis followed with a fly ball to right, and in a veteran move, Griffey got a good read on the ball and tagged up to third. He was stranded, however, as Stewart got Darnell Coles on a groundout.

Griffey took his next at-bat leading off the fourth with the Mariners down 3–0. He caused some anxious moments for A's fans as he flew out to the warning track in left field for the first out, as it was clear Stewart was now in a groove; however, the Mariners would finally get to Stewart in the fifth, when Martinez singled right to drive home Jeff Leonard to make it 3–1.

After Langston retired the top of the A's lineup in order in the bottom of the fourth, the Mariners inched closer in the bottom half of the inning. Reynolds led off with a strikeout before Griffey came up for his third at-bat. He coolly worked out a walk to get things started for Seattle. Davis then reached on an error, and Coles followed by grounding a single to left, driving home the speedy Griffey to make the score 3–2, knocking Stewart from the game.

Griffey's next at-bat came against A's reliever Rick Honeycutt, with the Mariners still down 3–2. Griffey fell behind 0–2 on Honeycutt but again played the part of a veteran. Griffey fouled off pitch after pitch before launching the ninth pitch to deep center field. A's center fielder Dave Henderson ran the ball down in the deepest part of the park for an out, but the at-bat left an impression on everyone nevertheless.

In the ninth, the A's called on Hall of Fame closer Dennis Eckersley to finish the win, which he accomplished by retiring the side in order to seal a 3–2 victory. The A's were off to a fast start in a season in which they would lead the majors with 99 wins. They captured the World Series title in a Bay Area showdown against the Giants that was marred by the devastating Loma Prieta earthquake.

Even though the A's won the game, everyone was talking about the kid in center field for the Mariners. Lefebvre kept it simple, but his words were prophetic. In a *Seattle Times* article by Blaine Newnham, Lefebvre said, "The kid has God-given talent that comes, I guess, from being around the game . . . Ken Griffey knows what to do."

Vizquel, who along with Griffey would go on to play in four decades, had a tough time, going 0-for-3 with an error on his first chance of the year. Martinez fared better, going 1-for-3 with an RBI. The Mariners wouldn't have the success they wanted in 1989, however, as the team went through growing pains associated with having such a young team. "We'd go out and beat the A's and Yankees, but then lose to some of the bottom teams. It was all part of our youth, but what a great time it was. I have nothing but great memories," said Holman, who says that a large number of his teammates still remain close friends.

The Mariners finished 73–89 in 1989 but had their share of highlights. Griffey got off to a hot start, as he batted .325 in his first month in the bigs, while belting three home runs. He batted .274 for the year and finished third in the AL Rookie of the Year voting, behind pitchers Gregg Olson and Tom Gordon.

In the offseason, the team was sold to a group led by Jeff Smulyan, founder and CEO of Emmis Broadcasting. This again injected more life into the up-and-coming franchise. Holman recounted their Opening Day win in 1990, a game in which he started and outpitched future Hall of Famer Bert Blyleven. "After the game we gave Mr. Smulyan the game ball for his first win as a major-league owner. He just had the biggest smile and looked like a little kid. He loved it; they were special times," recalled Holman.

The Mariners would finally put together their first winning season in 1991, as the seeds sown during the '89 season began to flourish. In addition to the four rookies who started on Opening Day in 1989, young stars Jay Buhner, Randy Johnson, and Erik Hanson got their starts and would eventually form the backbone of the team as it began a successful run in the late '90s. Unfortunately, Holman, who won 32 games in three seasons and came within one out of pitching a perfect game against the A's in 1990, underwent three separate arm surgeries and didn't pitch in the majors after the 1990 season.

Holman's injury aside, it was clear Seattle was the place to be on the baseball landscape in the early 1990s: "I was traded from the Yankees to the Mariners in 1992, and I couldn't have been more excited," said Tim Leary, a World Series champion with the Dodgers who pitched 13 years in the bigs. "I was part of that great young staff in '93, when Randy Johnson broke out for his first big year. It was exciting to watch."

While the Mariners had their ups and downs in subsequent years, they were no longer looked at as the doormats of the American League, and Griffey's career speaks for itself. He played 22 years in the majors, and despite fighting through injuries in nearly a third of his seasons, he clubbed 630 home runs, including 56 each year in '97 and '98. He was a 13-time All-Star and 10-time Gold Glove winner. Like most people, his manager had him pegged as a superstar from the start: "We saw the debut of a great talent tonight," said Lefebvre in the *Times* article. "That's a great talent."

Veteran major-league umpire Ted Barrett respected Griffey tremendously as a player and a person.

"I can't say enough good things about Ken," started Barrett. "He had an incredibly sweet swing, and anything in the air you just knew he was going to track down. He just had so much fun on the field as well."

Barrett continued,

I remember one time the Mariners asked to check Albert Belle's bat for cork, so we had to remove it from the game. Belle was furious, as were the Indians. In return, the Indians asked us to check A-Rod's bat. It turned out that A-Rod was using one of Griffey's bats at the time, and he was in the on-deck circle. A-Rod was young, and he just had this stunned look on his face. Meanwhile, Griffey was in the on-deck circle laughing and joking. He got the biggest kick out of the whole thing.

Foote puts Griffey among the best to ever play the sport, despite his injuries: "If he didn't have all of those injuries, I believe you could have placed him among the top five players or so of all time," said Foote. "Even with his injuries, I'd still put him somewhere in the top 20."

DEREK JETER AND JOE TORRE: THE START OF A NEW DYNASTY

April 2, 1996

The tradition and history surrounding the New York Yankees franchise is undeniable. Their success is unmatched, as their 27 World Series championships as of 2015 are more than twice that of their nearest competitor. The names of players who have put on the pinstripes read like a roll call of Major League Baseball's immortals. From Babe Ruth and Lou Gehrig to Joe DiMaggio and Mickey Mantle, an almost continuous 100-year run has seen baseball royalty call Yankee Stadium home. "I was sold to the Yankees by the Angels in 1974," said Rudy May, who had two stints in New York during his 16-year career. "What I learned when I went to that team was that nothing else mattered there except winning. It was expected of you to be a winner. I learned to have that winning attitude during my time there."

To get an idea of how many legends have suited up for the Yanks, one just has to take a look at the wall in the stadium's Monument Park. As of the end of the 2015 season, 21 players have had their numbers retired by the Yankees, and the only single-digit number not retired is 2. The numbers of the other single-digit Yankees are very well known: 3 for Ruth, 4 for Gehrig, 5 for DiMaggio, and 7 for Mantle. Billy Martin's 1 is retired, as is number 8 for Yogi Berra and Elston Howard. Roger Maris had his number 9 retired, and Phil Rizzuto, who spent more than 50 years in the organization as a player and announcer, had his number 10 retired in 1985. Joe Torre's number 6 was the second-to-last single-digit number retired in a ceremony on August 23, 2014. It won't be too long before Derek Jeter's number 2 will go down as the last single-digit number in Yankees history.

In the mid-'90s, the Yankees were beginning to come out of one of the longest down periods in their history. After the storied championship teams of 1977 and 1978, the Yanks hit the skids and, despite routinely spending money on big-name free agents, could not recapture that glory the team had experienced through the '80s. Although the Yankees won more regular-season games in the '80s than any other team, their only postseason appearance of the decade came in 1981, when the Dodgers topped them in the World Series. Between 1981 and 1995, the Yankees failed to make the postseason once.

Things started to turn around in the mid-'90s. The 1994 Yankees, managed by Buck Showalter, had the best record in the American League, but the remainder of the season was canceled by a players' strike. The 1995 Yankees featured veterans like Wade Boggs, Don Mattingly, David Cone, and Darryl Strawberry. Young up-and-comers like Bernie Williams, Andy Pettitte, and Mariano Rivera emerged, and it was clear the Yankees had the makings of a contender.

The Yankees finished second to the Red Sox in the AL East but qualified for the playoffs when they beat out the Angels for a wild-card spot. They then fell in dramatic fashion to the Mariners in the first American League Division Series of the wild-card era, 3–2. This didn't sit well with George Steinbrenner, who had higher hopes for his squad. He fired Buck Showalter and searched for someone who he hoped would take the Yankees to the next level.

The search for a manager didn't go as Steinbrenner had planned, as some of the top candidates didn't want to work under the mercurial boss. Legend has it that with his search going so poorly, Steinbrenner thought about reneging on the firing of Showalter; however, he opted for Joe Torre, in what was an unpopular move at the time. Torre had managed the Mets, Braves, and Cardinals to minimal success. Most felt that Steinbrenner hired Torre because he felt Torre's laid-back personality and general lack of success would make him subservient. The *New York Post* was the bluntest of the local papers, as the headline after his hiring on November 2, 1995, screamed out, "Clueless Joe."

On April 2, 1996, five months after Torre's press conference, the Yankees were set for Opening Day and ready to take on the Indians at Jacobs Field. The Indians had won the AL Central in '95 and had the most wins in the league, with 100. Their star-studded lineup was built around feared slugger Albert Belle and had young superstars Manny Ramirez, Jim Thome, Carlos Baerga, and Kenny Lofton. Their pitching staff was equally impressive, led by All-Star veterans Orel Hershiser, Charles Nagy, and Jack McDowell, plus Opening Day starter Dennis Martinez.

The Yankees also posted a formidable lineup as Boggs, Williams, and Paul O'Neill returned. The team had acquired All-Star Tino Martinez in the offseason to replace the retired Mattingly, and Torre topped it off by making a key decision prior to spring training: He named 22-year-old rookie Derek Jeter as the starting shortstop.

Despite the fact that Jeter was the sixth overall draft pick in the '92 draft, this was not the "no-brainer" move you'd think it would be. Questions about his defense arose after he made 131 errors in four seasons of minor-league ball. Others also wondered if it was smart to start a young, unproven player in such a key position, especially since they had sure-handed All-Star Tony Fernandez there in '95. They originally planned on moving Fernandez to second in '96, but a spring training injury to the veteran ended that.

By Torre's admission, Jeter had a poor spring training in '96. In an article by Seth Livingstone in *USA Today*, Torre admitted that veteran baseball executive Clyde King even recommended sending Jeter back to the minors. Torre ultimately decided that it was too late in the spring to make such a crucial move and he would take the gamble with the rookie. Torre's risk paid off, as Jeter immediately became a key piece for the Yankees and unanimously won Rookie of the Year in '96. On April 2 of that year, Jeter became the first rookie shortstop to start for the Yanks on Opening Day since 1962, when Tom Tresh took over for Tony Kubek.

David Cone faced off against Dennis Martinez in front of 42,289 people on Opening Day of the '96 season, and both pitchers looked like they had great stuff early. Neither team broke through until the third, when Mariano Duncan singled to right for the Yanks. O'Neill then laced his second double of the day to drive home Duncan and give the Yanks a 1–0 lead. Martinez settled down, however, and tangled with Cone, who hadn't allowed a hit through the first four innings.

With the Yanks still up 1–0, the rookie shortstop was set to lead off the fifth. Jeter wasn't considered to be an offensive threat just yet and was batting ninth in the order. In 48 at-bats as a September call-up in 1995, Jeter had just 12 hits for a .250 batting average. In his first at-bat of the season in '96, he struck out looking. Unexpectedly, Jeter smoked a line drive over the left-field fence for his first career home run to extend the Yankees' lead to 2–0.

Cone continued his mastery of the dangerous Indians lineup and didn't allow a hit until a sixth-inning single by Julio Franco. Martinez continued to match Cone, as the game stayed 2–0 until the eighth. With Alan Embree now pitching for the Indians, O'Neill drew a one-out walk, and Ruben Sierra singled to left. After a fielder's choice, Williams hit a two-out, three-run homer to blow the game open.

Torre opted to lift Cone from the game after 118 pitches, even though he'd given up just two hits. He brought in Bob Wickman, who gave up a leadoff walk to Kenny Lofton. Lofton stole second and third, and came home to score on a groundout for what would be the Indians' only run of the game.

The Yankees tacked on two insurance runs in the eighth on an O'Neill single and a Sierra double. Torre then turned to John Wetteland to close out the ninth and seal the Opening Day win.

The game was the precursor for a magical season for the Yankees. O'Neill led the way with a 3-for-4 effort, driving in two runs and scoring another, and Sierra recorded a multihit game for the Yanks as well. Torre recorded a win in his first game as Yankees manager, and Jeter finished 1-for-4, with a solo home run. Torre would later say in Livingstone's *USA Today* article that "he became Derek Jeter, forever, right there."

The Yankees went on to finish 92–70 in 1996, to take first in the AL East, ahead of the Orioles, who had enough wins to qualify as the wild card. The Indians again led the AL in wins, this time with 99, but were upset by the Orioles 3–1 in the Division Series. The Yankees topped the Rangers 3–1 in the other ALDS and met up with the Orioles in the American League Championship Series.

In the first game of the ALCS, Jeter hit one of the most controversial home runs of the era when he launched a long fly ball to right with the Yankees trailing 4–3 in the eighth. As Orioles right fielder Tony Tarasco settled under the ball, Jeffrey Maier, a 12-year-old Yankees fan from New Jersey, reached out of the stands and clearly pulled the ball into the seats before it landed in Tarasco's glove. Despite the fact that umpire Richie García was deep down the right-field line, seemingly in good position to make the call, he ruled the shot a home run, against vehement protest from Tarasco and Orioles manager Davey Johnson. The Yanks would go on to win the game on a walk-off homer from Williams in the 11th and took the series 4–1.

Jeter, the inexperienced rookie, grew up fast in the postseason, as he hit .417 in the ALCS to help the Yankees win the AL pennant. They then topped the Braves 4–2 in the World Series to nail down the Yankees' first championship in 17 years.

In baseball, people like to play the percentages. Whether it's in the middle of a game or in making decisions off the field, it takes guts to take risks. The Yankees would go on to win four World Series titles in five years and fully establish themselves once again as the predominant power in all of baseball. Two of the main keys to that dynasty got their chance from the organization despite backlash from just about everywhere.

Torre, the unpopular managerial choice, went on to become one of the most revered managers in Yankees history and a Hall of Famer in 2014. He certainly had the talent to work with, but the way he handled the New York media and the respect he carried among the players made a big difference as well. "I admired Mr. Torre and loved playing for him," said Aaron Small, whose 10–0 record in 2005 spurred the Yankees to an AL East championship. Small added,

> When I got to the Yankees in 2005, he approached me in spring training and said that one of his rules was that he wanted players to hear things from him first rather than through the media. During the season I was 4–0, but Jaret Wright was coming off the disabled list and some media members told me I might be headed to the bullpen.

Small continued,

> Mr. Torre approached me and asked if I heard the speculation about a move to the bullpen. I told him that I had some discussions with some media members, and they told me I might be headed to the pen. Mr. Torre was straight with me. He first apologized and then told me it was true, that I was going to the bullpen, and he'd understand if I was upset. I told him, "Mr. Torre, three or four weeks ago I was in the minor leagues thinking about calling it a career. I'd stick around and shine shoes if I meant I got to pitch on your staff."

Small ended up back in the starting rotation and won all five of his September starts, including four wins against AL East foes. The Yankees ended up with an identical 95–67 record as the Red Sox but won the AL East on tiebreakers through percentage points. Said Small, "To this day, every time I see Mr. Torre he tells me, 'Smalley, we wouldn't have won it without you.'"

Jeter became the face of the franchise going into the new millennium, retiring in 2014, with 3,465 hits, the sixth most in major-league history. Almost as important, Jeter conducted himself impeccably on and off the field under the brightest of spotlights in the game's biggest media market. Despite coming up on a team that had more than its share of veteran leaders, Jeter established himself in the clubhouse at a young age. "Derek Jeter was a class act from day one," said Scott Pose, who was a teammate of a 23-year-old Jeter. "He carried himself extremely well for such a young player that had many potential off-field distractions in New York. I am not surprised by Derek's success; he relished clutch situations and always stayed focused."

Pose continued,

> What many don't talk about is that he always had an intrinsic sense of the pecking order in the clubhouse, meaning he deferred to the leadership that was earned by seasoned veterans at the time, [players like] Cone, O'Neill, Martinez, and Girardi. When it came time for him to assume that role, he reluctantly, but deservedly, accepted the captaincy. His humility made him a great teammate and leader and, in my opinion, is why he garnered so much respect from so many.

Small was Jeter's teammate during his two seasons in the Bronx and agreed:

> Derek Jeter was an amazing teammate, and baseball is going to miss him. I remember in the '05 postseason, I was sitting in the dugout before a game just kinda rubbing my hands down my legs nervously. Derek came by and said, "Hey Smalley, you getting nervous? We're here playing a kids game and getting paid, let's go have some fun." That's the kind of leader and captain he was.

Ted Barrett, who was a major-league umpire for Jeter's entire career, first met the shortstop not long after he was drafted.

"I first met Derek in the fall league very early on in his career," said Barrett.

> Nomar and A-Rod were in that league too. Derek never changed. He was a class act right from the start. If he disagreed with you, he argued respectfully. He was just a great player who played hard. He had never been thrown out of a game, and he joked with me in his final season that he wanted me to eject him. I said, "No! No! No!" I had already been the only umpire to eject Edgar Martinez from a game, I wasn't about to be the only one to eject Derek too.

Don Slaught, who spent 16 years in the bigs as a catcher and played for the Yankees in '88 and '89, spoke about the impact of Jeter's career: "Jeter was a class act for so long," said Slaught. "He played with so many stars on his own team and in the American League, and he stood out among them. He was a great role model and knew how to carry himself on and off the field. There were many superstars who played in that era who weren't like that."

Slaught, who founded RightView Pro, a video swing-analysis company, talked about his company's participation during Major League Baseball's All-Star weekend: "We have software that can take someone's swing and superimpose it over another as a comparison," said Slaught.

We took it to the fan fest during All-Star weekend and had it set up for kids to take a swing and compare it to a major leaguer. The overwhelming majority of kids wanted to compare their swing to Derek Jeter's. It showed how many kids out there look up to Derek Jeter probably more than any other player.

Jeter's final game in Yankee Stadium came on September 26, 2014. The game followed the typical storybook formula that most of Jeter's career previously had. Jeter belted a double off the left-field wall in his first at-bat against the AL East champion Orioles and drove in another run with a fielder's choice in what looked like his last at-bat in his home stadium; however, after All-Star closer David Robertson gave up three runs in the top of the ninth to allow the Orioles to tie the game, Jeter was given one more at-bat.

José Pirela led off the ninth with a single and was pinch-run for by Antoan Richardson. After Bret Gardner sacrificed Richardson to second, Jeter came up with a chance to win it. With the capacity crowd on its feet and to nobody's surprise, Jeter lined a single to right field, as he had done so many times before, to plate Richardson with the winning run, setting off a chaotic and teary celebration.

"I didn't get to know him personally, but as an opponent, I was always just like, 'Wow, what a career,'" said Adam Melhuse, who played against Jeter frequently as a member of the A's and Rangers. "Day in and day out, he was just unbelievable. What goes a long way with me though is that he was just a quality guy. He wasn't out there getting DUIs or getting into trouble. He's just a stand-up guy, and the career he had on and off the field was just so impressive."

Joe Torre's and Derek Jeter's legacies began on April 2, 1996, with a win over the powerful Indians. Torre, who was working as executive vice president for baseball operations for Major League Baseball in 2014, was on the field to celebrate and congratulate Jeter on his stellar career and game-winning hit. It was only fitting that Torre, the man responsible for giving Jeter his starting position as the Yankees' shortstop, was there to walk Jeter off the field for the last time at Yankee Stadium.

THE FIRST ALL-STAR GAME: THE "GAME OF THE CENTURY"

July 6, 1933

More than any other sport, baseball is a game of tradition. From the ivy-covered walls of Wrigley to Yankees pinstripes to Fenway's Green Monster, many great traditions have endured the decades. Every July, the sport takes a brief vacation from the regular season to revisit a tradition that started on July 6, 1933: the Major League Baseball All-Star Game.

The idea came about when Chicago was slated to host the World's Fair in conjunction with the celebration of the city's centennial. Arch Ward, sports editor of the *Chicago Tribune*, came up with the idea of an All-Star Game, billed it as the "Game of the Century," and pitched it to his boss, as well as the presidents of the American and National Leagues. He was so convinced that the game would be a success that he offered to cover any financial losses from his own paycheck. Eventually, Commissioner Kenesaw Mountain Landis agreed to the event, and it was set for July 6, 1933, at Comiskey Park.

In a tradition that still stands today, fans were able to cast votes as to who they wanted to see in the game, and 55 newspapers from throughout the country published ballots. The United States was in the midst of the Great Depression, and attendance had fallen off at ballparks. Fans also were beginning to become critical of baseball, as teams spent hundreds of thousands of dollars a year and players were drawing big salaries for the time despite the fact that the average American family was having trouble finding employment. Letting the fans vote created a way for turned-off fans to interact personally with the league.

Ward hyped his "Game of the Century" with numerous articles in the *Chicago Tribune*, and his campaign was a success, as 47,595 fans turned up for the event. Participation in the balloting was also received well, as hundreds of thousands of votes were tallied.

The game featured 18 future Hall of Famers, and the lineups were so stacked that players like Pie Traynor, Carl Hubbell, Lefty Grove, and Jimmie Foxx weren't even starters. Among the all-time greats who were voted into the starting lineups were Lou Gehrig, Lefty Gomez, Al Simmons, and Babe Ruth. While Ruth was at the end of his career, he was still the major attraction, garnering the most votes.

Gomez was the starting pitcher for the AL, while Wild Bill Hallahan started for the National League. The game was a well-played affair and delighted the capacity crowd. Gomez started the game by retiring three all-time greats. Hallahan got Ben Chapman on a groundout to third to start the bottom of the first but walked Charlie Gehringer to bring Ruth to the plate. After Gehringer stole second, fans anticipated Ruth would drive in the first run of the game; however, Babe struck out looking and Gehrig was retired on a groundout to first to end the threat.

The AL jumped on the board first, as Jimmy Dykes and Joe Cronin drew one-out walks, bringing up Gomez, who was a .147 lifetime hitter. Gomez drove a single to center to bring home Dykes with the first run in All-Star

Game history. Gomez then retired the NL in the top of the third, and the AL would come to bat with Gehringer, Ruth, and Gehrig due up.

Gehringer worked out a walk, and Ruth stepped up to the plate with great anticipation from the fans. Ruth launched one of his trademark long home runs into the right-field stands to give the AL a 3–0 lead. Gehrig then drew a walk, and Hall of Fame NL manager John McGraw called for Lon Warneke to replace Hallahan. Warneke retired the side without further damage.

The game stayed at 3–0 until the sixth, when the NL mounted its best rally of the day. Warneke hit a one-out triple and came around to score the NL's first run on a groundout by Pepper Martin. Frankie Frisch followed with a home run to right to bring the NL within one run. Chuck Klein then singled, but the AL got out of the inning without further harm.

The American League got one of the runs back in the bottom of the sixth, when Cronin led off with a single, was bunted to second by Rick Ferrell, and came in to score when pinch-hitter Earl Averill singled to center to make the score 4–2.

However, the National League wasn't done. In the top of the seventh, with Grove now on to pitch for the American League, Bill Terry led off with a single and Traynor knocked a pinch-hit double to left to put runners on second and third with one out. But Grove got out of the jam by retiring Gabby Hartnett and Woody English.

With the AL unable to get an insurance run against Hubbell in the eighth, it was up to Grove to nail down the win against the 4–5–6 batters of the Senior Circuit's lineup. He retired Terry, Wally Berger, and Tony Cuccinello without incident to pick up the save in the AL's win in the inaugural All-Star Game.

As Ward predicted, the game was a huge success. With backing from the *Chicago Tribune*, media coverage of the event was extensive and played a big role in helping the game meet expectations. A defining moment like Ruth's home run added to the lore of the game and allowed for the event to be played the following year at the Polo Grounds.

Artifacts from the first All-Star Game are highly valued collectibles now. Ticket stubs from the game still exist and, despite the initial $1.10 admission fee, are now worth thousands of dollars. As expected, Babe Ruth's home run ball was the most prized possession from the game. The ball landed in the hands of a fan named Earl Brown. Brown was mentioned by name in the game article the next day, and when the Yankees returned to Comiskey later in the year, Brown had Ruth autograph the ball. He had the ball and signature authenticated, and it would eventually sell at an auction in 2006 for $805,000.

Despite the fact that the MLB All-Star Game was originally meant to be a one-time-only "Game of the Century," its popularity endured. In fact, the game became so popular that two All-Star Games were played yearly between 1959 and 1962. The only year the All-Star Game would not be played was in 1945, due to travel restrictions brought on by World War II. The game returned to Comiskey Field twice (1950 and 1983) before the famed ballpark was torn down in 1991.

Like Opening Day and the World Series, the MLB All-Star Game marks a milestone on the baseball calendar. The regular season stops for a brief hiatus, allowing the game to stand alone, as no other major sports are in action at that time. This gives fans and players a break from the everyday rigors of the 162-game schedule and allows everyone to enjoy the best-of-the-best playing the national pastime on the grand stage. "Growing up in the '60s and '70s, you had the Game of the Week, but not much else," said Jeff Montgomery, a three-time All-Star closer for the Royals in the '90s. "Then you had the All-Star Game. It's always one of those games that you just had to watch, even as a 10-year-old kid. You had to stay up late to watch every inning."

Shawn Estes, who made the All-Star Game as a 24-year-old in '97, has similar memories: "Looking around and seeing all these stars like Greg Maddux, Pedro Martinez, and Tom Glavine was just amazing," said Estes. "It felt like the whole thing was a dream. Being there with my teammates, Rod Beck and Barry Bonds, was special too." Estes actually took the loss in the '97 game when he gave up a home run to Sandy Alomar in his home ballpark to break up a 1–1 tie in the bottom of the seventh. "It didn't bother me at all," said Estes. "It was a 2–2 low changeup, and he went down and hit it out to left. It was just an amazing atmosphere, and to be involved in the All-Star Game, especially at such a young age, was just incredible."

It's been the showcase for the best baseball has had to offer. Stars like Ted Williams, Carl Hubbell, Jackie Robinson, Ken Griffey Jr., and Mariano Rivera have enduring legacies from the Midsummer Classic. The precedent was set by an aging Babe Ruth and the big home run in the third inning of the MLB All-Star Game of '33.

PUMPSIE GREEN: YEARS OVERDUE, INTEGRATION IN BOSTON

August 4, 1959

Baseball took a big leap forward on April 15, 1947, when Jackie Robinson made his debut for the Brooklyn Dodgers. Robinson's story is well known, and his success on the field, along with the dignity with which he faced unspeakable discriminatory defamation, paved the way for other teams to follow suit. Less than three months after Robinson's debut, the equally classy and talented Larry Doby got his start with the Cleveland Indians. Soon, many major-league clubs recognized the talent they were missing out on, and legends like Minnie Miñoso, Roy Campanella, Don Newcombe, and Monte Irvin debuted.

Baseball's integration hit full stride by the end of the '54 season, as all but four clubs featured black players. Although it took seven years, some of the brightest stars in the game in the mid-'50s would not have been allowed to play in the majors just a decade earlier. In 1955, the Brooklyn Dodgers finally broke through to win the World Series, thanks to the pitching of Newcombe, who went 20–5, and the play of Campanella, who was named MVP for the third time in his career. Although older, Robinson was also a key player for the '55 team. It was clear that any team not willing to integrate was falling behind and playing at a major disadvantage.

"Racism was still present in the game, even after Jackie Robinson broke into the majors," said Fred Valentine, who first received recognition by major-league teams in 1953, at a time when only seven major-league teams were integrated. "Although teams were integrated by the time I reached the majors, many teams hadn't really accepted integration. The minor leagues were even more harsh towards blacks."

The Yankees, Phillies, and Tigers received criticism for not being as open to integration, and their on-field product suffered because of it. The Yankees added Elston Howard in 1955, but many criticized them for stopping there.

The main culprit in the failure to integrate their team was the Boston Red Sox. By the time Pumpsie Green stepped onto the field for the Sox on July 21, 1959, it had been 12 years since Robinson broke the color barrier. In fact, the Red Sox were so far behind that Robinson had been retired for three years by the time Green made his debut.

Despite the fact that it had been more than a decade since Robinson debuted for the Dodgers, Green's journey to the majors was anything but easy. Green was playing for a minor Pacific Coast League affiliate team when he was given the surprising news that the Red Sox had purchased his contract mid-season. While that would be great news for some, he was supposed to report to the Red Sox minor-league affiliate team in Montgomery, Alabama. With the Deep South still far behind on race relations, Green was apprehensive about playing there. In Herbert F. Crehan's book *Red Sox Heroes of Yesteryear*, Green says, "I don't think there was a black man in America who wanted to go to Montgomery, Alabama, in 1955." He was allowed to finish out his season on his PCL team and reported to spring training in 1956.

Green developed in the minors during the next few seasons and was in spring training with the big club in 1959, and had a chance to make the squad.

He was well liked among the big leaguers and widely accepted by the team, especially Ted Williams. Williams would become Green's warm-up partner upon his arrival in Boston, and many thought that his public showing of support for Green helped ease the transition.

By his own accounts, Green dominated spring training in '59 and expected to make the trip north with the Red Sox. He said he outplayed everyone, including Williams; however, he was sent back to Minneapolis to start the season in the minors. It was at that point that the talk about Red Sox owner Tom Yawkey's alleged racism grew much louder. National newspaper editorials picked up on the story, and it became a major hot-button issue in Boston.

Green's demotion was met with such outrage that numerous civil rights groups contacted Green to try to take up his cause. The Boston NAACP ordered a boycott of Fenway Park and organized protests outside the stadium. The Red Sox manager at the time was Pinky Higgins, an old-timer who played from 1930 to 1946 in an era well before integration.

During this controversy, Green, who was a reluctant trailblazer, was getting fed up with the attention that was being paid to his race. He just wanted to be a successful ballplayer, not a pioneer. He didn't want his demotion or the perception of racism from the Red Sox to play any part in his baseball life. He felt that if he supported the claims from the civil rights groups, it would set him back even further. So, instead of sulking after his demotion, Green went to Minneapolis and continued to dominate. He was hitting over .330 through mid-July and was finally called up to the Red Sox on July 21. Green's call-up came when the Red Sox were already 12 games out of first place, sitting in eighth place in the AL East. Green's debut coincided with a long road trip, as his first nine games would be played on the road. This gave the media and fans time to calm down before he made his Fenway Park debut.

Higgins was not around to see Green's debut, as he was fired in early July.

Green got off to a decent start in his first nine games, as he batted .292 during that time, with seven walks and two stolen bases. He also struck out just twice in 40 plate appearances. Playing second base, the 25-year-old also showed great promise as a fielder and brought excitement to the moribund Red Sox franchise.

On August 4, 1959, Green was set to make his Fenway Park debut against the Kansas City A's. The Sox had now fallen 17 games out of first, and fans had little to cheer about and even less reason to attend games. Despite this, Green recalled that the park was full for his debut, and many black fans wanted to attend the game. The Sox were not known for drawing black fans, but for this game they appeared. To the organization's credit, because there were only a limited number of tickets available for the game, the Red Sox created a standing-room-only section in center field for any black fans who wanted to watch Green's debut. They filled the section and were boisterous in support of Green and the Sox.

Tom Brewer was the starting pitcher for the Red Sox in game one of the doubleheader, and he got through the top of the A's lineup in order in the top of the first. Green was batting leadoff, so he would be making his Fenway debut immediately. As Green grabbed his bat and walked up to the plate, the crowd rose to its feet and gave him a standing ovation.

Green slowed as he walked to the plate to take everything in, and even home plate umpire Eddie Rommel wished him luck. Green worked the count to 2–1 against A's starter John Tsitouris and then launched a shot into deep left-center field. The ball caromed toward center as it hit off the wall, and Green hustled around the bases for a triple. The already-raucous crowd got even louder. Green came in to score on a groundout by Pete Runnels to give the Sox a 1–0 lead.

Green's second at-bat came in the third but resulted in a fly out to left. He next came up in the fifth with runners on first and second with two outs but could not come through in the clutch that time either.

Brewer and Tsitouris engaged in a pitchers' duel from there, as the game remained 1–0 into the sixth. Jackie Jensen doubled home a run in the sixth to make it 2–0, and Brewer retired the side in order in the top of the seventh to move the game to the eighth. Red Sox shortstop Don Buddin led off the inning with a single, and Brewer followed with a walk to bring Green up to bat for the fourth time. The shortstop laid down a perfect sacrifice bunt to move the runners up for the heart of the Red Sox order. His sac worked perfectly, as Runnels singled both runners home to move the lead to 4–0.

The A's finally broke through with a run on a single by Preston Ward in the eighth, but that would be all they'd get and the Red Sox would go on to win in Green's Fenway debut by a score of 4–1.

Through late August 1959, Green's average was over .300, as he provided a big lift to the top of the Red Sox batting order; however, a late-season slump dropped his average nearly .070 points and he finished the season batting just .233. Green appeared in 133 games for the Sox in 1960, but many of those were as a pinch-runner, pinch-hitter, or defensive replacement. He would record 260 at-bats and hit .242 that season. His role diminished during the next two years, as he played in just 144 games in that time and was never really given a full-time chance as a starter to prove himself.

On December 11, 1962, Green was traded to the New York Mets, who'd just completed their historically awful premiere season in the National League. Green played in just 17 September games for the Mets in '63. He spent '64 and '65 playing in the minors in Buffalo before retiring from baseball permanently.

During the 15-year period between 1945 and 1960, the game of baseball underwent significant changes. It was dominated by such all-time legends as Willie Mays, Hank Aaron, Mickey Mantle, Stan Musial, and Frank Robinson. But black baseball pioneers of the era were just as important to the progress of the game. Whether the player was someone who transcended the sport like Jackie Robinson or Larry Doby, or an unwilling trailblazer like Pumpsie Green, they hold a special place in baseball history as a brotherhood that changed the game forever.

· 2 ·

Magic Numbers

PETE ROSE: THE 4,000-HIT CLUB

April 13, 1984

Judging by how far Pete Rose has fallen since his 1989 banishment from baseball, it's hard to recall a time when he was a true treasure of the sport. Always a symbol for the way the game should be played, Rose's late career was a celebration of his years of excellence. On the night of April 13, 1984, Rose was set to join such an elite club that there was only one other member: the 4,000-hit club.

The Expos were a promising team led by Hall of Famers Gary Carter and Andre Dawson, and young All-Stars Tim Raines and Tim Wallach, and were hoping Rose's leadership would help them reach higher levels. They also had a balance of solid veterans like Jim Wohlford and Terry Francona, and solid pitching, led by Steve Rogers, Bill Gullickson, and Jeff Reardon; however, they needed some real veteran star power to get over the top. That leadership came in the form of Pete Rose. "Pete was a winner and brought that winning attitude to the field every day," said Wohlford. "I learned more from Pete Rose than anyone else in all my years in the game. I loved him; he was a great teammate."

Needing just 10 hits to reach 4,000, it appeared Rose would be on track to approach that feat in an early-season matchup against the Cincinnati Reds, the place where Rose recorded the first 3,164 hits of his career. Rose approached the three-game set needing five more hits. He recorded two hits in each of the first two games but was walked four times in the third game as he went 0-for-1 on the night, leaving him one hit short.

On April 13, Rose's Expos returned home to Olympic Stadium for a quick two-game series against the Phillies. The game was the home opener for the Expos, and with the chance to see baseball history, 48,060 fans showed up in what would be the Expos' largest crowd of the season.

Jerry Koosman was the Phillies' starting pitcher that night. Koosman was reaching the end of a very good career and had faced Rose numerous times in the '70s, when he pitched 12 seasons for the New York Mets.

Rose batted leadoff that night and was hitting a respectable .273 in the early part of the season. In his first at-bat against the lefty in the bottom of the first, Rose grounded out to second. The Expos mounted a rally against Koosman in the second and would get Rose a quick second chance at hit number 4,000. With a 1–0 lead and pitcher Charlie Lea on second, Rose hit a comebacker to Koosman, who committed an error. Rose reached first, but his chance for 4,000 would have to wait.

In the top of the fourth, the Expos led 2–0, but Glenn Wilson scored on a single by Bo Diaz to cut the lead in half. Rose was due up second in the bottom of the fourth, and the crowd anticipated the historic moment. Lea led off with a walk, bringing Rose to the plate for his third at-bat. Batting righty, Rose hit an opposite-field double to reach a milestone only Ty Cobb had reached before. Cobb recorded his 4,000th on July 18, 1927. "Nobody will ever accomplish 4,000 hits again," said Wohlford. "You'd have to start when you're 20 and average 200 hits a season for 20 years. It'll never happen."

Always a competitor, Rose accepted his congratulations from the Expos fans and then got back to trying to win the game. Bryan Little grounded out after Rose's hit, but Raines drove home Lea and Rose with a single to center to make the score 4–1.

Lea kept the strong Phillies lineup at bay for the remainder of the game, and the Expos tacked on an insurance run when a double to left by Carter scored Dawson in the seventh on the way to the win.

The Pete Rose experiment in Montreal did not last long, however, as Rose hit just .259 in 95 games with the team. Wohlford had a sense that Rose's time in Montreal would be short-lived. "He told me that he'd be leaving soon, but I said, 'Come on Pete, everyone says they'll be leaving Montreal.' But sure enough, he was gone soon after."

On August 15, Rose was traded back to Cincinnati for infielder Tom Lawless. Not only did the Reds hope Rose's play on the field would help them improve, but they also fired manager Bill Virdon on the same day and named Rose their player-manager. In 26 games with the Reds in 1984, Rose enjoyed a renaissance. He hit .365, with nine of his 35 hits going for doubles. Rose ended the 1984 season with 4,097 career hits, putting him well within reach of Cobb's all-time record of 4,191. Rose played two more years for the Reds, accumulating 159 hits on a .248 batting average. He surpassed Cobb's all-time mark with a single to left-center off the Padres' Eric Show on September 11, 1985.

Andy McGaffigan, who pitched in 363 games in 11 seasons, was a teammate of Rose's both when he recorded his 4,000th hit in Montreal and when he broke Cobb's record in Cincinnati. "Pete was unbelievable," said McGaffigan. "He was just so driven to get that record. He was a man on fire, a man on a mission."

Ted Power, who pitched in 564 games in his 13-year big-league career, recorded the save in the game when Rose passed Cobb in 1985. "It was an awesome experience the whole season, but that night is a great memory," said Power. "The last out was a grounder to Pete at first base, and he flipped me the ball for the out. I still have that ball."

Ron Oester, who played his entire career with the Reds from 1978 to 1990, played second base on the night that Rose broke Cobb's record and echoed the statements of Power. "Pete Rose was my idol growing up in Cincinnati," started Oester.

I loved the way he played the game, and I tried to play the same way. He gave everything he had every out, every inning, every pitch, every day. His breaking of Ty Cobb's record and playing in the game next to him was one of the best memories I had in the game. To see him look up to the sky thinking about his dad and getting emotional will stick in my mind forever.

Rose retired from baseball in November 1986, but continued to manage the Reds through 1989. He became the subject of an investigation by Commissioner Bart Giamatti on allegations that he bet on baseball. The final conclusion was that he placed himself on baseball's "permanently ineligible list" with the chance to appeal that decision one year later; however, just eight days after Rose's banishment, Giamatti suffered a fatal heart attack at the age of 51.

In the subsequent years, Rose has used all forms of promotion to campaign for his reinstatement and for election to the Baseball Hall of Fame. He formally applied for reinstatement in September 1997, but commissioners Fay Vincent and Bud Selig chose not to act on his application.

As the years went on, public sentiment and support from his former teammates began to grow. Wohlford is among Rose's biggest supporters: "Absolutely he deserves to be in the Hall of Fame," said Wohlford. "He's an all-time great, went out there every day, played hurt, and was a winner. The game loses out without him involved. What would golf be without Jack Nicklaus?"

Despite his troubles off the field, nobody can argue Rose's prowess on it. He was a 17-time All-Star and won three World Series championships. He was the NL MVP in 1973, and the World Series MVP in 1975. Rose was even one of the 10 outfielders named to Major League Baseball's All-Century Team in 1999.

Pete Rose is a polarizing figure in modern-day sports. He broke one of the most sacred rules regarding the integrity of the game of baseball, spent time in jail on tax evasion, publicly lied about his gambling, and only came clean when he wrote a book in which he expected to profit greatly from his admissions; however, on the field Rose was revered. Whether it was winning a World Series with the Big Red Machine or with the Phillies, or on the night of April 13, 1984, when he recorded his 4,000th hit in his brief tenure with the Expos, fans were always willing to give Pete Rose the recognition he deserved.

TED WILLIAMS: .406 THE HARD WAY

September 28, 1941

Among everything you can say about Ted Williams, the simplest way to describe the man is that he had unflappable confidence and guts. Nothing in Williams's life proved this more than his military accomplishments. He was a fighter pilot during World War II and in the Korean War, where his skill was greatly documented. On the baseball field, the greatest display of his fortitude may have come on September 28, 1941, the final day of that year's baseball season.

The 1941 season is considered to be one of the greatest in MLB history. It's most famous for being the season that Joe DiMaggio hit in 56 straight games and Williams finished the season with a .406 average. Two other Hall of Famers reached personal milestones, as Mel Ott became the fourth player to hit 400 home runs (Babe Ruth, Lou Gehrig, and Jimmie Foxx had done it previously), and Lefty Grove earned his 300th career win, which was also his final win. It was also the year that Lou Gehrig died from the disease that now bears his name.

As great a season as 1941 was, it's only fitting that the season had one of the great endings as far as personal statistics went. A 22-year-old Williams was enjoying one of the best offensive seasons of the modern era and was remarkably consistent. Through May, Williams was hitting .429 and had 51 hits through the first 35 games of the year. His average never dipped below .400 during June, and except for a brief three-week "slump" in which he hit .364 to drop his average to .393, he stayed above .400.

On September 14, Williams's average sat at .411 as he attempted to become the first player to hit .400 since Bill Terry in 1930. Williams had just 13 games left in the season to accomplish that feat; however, he hit .310 in the next nine games and stood at .402 going into the second game of a double-header against the Senators. He went 1-for-4 to drop his average to .401.

After a three-day break, Williams's Red Sox were set to take on the Philadelphia A's for a three-game set to close the regular season. In the opening game of the series, Roger Wolff, a 30-year-old rookie pitching in just his second major-league game, held Williams to a 1-for-4 effort. A quick calculation showed that Williams's batting average stood at .39955, which would be rounded up to an even .400 if the season ended that day.

September 28 was the final Sunday of the season, and the Sox were to face the A's in a doubleheader. Red Sox manager Joe Cronin gave Williams the option of sitting the games out to preserve his .400 batting average. Williams refused and went out to earn his final average.

In the first game of the doubleheader, rookie Dick Fowler was the starting pitcher for the A's. He had started just two games prior to that and would eventually go on to an unremarkable 10-year career. The game was a slugfest in which the Red Sox won 12–11, as the teams combined for 31 hits. Williams went after Fowler and two relievers aggressively and didn't give fans much doubt as to whether he would maintain the .400 average. He singled in his first at-bat and homered in his second. Williams followed with two more singles to go 4-for-4 on the game to raise his average to .405 on the year. In his final at-bat of the game, Williams reached first on an error, dropping his average to .404.

With the option of sitting out the next game still available, Williams didn't even address Cronin about it, and the veteran player-manager wrote Williams into the lineup in the cleanup spot without asking. Williams again responded quickly by singling in his first at-bat and followed that up with a double in his second trip to the plate. In his final at-bat of the season, Williams flied out to left. He ended up 6-for-8 with two runs and two RBIs on the day, to post a final batting average of .406, which stands as one of the magic numbers in baseball history. The game was also the final game in the legendary career of Lefty Grove, as the Hall of Famer took the loss to fall to 7–7 on the year and 300–141 for his career.

While the Red Sox had a good year, finishing at 84–70, they were far behind the first-place Yankees, who went 101–53 that year. Led by DiMaggio, Bill Dickey, and Phil Rizzuto, the Yankees went on to beat the Brooklyn Dodgers in the World Series, 4–1.

Williams ran away with the batting crown in 1941, outdistancing himself from Cecil Travis of the Senators by .047 points. He also led the American League in homers, with 37, and his .553 on-base percentage stands through 2015 as the AL record. In addition to his high average and on-base percentage, Williams wasn't just someone looking for a single. He wanted to drive the ball, and it showed in his .735 slugging percentage. That total topped DiMaggio by .092 points and remained in the top 20 in baseball history through 2015.

One final note to Williams's remarkable season is that between 1940 and 1954, sacrifice flies were actually counted as outs. Years later, it was approximated by Cronin that Williams had an estimated 14 sacrifice flies in 1941, which means that by today's standards, his .406 would have actually been .419. Since Williams hit .406 in 1941, few players have even flirted with the mark. In fact, only Rod Carew (.388 in 1977), George Brett (.390 in 1980), and Tony Gwynn (.393 in 1994) have topped .380 for a full season.

Carew reflected on whether someone could top the .400 mark again: "I will never say never," he said. "A few years ago I thought Ichiro had a chance. It will take another hitter like Ichiro, a guy who is fast, can bunt, puts the ball in play, and uses the entire field."

One of the great debates of the 1941 season is which accomplishment was greater: Williams's .406 or DiMaggio's 56-game streak? While DiMaggio's streak hasn't been broken or even threatened through 2015, Williams's .406 average marked prolonged excellence throughout the 154-game schedule. After the season, DiMaggio was the one named AL MVP, as he received 15 first-place votes to Williams's eight. While Williams had the overall more dominant offensive season, DiMaggio's Yankees were the AL champs, thus clinching the vote for DiMaggio.

After 1941, Williams went on to become arguably the greatest hitter who ever lived. Despite the fact that he missed three years to World War II, was sidelined for most of 1952 and 1953 for the Korean War, and only played a combined 187 games in 1950 and 1955, Williams led the AL in batting six times, home runs and RBIs four times each, and runs six times. He hit 521 career homers and finished with a .344 career average. He was an All-Star in every year that he played except his rookie year (he did end up fourth in the MVP voting that year) and received MVP votes in each of his 18 seasons, including 1953, when he played just 37 games.

However, of all the accomplishments Williams had on the field, the one that best embodies his boldness and confidence happened on September 28, 1941, when he opted to earn his .400 batting average by playing instead of watching it happen from the sidelines.

WALTER JOHNSON: CLOSING THE 400 CLUB

April 27, 1926

On April 27, 1926, Walter Johnson took the mound for the 755th time in his big-league career. At the time, the 38-year-old was showing no signs of slowing down, as the previous two seasons he combined for a record of 43–14. Modern-day fans have become accustomed to veteran star pitchers sputtering toward 300 wins, some hanging on well past their days of effective pitching to accomplish the feat. That wasn't the case with Johnson. On that day, Johnson wasn't chasing after the magical 300; he had blown by that total nearly six years earlier, on May 14, 1920. In this game against the Boston Red Sox, Johnson was ready to become the second pitcher to reach 400 wins.

Johnson's place in baseball history is reserved among the very best of all time. One of the first great fastball pitchers, batters at the time hadn't encountered anyone like Johnson. In an era where pitchers threw to contact and didn't strike out many batters, Johnson came at hitters with an intimidating sidearm delivery and was said to have possessed a fastball that topped 90 miles per hour at a minimum. As a comparison, Johnson's contemporary, Cy Young, accumulated 2,803 career strikeouts in 7,356 innings pitched. It took Johnson just 4,469 innings to reach that total.

Johnson got his start with the Washington Senators in 1907, when he was signed as a 19-year-old out of the Idaho State League. It took Johnson a few years to get settled in the major leagues, as he went 32–48 in his first three big-league seasons, averaging just fewer than 5½ strikeouts per nine innings; however, during the next four seasons as Johnson reached his prime, he won an incredible 119 games, while losing just 49. Despite the slow start to his career, Johnson's lifetime ERA to that point was an astonishing 1.60 in 273 games. Just as impressive was that of the 230 games he started, he completed 198 of them.

Johnson's best season came in 1913, as a 25-year-old, when he went 36–7 for the Senators, with a 1.14 ERA. He won the AL MVP that year over Shoeless Joe Jackson, after leading the Senators to a 90–64 record. Johnson topped the 20-win mark in each of the next six seasons to make it 10 straight years in which he topped 20 wins. By age 31, he had won 297 major-league games and, if he could hold on long enough, was thought to have a chance at Young's record of 511 wins. Johnson actually far outdistanced Young's win total by the age of 31, as his 297 topped Young's 241 easily.

However, in 1920, Johnson began a four-year stretch where he failed to top 17 wins in any season. His overall record from 1920 to 1923 was just 57–52, and while he had easily eclipsed the 300-win mark, it seemed that 500 might be out of the question. Johnson's rebound years in '24 and '25 gave him 397 wins by the age of 37, compared to Young's 405. While he was now behind Young, it was just a matter of Johnson's ability to stay effective into his 40s.

Before Johnson could think about 500, however, he had to get to 400. He got win number 398 on an Opening Day, 1–0 shutout in 1926 over the Philadelphia A's and recorded his 399th against the A's 10 days later. In his next start, Johnson was set to take on the Red Sox in search of win number 400.

Washington was off to a good start that year and stood at 8–6 on April 27. They were in third place, just two games behind the Yankees, who fielded basically the same lineup as their "Murderers' Row" team of 1927. The Red Sox didn't have much star power in the post–Babe Ruth era and would go on to be the worst team in the majors in 1926. The Senators' offense was led by Hall of Famers Sam Rice and Goose Goslin. Goslin, a 25-year-old outfielder at the time, enjoyed a great season in which he hit .354, with 17 home runs and 108 RBIs. Although Babe Ruth hit 30 more home runs than Goslin in '26, his total of 17 was good for fourth in the American League.

The Senators finally broke through against Tony Welzer in the bottom of the third. Washington plated five runs in the half inning to stake Johnson to a 5–1 lead. From that point onward, the dominant righty would not look back. Washington eventually added four more runs in the sixth to take an easy 9–1 victory from the Sox for Johnson's 400th.

After some early bumps in the game, Johnson settled in and continued his dominant stretch of pitching. He hurled a complete game four-hitter and struck out three batters along the way. The Senators pounded out 13 hits and were led by Goslin, who went 3-for-5 with two runs and an RBI. Third baseman Ossie Bluege, who went on to play 18 years for Washington, had the game's only home run.

The win moved Johnson's record on the early season to 3–1, with his only loss coming at the hands of the Yankees in an 18–5 drubbing. In that game, Johnson lasted just three innings, and Ruth and Lou Gehrig combined to go 7-for-10 with nine runs scored and eight RBIs. Johnson won his next three starts and stood at 6–1 after the season's first month of games; however, the Big Train began to show his age soon thereafter, as he lost seven of his next eight starts.

That stretch would become the beginning of the end for Johnson, and it became apparent that he was not going to be able to pitch into his mid-40s like Young to chase 500 wins. Johnson ended the 1926 season with a 15–16 record, just the second time since 1906 that he had a losing record in a full season of starts. Johnson returned for the 1927 season but continued his steep decline, as he started just 18 games, while posting a 5–6 record. His last major-league win came against the White Sox in a July 28 complete game 12–2 win. In his final career start, Johnson was shelled for five earned runs on nine hits in a game the Senators went on to win 10–7 against the Browns.

The sharp end of Johnson's career notwithstanding, the righty was truly the dominant pitcher in the majors during the 1910s and '20s. By the time he finished his career, his final record stood at 417–279, and he had accumulated 3,509 strikeouts. Johnson was so far ahead of his time that no pitcher surpassed the 3,000-strikeout total until Bob Gibson in 1974. Although Gibson passed

3,000 strikeouts, he could not catch Johnson, whose record stood for 55 years, until it was broken by Nolan Ryan in 1983.

Johnson's accomplishments far surpassed any of his contemporaries, as he topped 20 wins 12 times and 30 wins twice, and pitched in 64 games that ended with a final score of 1–0 (he went 38–26 in those games). As of 2015, Johnson still held the American League record for consecutive scoreless innings, with 55.2, and also had a streak in 1918, in which he hurled 40 consecutive scoreless innings. He is the only pitcher to have multiple scoreless inning streaks of 40 innings or more. Johnson's 110 shutouts are an all-time major-league record, 20 more than his closest competitor, Pete Alexander. With the way the game has changed throughout the years, it is possible that he will be the last pitcher to surpass 100 shutouts, and on April 27, 1926, he probably became the last pitcher to reach the 400-win milestone.

ROBERTO CLEMENTE: ENDING ON 3,000

September 30, 1972

September 30, 1972, was a historic night at Three Rivers Stadium in Pittsburgh. Tragically, it was a night that would grow even bigger in proportion three months later. On the night of September 30, Roberto Clemente became the 11th player in Major League Baseball history to record his 3,000th career hit. Three months later, he was dead.

Clemente's story is well known. He was scouted playing in the Puerto Rican Professional Baseball League and signed by the Brooklyn Dodgers. He reported to their AAA team right away but wasn't getting much playing time. On the advice of scout Clyde Sukeforth, the Pirates selected Clemente in the Rule 5 Draft in 1954, and the rest is history.

Clemente played 18 seasons in the bigs and was a 12-time All-Star. He finished in the top 10 in MVP voting eight times, winning the honor in 1966. In addition, Clemente was a tremendous defensive outfielder with one of the best arms in baseball history. The right fielder won the Gold Glove Award 12 years in a row.

"I grew up in Butler, Pennsylvania, which is 30 miles north of Pittsburgh," said John Stuper, who pitched 111 games in the majors in the '80s and was on the 1982 World Series champion Cardinals. "I got to see Roberto Clemente in his prime. I thought then and still think now that he was the greatest player I have ever seen. A throwing arm that no one, past or present, could rival. He played hard; played the right way. Power, speed . . . he had it all."

Juan Padilla, who pitched for the Yankees and Mets in 2004 and 2005, respectively, and is a native of Puerto Rico, mentioned how much Clemente meant to his fellow countrymen: "I never got to see Clemente play in person, as he died before I was born, but my dad told me many stories about him," said Padilla. "I look up to him as a role model and still try to keep the Puerto Rico name high in the baseball world."

As Clemente maintained his greatness throughout a long period of time, it became apparent that he was likely to eventually join one of the most elite clubs in MLB history: the 3,000-hit club. To that point, only 10 players had reached that milestone. In July 1971, Clemente gave an on-camera interview in which he was asked about the pursuit of his 3,000th hit. Clemente gave a somewhat cryptic response: "You never know because God tells you how long you'll be here," said the Hall of Famer. "You never know what can happen tomorrow."

But Clemente did estimate that "if everything went well" he could reach the goal by the 1972 All-Star break. Things did not go well for Clemente, however, as he battled injuries from that point onward, pushing his pursuit to the late stages of the 1972 season. He enjoyed a hot streak from mid-May to mid-June but cooled off considerably when his broken-down body allowed him to play just 23 games in July and August.

Clemente entered the final month of the regular season needing 30 hits to reach 3,000. In July and August, he had just 19. May was the only month in 1972 that Clemente topped 30 hits; however, he would go on to hit .330 in September, as the Pirates ran away with the NL East. He had 29 hits coming into a three-game series against the New York Mets and needed just one hit in the final five games of the season to reach the milestone.

On the opening night of the series, he faced off against Mets ace Tom Seaver. The future Hall of Famer was 28 years old and just entering the peak of his career. Clemente went 0-for-4 as Seaver hurled a two-hit shutout. Clemente did hit a ball up the middle that was mishandled by Mets second baseman Ken Boswell, but the play was ruled an error. Clemente would have to give it another shot on September 30.

That Saturday afternoon, 13,000 fans showed up to Three Rivers Stadium (about half of the previous night's total) to see if Clemente could get number 3,000. Jon Matlack and Dock Ellis faced off in an otherwise meaningless game. Clemente took his usual spot batting third and played right for the Pirates that day.

In his first at-bat, Clemente struck out. Matlack and Ellis hooked up in a pitchers' duel and had allowed just one hit combined through the first 3½ innings. Clemente led off the bottom of the fourth, looking for hit number 3,000 and hoping to start a Pirates rally. He accomplished both.

Clemente drilled a Matlack offering deep into the left-center gap for a no-doubt double to send the Three Rivers crowd to its feet. As had been his demeanor, Clemente humbly acknowledged the standing ovation with a tip of his cap.

He became the third active player to notch 3,000 hits. Hank Aaron and Willie Mays were both active at the time, and each recorded hit number 3,000 in 1970. Stan Musial reached the milestone in 1958, and before that, the club featured such legends as Cap Anson, Ty Cobb, Tris Speaker, and Honus Wagner. Mays was in the visiting Mets dugout to see Clemente's hit firsthand, as he was playing out the end of his career in New York. Mays came out of the Mets dugout between innings to personally offer his congratulations.

After the ovation, there was still a game to be played. Manny Sanguillén drove home Clemente with the game's first run, and a triple by shortstop Jackie Hernandez drove home Sanguillén and Richie Zisk to make it 3–0. After Dock Ellis got the side in order in the top of the fifth, Clemente was due up third to bat in the bottom of the fifth; however, the star chose to remove himself from the game to rest for what was going to be a tough playoff series against the Reds.

With two outs and nobody on, manager Bill Virdon elected to send future Hall of Famer Bill Mazeroski up to pinch-hit for Clemente. The move was significant because Mazeroski had been Clemente's teammate for the previous 16 seasons and was playing in the final season of his career. Mazeroski popped up for the third out and would record just four more hitless at-bats in '72 as his career wound down.

The Pirates tacked on two unearned runs in the bottom of the sixth on an error by Mets shortstop Jim Fregosi, and Ellis gave way to Bob Johnson, who came on to close out the 5–0 shutout win. Clemente would not get another regular-season at-bat in his career and appeared in just one of the Pirates' final three games as a defensive replacement.

The Pirates took on the Reds for the right to go to the World Series in an epic five-game playoff series in 1972. They took a 3–2 lead to the ninth in a deciding fifth game, but a Johnny Bench home run and a wild pitch with two outs allowed George Foster to send the Reds to the World Series. Clemente went 1-for-3 that game and hit .235 for the series.

Despite his physical breakdown and postseason slump, Clemente planned on returning for the 1973 season; however, the 38-year-old would never make it that far. A major earthquake struck Nicaragua on December 23, killing 5,000 people and leaving an estimated 250,000 homeless. Clemente organized a personal relief effort, and aid poured in from throughout the world. But reports surfaced that Nicaraguan dictator Anastasio Somoza was misusing and stealing relief supplies. Clemente decided to personally accompany the fourth flight of his mission to Nicaragua to see that the supplies went to those in need. The plane crashed shortly after takeoff on New Year's Eve, and Clemente's body was never found.

In late September each year, the baseball season winds down. There is a palpable emptiness as the final games tick off the calendar. Nostalgia runs deep as many veterans take the final at-bats of their careers. On the night of September 30, the night of his 3,000th hit, Clemente received a standing ovation from his hometown crowd. While nobody knew it at the time, it ended up being the perfect sendoff for one of the greatest to ever play the game.

LOU GEHRIG: 5,084 DAYS

April 20, 1939

Part of the charm of baseball is that it is always there. From spring training to Opening Day, through the All-Star break and into the postseason, baseball provides a reliable backdrop that takes a fan from early spring through the summer and into the fall. The local announcers, who seem to last for a generation, have a voice as familiar as an old family member, and the players return every year like old friends. Of course there's change from year to year, especially with free agency and financial standing, but it's always familiar and reliable.

During the pre–World War II era, one of the reliable sure things about baseball was that when Opening Day came (or any game for that matter), Lou Gehrig would be batting fourth and playing first base for the Yankees. April 20, 1939, was no different, as Gehrig led his Yanks against the Red Sox on Opening Day, but shockingly it would be the last Opening Day Gehrig would play.

Coming into 1939, Gehrig was 36 years old. He was on the downside of his career but still remained productive. In '38, he hit 29 homers, with 114 RBIs, off from his peak for sure, but still more productive than most players. He reported a decrease in his power and stamina as the season went on, but what may have been early signs of the disease that now bears his name could have been dismissed as the ailments of an aging veteran. In the spring of 1939, Gehrig's game was way off. He struggled on the field and on the bases, and didn't hit a homer all spring. It wasn't just his age showing; there was a visible lack of coordination, strength, and basic motor skills.

However, when Opening Day came, Gehrig was there as expected. For the 2,123rd game and the 14th straight Opening Day, Gehrig was on the field in active duty, despite concerns that something was seriously wrong.

Gehrig's final Opening Day game was historic for other reasons, too. Someone would be hard-pressed to find a regular-season game that featured more baseball immortals on the field at the same time. Gehrig was in the lineup, generally considered the greatest first baseman ever. Joe DiMaggio roamed center field that day for the Yanks and batted cleanup. The Yankees' catcher was Bill Dickey, who was considered one of the top catchers in baseball history by the end of his career. The Yankees lineup was so good their eighth hitter, Joe Gordon, is a Hall of Famer.

The Red Sox lineup was about equal to the Yankees. The centerpiece of the lineup was Jimmie Foxx, who at the time had 429 career homers, behind only Babe Ruth and Gehrig. Hall of Fame player-manager Joe Cronin batted cleanup for the Sox, and like the Yanks, the bottom of the Boston lineup featured a Hall of Famer in seventh-place hitter Bobby Doerr.

But as notable as this game is for its legendary lineups and for being one of Gehrig's final games, there is more historical significance: The game marked the major-league debut of a highly touted 20-year-old rookie named Ted Williams. This would be the only game that ever featured both Williams and Gehrig.

For good measure, the pitching matchup was Red Ruffing versus Lefty Grove, two Hall of Famers who combined to win 573 games in their careers. Ten of the 18 starters were eventual Hall of Famers, and four others were All-Stars.

The Thursday night game took place on the season's second day but was the opener for both the Yanks and Sox. There were 30,278 fans at Yankee Stadium to see the top two teams in the AL from the previous year battle it out. The last time the Yanks were seen on the field, they were finishing off the Cubs in a four-game sweep to take home their seventh World Series title on October 9, 1938, a game won by Ruffing.

This game would be one of the more extreme tests of the old adage "good pitching beats good hitting." The saying was ramped up a bit, as it would be immortal pitching against legendary hitting. On this day, despite the firepower and depth in both lineups, the saying held true.

The first inning went by scoreless, and Ruffing pitched out of a jam in the top of the second to keep the game that way. The top of the second included the first career at-bat of Williams, which ended in a strikeout. The Yanks got on the board first when Dickey cracked a solo homer to make it 1–0. Dickey batted fifth in the lineup and was the third hitter in the lethal combination of DiMaggio–Gehrig–Dickey.

The game stayed scoreless until the fifth, when the Yankees would tack on another run against Grove after Jake Powell drove home Red Rolfe with an error by Foxx, making the run unearned. Ruffing pitched in and out of trouble the rest of the way but always got through the vaunted Sox lineup to preserve the 2–0 win.

With all the legends in the lineup, it was Powell, one of the few players in either starting lineup to never be an All-Star, who had the only three-hit game. DiMaggio ended 1-for-2 with two walks, and Dickey was 2-for-3 with the key solo homer. Gehrig, still not feeling himself, hit into two double plays, went 0-for-4, and committed an error.

For the Sox, their fearsome 3–4 combination of Foxx and Cronin went 0-for-8. Even given all the stars in the Sox lineup, it was Joe Vosmik who had the only multihit game, as the left fielder was 2-for-4 with a double. Williams struck out in his first two at-bats but finally broke through against Ruffing with a double for his first career hit.

While the Yankees' win over the Red Sox made news in New York, the real headline was the continued disintegration of Gehrig. His struggles in the spring continued to Opening Day, as again he just didn't seem the man they called the Iron Horse. Gehrig was out there the next day for consecutive game number 2,124 and had a brief resurgence, going 1-for-2 with a run and two walks.

Gehrig then went 0-for-11 and looked worse with each passing day. Manager Joe McCarthy, despite pressure from fans and the media, kept putting Gehrig's name in the lineup right underneath DiMaggio, hoping that one day Gehrig would break through. It never happened.

The Yankees played eight total games in April, and as the month ended, Gehrig was 4-for-28 for a .143 average. In May, Gehrig finally relented and approached McCarthy to ask to be taken out of the lineup. McCarthy approved the decision and inserted Babe Dahlgren. It marked the first time since May 31, 1925, that Lou Gehrig wouldn't appear in a game for the Yankees, a span of 2,130 games in 13 years, 11 months, and two days—5,084 days.

In their first game in nearly 14 years without Gehrig, the Yankees beat the Tigers 22–2. Dahlgren went 2-for-5 with two runs, two RBIs, and a home run. It would have been easy for McCarthy to insert Gehrig, just to keep the streak going, but he didn't. It was as if both men knew that what was going on with Gehrig was much bigger than the game or the streak.

As Gehrig's coordination deteriorated rapidly, he and his wife Eleanor sought answers. Finally, Gehrig went through six days of extensive testing at the Mayo Clinic in Rochester, Minnesota. He was diagnosed with amyotrophic lateral sclerosis on his 36th birthday, June 19, just two months after he was on the field for Opening Day.

Within two days, the Yankees announced they would hold "Lou Gehrig Appreciation Day" on July 4 that year and host a ceremony between games of a doubleheader versus the Washington Senators. The ceremony featured former teammates, dignitaries, and a 44-year-old Babe Ruth, who also spoke for a brief time. The ceremony itself is best remembered for Gehrig's "Luckiest Man on the Face of the Earth" speech.

Needless to say, emotions ran high that day, as it became widely reported that Gehrig's condition had no cure and that he was about to face horrific deterioration. McCarthy broke down giving a speech, and when the Yankee Stadium crowd gave Gehrig a standing ovation, he broke down as well. Yankees personnel adorned Gehrig with gifts, many of which he didn't have the strength to hold, and in a final gesture the Yankees retired Gehrig's number 4, never to be worn again. It was the first number retired in baseball history.

In October 1939, the Yankees took home another World Series championship, this time in a sweep of the Reds. In December of that year, knowing full well what Gehrig's future held, Major League Baseball waived the waiting period for Hall of Fame induction and put Gehrig on the ballot. He was elected unanimously.

Lou Gehrig died on June 2, 1941, exactly 16 years after he replaced Wally Pipp in the Yankees lineup. His death was mourned by the city of New York and throughout the country. Flags were flown at half-mast, and upon hearing news of Gehrig's death, Babe Ruth went to Gehrig's home to console his family.

From the mid-'20s until the end of the '30s, Lou Gehrig was always there. He was reliable, consistent, dynamic, and seemingly built of iron. For a decade and a half, Gehrig playing first for the Yanks was a sure thing.

The record stood as one of baseball's "unbreakable" records for 56 years, until Cal Ripken improbably passed Gehrig's mark on September 6, 1995. Ripken's accomplishment may have been more difficult, as he surpassed Gehrig while playing the physically demanding position of shortstop for most of the streak. According to Ripken's former teammate and fellow shortstop Kelly Paris, Ripken's streak was even more impressive when witnessed in person: "You had to be there to really appreciate it," said Paris. "He played with injuries, broken bones; it was just incredible. Day in and day out, he was just a warrior."

Umpire Ted Barrett saw Ripken's accomplishments from a different perspective.

"During the streak, Ripken was all business," said Barrett, who began his service in 1994.

> He didn't interact too much while the streak was active, he just focused on playing. Once the streak was over though, we saw a different person. He seemed to be enjoying himself more and was much more talkative in games. He's a genuine nice person, and it was good to see him enjoying the game and his accomplishments.

Stanley Jefferson played behind Ripken in the Orioles outfield in 1989 and 1990, and marveled at the way Ripken played and his carefree nature as a teammate: "Cal Jr. was just the best, he was the coolest dude," started Jefferson. "He had this incredible streak going and he'd come into the clubhouse and wrestle around with the guys. I'd be like, 'Come on Cal, go sit and relax over there,' but he wanted to just be one of the guys. What he did was just awesome." Jefferson continued about learning to manage your health through a season:

> I thought Cal's streak was amazing because I couldn't keep myself on the field. I realized in hindsight that because it's a marathon, you have to pace yourself. I played with maximum effort guys like Lenny Dykstra and Gregg Jefferies and their careers were cut short because of the way they played. Mike Cubbage and Sam Perlozzo talked to me about what percentage I felt health-wise some days. There are days where you only feel about 80 percent. On those days maybe you don't crash into the wall or go all out down the line on a groundout. On the days you're feeling 100 percent, that's when you go all out. That's the way to pace yourself for the marathon.

Jeff Ballard, Ripken's teammate in Baltimore for seven years, echoed those statements: "Cal Ripken was the shortstop for every single pitch I threw as a Baltimore Oriole," said Ballard, who pitched 773 innings for the O's. "Aside from his consecutive games streak, Ripken set the record for consecutive innings played. I believe it was somewhere up around 10,000 innings straight. He also took batting practice every day, took extra grounders. He was out there trying to make himself better every day."

Ballard continued,

> Finally, on the last day of the 1987 season, Cal's father took him out of the game for a pinch-hitter to put an end to the innings streak. It took a lot of pressure off of Cal to not have to worry about the innings streak and the games streak. Cal's just awesome. He's the role model I use whenever I'm talking to kids. He never used his celebrity as an advantage and didn't live in a glass house. He didn't try to protect his streak, he just went out and played every day, no matter how much he may have been tired or hurting.

The same could be said of Gehrig.

In a game that featured the greatest hitter of all time in Williams, the immortal DiMaggio, 573 wins combined between Grove and Ruffing, two Hall of Fame managers in McCarthy and Cronin, and the only other slugger of the era who could match Ruth, Jimmie Foxx, there stood Lou Gehrig. Referred to in his *New York Times* obituary as being "regarded by some observers as the greatest player to ever grace the diamond," Gehrig left a legacy of dignity, toughness, grace, and consistency. Like the game of baseball itself, Lou Gehrig's legacy will always endure.

• $\mathcal{3}$ •

Masterful on the Mound

SANDY KOUFAX: THE DAWN OF THE PHENOM

August 27, 1955

Sometimes baseball fans don't know they're watching history unfold. When Roger Maris cracked a homer off of Paul Foytack on April 26, 1961, nobody could imagine they were seeing the start of a trek to 61 homers that year. If you were at Yankee Stadium on May 15, 1941, and you saw Joe DiMaggio go 1-for-4 against Eddie Smith, you wouldn't know you were at the start of his 56-game hitting streak. Sometimes it can take years to appreciate what you witness. That was the case for the 7,204 fans in attendance at Ebbets Field on August 27, 1955, when they saw a 19-year-old lefty named Sandy Koufax earn his first major-league win.

While his talent was always undeniable as a teenager, Koufax wasn't a highly accomplished player as he grew up in Brooklyn, New York. He attended the University of Cincinnati, where he was given the chance to be an unrecruited pitcher. His big strikeout numbers (51 in 30 innings) were enough to draw the attention of professional scouts. Koufax wowed in individual workouts for the Giants and Pirates, but the Dodgers scheduled a tryout for the lefty as well. He would never pass up the chance to play for his neighborhood team and ended up signing with the Dodgers for $6,000, with a $14,000 signing bonus.

Because of the high value of the contract, the Dodgers would have no choice but to put the lefty on the major-league roster immediately and keep him there for two seasons, as per the "bonus baby" rule. The rule simply stated that if an initial contract exceeded $4,000, the team was bound to keep that player on their major-league roster for two seasons. In the era before the draft, this rule was in place to keep richer teams from going out and signing an excessive number of players and just stashing them away in their farm system.

In 1955, the Dodgers were just two years removed from losing to the Yankees in the 1953 World Series and anticipated being able to contend again. They were led by Hall of Famers Roy Campanella, Duke Snider, and Jackie Robinson, and they were a veteran team that had been together for years. For a 19-year-old to be thrust into the spotlight on one of the signature clubs in the majors was asking a lot of the young Koufax; however, the Dodgers had no choice.

The Dodgers were cruising along in the National League and enjoyed an 11-game lead over the Milwaukee Braves on August 27. They were even four games ahead of the Yankees for the best record in baseball. For nearly the first three months of the year, Koufax never entered a game and worked with his coaches on making a big jump to the top of the baseball world. On June 24, with the Dodgers losing 7–1 to the Braves in the fifth inning, they gave Koufax his first taste of the majors.

Koufax gave up a single to Johnny Logan and fielded a bunt by Eddie Mathews but threw the ball into center field and walked Hank Aaron in his auspicious start. He did, however, pitch out of the jam and go two innings without giving up a run. They later let him mop up the ninth inning of a 6–1 loss to the Giants. He loaded the bases again but pitched out of the jam with his ERA still spotless.

Finally, on July 6, the Dodgers needed a pitcher for the second game of a doubleheader. Already up 12½ games on the Braves, they figured they had little to lose by giving Koufax his first start. He pitched in and out of trouble again in 4.2 innings, walking eight batters and giving up three hits, but allowing just one run. Manager Walter Alston returned Koufax to the bullpen but continued to give him innings in relief during Dodgers losses. Alston decided to give Koufax another chance at starting on August 27, after putting up impressive numbers. He pitched 11 innings overall and had an ERA of 2.31. The only real concern was the 12 walks he posted as well.

The Dodgers were up against the Cincinnati Reds on August 27, a Saturday afternoon, and the team had surprisingly lost the first three games of the four-game series to the .500 ball club. The Reds featured Ted Kluszewski and Wally Post in their lineup, both of whom would top 40 homers in 1955, but they were far from a powerhouse team.

Koufax took to the mound to start the game and got through the top of the Reds order easily, allowing just a harmless single to Kluszewski. Along the way, he was able to strike out All-Star catcher Smokey Burgess. The Dodgers staked Koufax to an early lead when they jumped on Art Fowler for three quick runs in the first. Jim Gilliam doubled to right to lead off the game, and

Snider drew a walk. Campanella hit a sacrifice fly to score the first run, and Carl Furillo followed with a homer to make it 3–0.

From that point onward, Koufax took the lead and ran with it. He retired the side in the second, striking out two Reds, and repeated the feat in the third inning. Through three, Koufax tallied five strikeouts, allowed one hit, and, most importantly, didn't walk a batter. The Dodgers and Koufax cruised from there. Jackie Robinson hit a two-run homer in the bottom of the seventh to give Koufax a 7–0 lead. With the way Koufax was pitching, the game was clearly in hand, and the only question that remained was whether the Reds could even get another hit against the lefty.

Through seven innings, Koufax had allowed just the first-inning ground-ball single by Kluszewski and had a record 11 strikeouts. Koufax didn't fade in the late August Cincinnati heat; if anything, he got stronger.

In the eighth, Koufax sat down the side in order, including strikeout victims number 12 and 13 in the form of Burgess and Kluszewski. Having thrown 123 pitches, Alston left Koufax in to finish his gem. He got Post to ground out leading off the ninth and then struck out Bell for the fourth time of the day. With one out to go, Koufax allowed his second hit of the game, a double to left by Sam Mele. He then got a first-pitch popup from Rocky Bridges to fall in the glove of Pee Wee Reese for the final out of an incredible performance.

That day, Koufax's line read like that of a seasoned All-Star: 9 innings, 2 hits, and 14 strikeouts. He walked five batters, but that was lower than what he had been averaging in 1955. Between Kluszewski's first-inning single and Mele's ninth-inning double, Koufax faced 30 batters. He struck out 13 of them without allowing a hit. Knowing full well what the neighborhood legend Koufax was capable of, Dodgers fans had to be expecting that this would be the start of something incredible. They were right, in a way.

The next two seasons were the final seasons for the Dodgers in Brooklyn. Koufax went an unremarkable 7–8, with a 4.25 ERA. The move to Los Angeles didn't help the lefty at first, as he went 27–30, with a 4.14 ERA, in his first three seasons in which he was finally given the role as a full-time starting pitcher.

As the 1961 season started, the afternoon of August 27, 1955, seemed like ages ago in the career of the promising Koufax. Fans who were at Ebbets Field that day probably remembered the outing as a glimpse of "what might have been" for a lefty with great stuff who never materialized; however, all of that changed in the '61 season, which began a six-year stretch that many consider to be the most dominating in the career of any pitcher. Koufax went 129–47, averaging 22 wins a season, with an ERA of 2.19. He topped the 300-strikeout mark three times and recorded three seasons with an ERA under 2.00.

It all came crashing down for Koufax after the 1966 season. After pitching 658 innings in the '65 and '66 campaigns, Koufax developed arthritis in his left arm, and after what many consider his best season (27–9, 1.73 ERA, 317 strikeouts, plus his third Cy Young Award), he was forced to retire abruptly.

Sandy Koufax is often described as a shooting star across the night sky, so brilliant to see, but so quick to burn out. His career has left people wondering what his lifetime numbers could have been if he was able to stay healthy or if he had enjoyed immediate success in the bigs. On the afternoon of August 27, 1955, fans witnessed one of the greatest pitching performances from one of the best pitchers in Major League Baseball history. It just took them about a decade to realize it.

DAVE STIEB: NO MORE CLOSE CALLS

September 2, 1990

The baseball gods reached down and touched Dave Stieb on September 2, 1990, and this time it wasn't a cruel joke. The simple story is that Stieb channeled all of his greatness for one nine-inning stretch as he spun a no-hitter against the Cleveland Indians. Of note was that this was the first no-hitter in Blue Jays history, and it was the ninth no-hitter of the season in what became known as the "Year of the No-Hitter."

What made this no-hitter more special was how tantalizingly close Stieb had come so many times before. Previously, Stieb had four no-hitters broken up in the ninth inning, including a potential perfect game on August 4, 1990. He threw five one-hitters during his career.

Stieb's first glancing blow at baseball history came on August 24, 1985. Stieb's opponent that night was the White Sox, who had Tom Seaver on the mound. Ironically, before Stieb came along, Seaver was known as the tough-luck pitcher when it came to near no-hitters. Seaver had no-nos broken up in the ninth inning on three separate occasions before finally hurling one on June 16, 1978.

On the night of August 24, Stieb was ripping through the White Sox lineup with ease. Rudy Law, Chicago's leadoff batter, put an end to the drama when he hit a high-outside fastball out of the park for a leadoff homer in the ninth. Law would hit just 18 homers in his seven-year career. After the game, it was learned that Stieb was pitching through elbow pain and admitted he had nothing left after about the sixth inning.

The next heartbreak came on September 24, 1988. Stieb was taking on an Indians team that was 16 games out of first place as the season wore down.

He carried his no-hitter into the ninth when he got Andy Allanson on a strike-out and Willie Upshaw on an easy grounder to second. Julio Franco was the final obstacle, and Stieb got ahead on Cleveland's All-Star, 1–2. Franco fouled off three straight pitches before hitting what looked to be a routine grounder to Blue Jays second baseman Manny Lee. The ball appeared to hit the seam between the infield grass and dirt cutout, and shot directly over Lee's head for a bad-hop single.

Remarkably, Stieb found himself in the same position in his very next start. On September 30, Stieb mowed through the Orioles lineup, having faced the minimum number of batters through 8.2 innings. He hit Baltimore's leadoff hitter, Joe Orsulak, with a pitch leading off the fourth but got Pete Stanicek to ground into a double play on the next pitch.

Facing a lineup that featured six batters who were hitting .235 or lower, Stieb was not threatened as the Jays built a 4–0 lead. He got rookie Brady Anderson to ground out to lead off the ninth and handled Jeff Stone's come-backer himself. Playing with an expanded September roster, O's manager Frank Robinson sent up Jim Traber to pinch-hit. A .222 hitter that season, Traber looped a 2–2 pitch over a leaping Fred McGriff for a soft single to right. Traber would be out of baseball after just one more season.

Growing slightly more frustrated by this habit, Stieb threw his head back and stared at the Toronto night sky in exasperation. It would be Stieb's last win at Exhibition Stadium and the last complete game pitched there, as the Jays moved to the SkyDome in 1989. A little more than 10 months later, Stieb found the form again and took perfection into the ninth against the Yankees in front of nearly 50,000 fans on a Friday night at the SkyDome.

In a lineup featuring such All-Stars as Don Mattingly, Steve Sax, and former teammate Jesse Barfield, a young Roberto Kelly spelled doom for Stieb's bid for perfection. After the first inning, only Sax and Mattingly would hit balls out of the infield, as Stieb was masterful in retiring the first 26 batters of the game, 11 of which came on strikeouts.

Kelly was in his first season as the full-time center fielder and was the final obstacle between Stieb and perfection. He had already struck him out twice that night. Yankees manager Dallas Green pinch-hit for the first two batters in the ninth, but after Hal Morris and Ken Phelps each struck out, Green decided to stick with Kelly.

To that point, only nine perfect games had been pitched in modern base-ball history. Stieb threw a first-pitch curve to Kelly, which home plate umpire Terry Cooney ruled just inside. He missed again with another inside curve. Catcher Ernie Whitt, who had also been the catcher in the White Sox and Indians games, called for a third curve, but this one hung and Kelly drove the ball to left for a two-out double. "Holy cow he broke it up with two outs!

I don't believe it," exclaimed Hall of Fame announcer Phil Rizzuto as Stieb removed his cap, rubbed his head three times, and got himself back on the bump. Sax would follow with a single before Stieb retired Luis Polonia on a groundout to end the game.

Which takes us to September 2, 1990. Stieb faced off against the struggling Indians, who were 17 games out of first and again playing out the season. Stieb had little trouble with the young Indians lineup and took a no-hitter to the ninth for the fourth time in about two years.

Stieb got through pinch-hitters Chris James and Candy Maldonado with a fly ball and a strikeout, and again stood one out from history. Alex Cole walked on four pitches to bring up Jerry Browne. The scrappy second baseman with good speed was in the middle of a productive career and would not be an easy out. Stieb threw a 1–1 curveball and got Browne to hit a fly ball directly at Junior Felix in right field. Felix secured the out, pumped his fist, and began his sprint toward the pitcher's mound.

Stieb exhibited relief, as he bent over with his face in his pitching hand. It seemed as if he was holding his breath for the entire game, or at least for the ninth inning. The relief on Stieb's face was belied by the joy on his teammates' faces, as he had finally accomplished the feat.

For as much as the no-hitter is celebrated as an incredible accomplishment by a pitcher, it really is a team accomplishment. The defense obviously has to make plays behind the pitcher, the offensive support must be there, and the role of the catcher cannot be understated.

Matt Walbeck caught for 11 years in the majors and was the starting catcher for the Twins on April 27, 1994, when Scott Erickson threw the first no-hitter in the history of the hitter-friendly Metrodome.

"It was my rookie year and something I had never been a part of before on any level," said Walbeck, who went on to discuss the mind-set of a catcher during a potential no-hitter. "Once you get to the fifth or sixth inning you start to become aware that you have a chance. Then in the dugout you don't ever sit next to [the pitcher], don't ever talk about it. You just let the game play out." Incidentally, Walbeck was in the park for the only other no-hitter in Metrodome history. He was with the Angels in 1999, and there as a visitor when Eric Milton accomplished the feat.

Because each of the five masterful performances Stieb pitched happened in such a short period of time, the cast of characters was quite familiar. Tony Fernandez was the shortstop in all five games. Kelly Gruber and George Bell were in the lineup for four of them. Pat Borders was his catcher on September 2, and was also the catcher when his no-hitter was broken up against Baltimore. Cory Snyder was the only Indian to be in the lineup for the no-hitter and on September 24, 1988, for the Franco bad-hop game.

Stieb threw eight terrific innings in the start after his no-hitter to raise his record to 18–5, as Toronto rode a 12–2 streak to a one-game lead with 12 games left. The Jays, however, dropped eight of their next 12 games and finished the season two games behind the Red Sox in the AL East.

Stieb enjoyed one of the finest careers of anyone in Blue Jays history and retired as Toronto's all-time leader in almost every pitching category. In 15 years with the Blue Jays, he finished with 175 wins and, behind Jack Morris, was the second most-wins pitcher in the majors during the '80s. "Dave was talented, the best we had," said Barry Bonnell, who was Stieb's teammate from 1980 to 1983. "He had a great slider and a great change. He expected excellence on defense, and he usually got it."

After appearing in four games for the White Sox in 1993, Stieb was out of baseball before attempting a comeback for the Jays in 1998. He appeared in 19 games, winning one and saving two, before finally calling it a career.

Columnist Max Lerner once wrote, "Men are most deeply moved not by the reaching of the goal but by the grandness of the effort involved in getting there—or failing to get there." There is no doubt that Stieb was moved not only in his failures at reaching this pinnacle, but also on September 2, 1990, when he finally got there.

TOM SEAVER: THE FRANCHISE'S BEST

April 22, 1970

In the pitching-rich era of the late '60s and early '70s, the names at the top of the leaderboard contained some of the best hurlers in the game's history, and many were just getting started. Veteran intimidator Bob Gibson led the way in many categories and was followed closely by future Hall of Famers like Jim Palmer, Ferguson Jenkins, Gaylord Perry, Don Sutton, Phil Niekro, and Bert Blyleven. As impressive as that group is, the leader of the dominant young pitcher movement of the early '70s was Tom Seaver. "There's only one Tom Seaver," said Rod Gaspar, a teammate of Seaver's between 1969 and 1970. "What a stud. He and Jerry Koosman, as far as winning games, there was nobody better."

Seaver burst onto the scene in 1967, when he won the NL Rookie of the Year and was named an NL All-Star as a 22-year-old rookie for the Mets, on his way to winning 16 games, while sporting an ERA of 2.76. He followed it up with another 16-win season in '68 and then broke through for what was arguably his most dominant season in 1969, when he went 25–7, with a 2.21 ERA. In '69, he won his first Cy Young Award, receiving all but one first-place vote. Seaver finished second in the NL MVP voting behind Willie McCovey, who hit .320, with 45 homers and 126 RBIs. He also led the Mets to their miracle World Series victory over the Orioles.

Benny Ayala, a teammate of Seaver's in '74 and '75, noted Seaver's work ethic and determination as two key factors to his greatness: "Even back in spring training, Tom Seaver always worked very hard," said Ayala.

> He laughed and had a good attitude, but always worked so hard. He had great mechanics and was also a great family man off the field. The best thing about Seaver was, when someone got on base against him is when he was at his best. He really focused at that point and was determined not to let anything else happen.

Throughout his legendary career, Seaver had many signature performances on the mound. He lost three no-hitters in the ninth inning, including a near-perfect game against the Cubs in 1969. He threw five complete game one-hitters before finally breaking through on June 16, 1978, when he finished a no-hitter against the Cardinals. As dominant as those performances were, Seaver's signature performance may have come on April 22, 1970, in a game against the completely overmatched San Diego Padres.

Seaver was off to a good start in '70, as he stood 2–0 with a 2.55 ERA in the early going. He shut out the Phillies in his third start of the year on April 17, and was set to face off against the Padres, who were in just their second year of existence. The Padres finished with the worst record in the majors in '69, and would finish last again in the NL in 1970.

The game was the second in a quick two-game series that ended the first Mets homestand of the season. It was played on a Wednesday afternoon in front of 14,197 at Shea Stadium. Seaver imposed his will on the Padres right from the start, as he struck out two of the first three batters to retire San Diego in order in the first.

The Mets got Seaver a quick lead in the bottom of the inning, as Buddy Harrelson singled with one out and came in to score on a double by Ken Boswell; however, Al Ferrara, a role player with good power throughout his career, connected for a homer against Seaver in the second to tie the game. Whether the homer ticked Seaver off or forced him to become more focused, he was a man pitching against children.

After the home run by Ferrara, Seaver retired the next three batters and set himself on a path of destruction through the Padres lineup. The Mets gave Seaver the lead back in the bottom of the third, when Tommie Agee singled to lead off the inning and Harrelson tripled him home for a 2–1 lead. Through the middle three innings, Seaver allowed just one hit and struck out six Padres to bring his total number of strikeouts through six innings to 10.

Seaver's strikeout of Ferrara to end the sixth started a record-breaking run of dominance that baseball had never seen before and hasn't seen since. Seaver would go on to strike out the next nine batters he faced, as he and the Shea crowd fed off one another. After Seaver struck out the side in the eighth, his strikeout total stood at 16. At the time, the major-league strikeout record was 19, by Steve Carlton. To that point, only five pitchers had even struck out as many as 18 batters in a game in the post–1900 era. Even though Seaver was facing the Padres' three best hitters, he mowed them down with ease, striking out Ferrara for the last out of the game to seal the 2–1 win.

Seaver's pitching line was 9 innings, 19 strikeouts, 2 hits allowed, 1 earned run, and 2 walks. He also became the first pitcher to strike out 10 batters in a row. Aside from Ferrara's home run, the only other hit was a harmless two-out single by Dave Campbell. Seaver's performance also allowed Mets catcher Jerry Grote to set two major-league records. By official scoring rules, catchers are credited with a putout for each strikeout, so Grote set records with 10 straight putouts and 20 overall in a game, as he also caught a foul pop by Van Kelly in the sixth inning.

Seaver had 11 more double-digit strikeout games in 1970 but overall fell off from his early career domination. He ended the '70 season with an 18–12 record and didn't get much consideration for the Cy Young Award, finishing seventh, without any first-place votes. He bounced back in 1971 and began a stretch during which he was generally considered the best pitcher in the National League.

In the next six seasons, the remainder of his stint with the Mets, Seaver went 107–63 and pitched to an ERA of 2.46. He was an All-Star in five of those six seasons and won the Cy Young Award in 1973 and 1975. He also finished second in the 1971 Cy Young voting and had three top 10 MVP finishes. "Seaver was a big-time competitor," said Gaspar. "He was the nicest guy, but as tough as they came. He threw harder in the ninth inning than he did in the first."

Although Seaver was rolling through the National League and putting up a career that was drawing comparisons to Christy Mathewson, Mets management and Seaver never truly got along. With free agency pending for Seaver, he wanted to renegotiate his contract with the Mets, looking for a contract extension and a raise; however, Mets chairman M. Donald Grant refused to hear the pitcher's pleas. Seaver himself tried to bypass Grant and approach majority owner Lorinda de Roulet. She, however, would not move forward on the deal without Grant.

Unfortunately for Seaver, and in the long run the Mets franchise, the contract squabble played out through the media, particularly through *Daily News* columnist Dick Young, who wrote scathing anti-Seaver articles.

Finally, when Seaver's family began to get drawn into the mix, he felt he had no recourse but to approach Grant and demand a trade. Grant obliged and shipped him to the Reds in one of the most lopsided trades in major-league history, setting off a period of darkness for the Mets franchise that lasted nearly a decade.

Seaver went on to win 122 games after his trade from the Mets, including his 300th win in a memorable 4–0 shutout of the Yankees in which a 40-year-old Seaver seemed transplanted to his younger days with a 10-strikeout performance. It was one of the signature days for a pitcher who not only dominated, but also possessed that which makes stars Hall of Famers.

According to a story from former Expos pitcher Don DeMola, Seaver could be considered the best righty of all time, and Hall of Fame manager Sparky Anderson agreed: "Seaver was probably the best ever to walk out on the mound from the right side," said DeMola.

> I love Pedro, but Seaver, he played with teams. At the Baseball Writers' Association dinner after my first year, I was sitting next to Sparky Anderson and I asked him, "Who is the best pitcher in the league in your opinion?" He replied, "Tom Seaver, because nobody walks out on the mound with more confidence than him." Well, I started to watch him like that, and he was right. He was a control pitcher, hardly ever gave up more than 10 homers a year. Check 'em all out, Fergie, Catfish, Maddux all gave up dingers, but solos. Seaver gave up flukes, he made very few mistakes. Home run hitters hit mistakes, and Tom made very few.

Whether he was a 40-year-old pitching for the White Sox or a 25-year-old striking out 19 batters against the Padres, Seaver could command his amazing ability and will his way to victory more often than not during his 20-year career. It was evident many times throughout those 20 years, but maybe never more so than on April 22, 1970, when he struck out 19 Padres, including the final 10 of the game.

FERNANDO VALENZUELA: FERNANDOMANIA

April 9, 1981

Every so often, baseball creates a perfect storm of events to boost a player to folk hero status. It doesn't happen often, which means when those "lightning in a bottle" players come along, their legend tends to create tales that endure. One such instance began on Opening Day of 1981, for the Dodgers. It was April 9, and it was the start of "Fernandomania."

The Dodgers are one of baseball's marquee franchises and have a history that's as rich in pitching as any other team. With a pitching tradition that dates back to Dazzy Vance and his days as a Brooklyn Robin, the Dodgers' tradition of excellence includes an imposing list of Hall of Fame pitchers. Sandy Koufax, Don Sutton, and Don Newcombe all wore Dodger blue. Don Drysdale started seven Opening Days for the franchise, and Johnny Podres was always considered one of the top pitchers of his time.

Even into the new millennium, the Dodgers had the best pitcher in the National League in the early 2010s—Clayton Kershaw. In 2013, Kershaw became the first lefty to win two Cy Young Awards before the age of 26 and just the second pitcher to finish in the top two of Cy Young voting three years in a row. Incredibly, he took another step forward in 2014, when he put together his best career season, going 21–3, with a 1.77 ERA, to unanimously win his third Cy Young Award.

When it came time for the Dodgers, who were expected to be one of the top teams in the NL in 1981, to take the field for the first time that year, many were surprised to see this pitching-rich franchise send a rotund, somewhat unknown 20-year-old Mexican named Fernando Valenzuela to the mound.

Valenzuela wasn't a complete mystery to baseball fans. In 1980, with the Dodgers in a tight pennant race with the Astros, they turned to Valenzuela for help in their bullpen as a September call-up. Then just 19 years old, the lefty responded in a heated pennant race with 17.2 scoreless innings in 10 appearances. Valenzuela faced 66 hitters during that span and allowed just eight hits, only one of which went for extra bases. Despite having the second-best record in the NL in 1980, the Dodgers finished one game behind the Astros and missed the postseason.

Dodgers manager Tommy Lasorda was impressed by Valenzuela and saw the lefty with the devastating screwball as a potential weapon out of the bullpen in 1981. His September performance also boosted his profile, and Valenzuela became a top-shelf prospect for the club. Lasorda named Jerry Reuss, fresh off an 18–6 season in 1980, as the team's starter on Opening Day; however, an injury forced Reuss out of the rotation, so Lasorda had a decision to make. Veteran Burt Hooton was the Dodgers' most experienced pitcher, so the manager could have bumped him up a day. Instead, not wanting to throw off the rest of the rotation, Lasorda turned to Valenzuela for the assignment.

Ted Power, Valenzuela's teammate during his '81 and '82 seasons, got to witness the start of his career firsthand: "[Fernando was] just a phenomenal competitor. Very intelligent and a good hitter, too."

Because of the heated pennant race with Houston the year before, the Dodgers' Opening Day matchup with the Astros was even more hotly anticipated than a typical Opening Day. Both teams were expected to do well in

1981, and thanks to a rearranged schedule due to the divided season caused by the players' strike, both the Dodgers and Astros went on to make the post-season in '81.

The Astros' strength was their starting pitching, led by Joe Niekro, Nolan Ryan, and Sutton, who had come over from the Dodgers via free agency in the offseason. Although their lineup featured some speed and marginal stars like César Cedeño, José Cruz, and Art Howe, pitching was generally considered the strongest unit of the team.

Valenzuela faced off against Niekro to start the season, and 50,511 fans showed up for the Thursday afternoon opener. He got through the top of the Astros lineup easily to start the game, allowing a harmless single to center by Craig Reynolds. Niekro, who was fourth in the Cy Young voting the previous year after going 20–12, got through the Dodgers in the first with ease as well.

Neither pitcher gave way as the game remained scoreless through 3½ innings. Both pitchers played uniquely that day, working to their advantage. Niekro's famous knuckleball was fluttering, and he allowed just two hits to that point. Valenzuela matched the veteran with a devastating screwball and hadn't allowed a hit since the first-inning single to Reynolds.

The Dodgers finally broke through in the bottom of the fourth when Steve Garvey laced a one-out triple to right and came home to score on a sacrifice fly by Ron Cey to give the Dodgers a 1–0 lead. Valenzuela had an easy fifth and carried the 1–0 lead into the sixth, where he would run into trouble for the first time. Reynolds hit a one-out single to center, and Cedeño followed with a double to left as the Astros threatened with second and third, and one out. Valenzuela pitched out of it, however, getting Cruz to line out and Howe to hit a comebacker.

The Dodgers extended their lead in the bottom of the sixth when Pedro Guerrero hit a two-out double to left to drive home Garvey for a 2–0 advantage. That would be all the support Valenzuela would need as he retired nine of the last 10 batters to preserve the 2–0 Opening Day win, delighting the crowd with each batter he faced.

Valenzuela got Dave Roberts to wave at a screwball for strike three to seal the shutout win in the first start of his career. Catcher Mike Scioscia was the first out to the mound to shake the hand of the round-faced, floppy-haired phenom, and Lasorda practically bowled over the other Dodgers to get to the mound to congratulate him next.

That was just the beginning of the fun. Valenzuela held his spot in the rotation and in his next start pitched a complete game four-hitter in a 7–1 win over the Giants. He then shut out the Padres, Astros, and Giants in consecutive starts as "Fernandomania" was reaching incredible heights before the season was even a month old. In April, Valenzuela was 5–0 with five complete games, four of which were shutouts. He pitched 45 innings, allowed just 28 hits, and struck out 43 batters. He allowed just one run all month.

Valenzuela's mystique reached well beyond his on-field dominance. In a story verified by longtime Spanish radio announcer Jaime Jarrín, ever since Walter O'Malley moved the Dodgers from Brooklyn to Los Angeles, he dreamed of finding a "Mexican Sandy Koufax" who he knew would capture the interest of the huge Mexican population in the Los Angeles area. It may have taken 24 years, and O'Malley wasn't alive to see it, but it happened in 1981.

The story of Valenzuela gained national attention quickly. Seemingly from out of nowhere, he was dominating the National League. Valenzuela's appeal was more than just his on-field performance. He was a charismatic lefty who was easy to root for with a body that was more like Babe Ruth than Don Drysdale.

With his belly hanging over his belt and his hair pouring out of the back and side of his cap, Valenzuela looked like a cartoon character. His windup added another twist to his lore. As he stepped back and raised his hands over his head, Valenzuela rolled his eyes skyward. Kids imitated his unique traits on ball fields throughout the United States, while opposing batters were wondering why he was looking nowhere near the strike zone as he was about to pitch. It was similar to Luis Tiant turning his back in the middle of his delivery, but it was a much more subtle trait. And the media ate it up.

As O'Malley dreamed, the Mexican fans and L.A. natives flooded Dodger Stadium, bringing sellouts whenever he pitched. Attendance typically doubled in Los Angeles on the days he was on the mound, and fans of other teams hoped the Dodgers rotation would be set up so he could pitch in their town. He became so in demand that the Dodgers had to set up press conferences featuring Valenzuela every time they reached a new city. The amazing thing is, he created this following and barely spoke a word of English.

Valenzuela's incredible run to start his career lasted through May 14. At that time, he had started eight games, gone 7–0, and pitched nine innings in every single game. He threw 5 shutouts, had an ERA of 0.50, and allowed 4 runs in his first 72 innings. The Phillies were the first team to finally beat him, and even in that game, he pitched seven innings and allowed just three hits.

Valenzuela would go on to become the first pitcher to win the Rookie of the Year and Cy Young Awards in the same season when he finished with a 13–7 record in the strike-shortened season. He led the league with 8 shutouts, 11 complete games, 180 strikeouts, and 192 innings pitched. He also finished fifth in the MVP voting and topped it off with a Silver Slugger Award for good measure after hitting .250.

In 1981, the Dodgers went on to win the World Series for the first time since 1965, and Valenzuela continued his dominance by posting a 3–1 record in the postseason. He made the NL All-Star Team in each of the next five seasons and remained one of the top pitchers in the league throughout the '80s; however, his career began a sharp decline in 1987, as the screwball put great strain on his elbow and began to cause a series of injuries. Many point to overuse in the early part of his career as a cause of great strain, as by the age of 25 he had already thrown more than 1,500 innings. Valenzuela did, however, manage to stick around for 17 years while pitching for four other teams through the '90s.

Ron Oester, a member of the Reds Hall of Fame and a stalwart second baseman in the '80s, faced Valenzuela 60 times during the course of the decade. Oester came up one year before Valenzuela and reflected on his emergence and subsequent career: "When Fernando Valenzuela came up to the big leagues, he was probably the top prospect in baseball," said Oester.

> He was so mature and confident for his age, the talk of Los Angeles. He had a good fastball, a good curve, and a great screwball, along with great command of each pitch. He was a tough competitor, never giving in to the hitter. It didn't take him long to win the hearts of Dodgers fans.

While Valenzuela was effective through the early part of his career, nothing he did ever matched the initial explosion of "Fernandomania." It was a perfect storm of a lovable 20-year-old Mexican pitching in Los Angeles, just 200 miles from the Mexican border.

He had a round, smiling face, a bowl haircut, a belly that hung over his belt, and the best promoter anyone could ask for in Lasorda. He captured the imagination of the baseball world and created many new Dodgers fans. The start of his career was as dominant as that of any pitcher who ever took the mound, and his fun-loving ways may have even made a few Giants fans love him. He led the Dodgers to their first World Series since the '60s and amazed every time he took the mound. Even if it was for just one brief stretch, he was the Mexican Sandy Koufax Walter O'Malley dreamed of.

NOLAN RYAN: AN EARLY FLASH FROM THE EXPRESS

April 14, 1968

Potential is one of the toughest things to gauge in a baseball prospect. "Can't miss" prospects fail to make it more often in baseball than any of the other major sports, while players drafted in the lower rounds become superstars with regularity. The way clubs treat their youngsters varies from player to player. Some are given just a couple of chances, while others are given years to prove their worth. The one thing that is certain about the potential in professional baseball players is that there is no formula in measuring how a player will turn out to be.

An examination of how the Mets handled Nolan Ryan's career justifies just how unpredictable a person's baseball career can be. In his Hall of Fame speech, Ryan mentioned how he was 6'2" and 140 pounds as he was about to venture into a professional career. Without the prototypical body, few teams were willing to take a chance on the 18-year-old. The Mets, however, chose him in the 12th round of the 1965 draft, and although Ryan was not a particularly high pick, the Mets called him up to the big club for two games in 1966. He responded by pitching three innings and giving up five runs. He was given a start on September 18, 1966, and lasted just one inning. He faced nine batters and allowed four runs, but he did strike out the side. He would spend the entire 1967 season back in the minors.

On April 14, 1968, Ryan found himself in the starting rotation as the Mets broke camp for the season. The rookie was the fourth starter for the team, behind fellow youngsters Tom Seaver and Jerry Koosman. After the Mets split a two-game series with the Dodgers, Ryan was on the mound for his second major-league start against the Astros in the Mets' fourth game of the year.

The Mets and Astros came into the league together in 1962, and neither had experienced much success in their first six seasons. The youngsters of the '68 Mets team would become the cornerstone for their amazing 1969 World Series victory and their equally incredible run to the 1973 World Series. "We were all young guys, most of us younger than 25," said Rod Gaspar, who played 118 games as an outfielder for the Mets in 1969, as a 23-year-old.

Holding those youngsters together was Gil Hodges, the legendary Brooklyn Dodger who took over as manager of the Mets in 1968. The Mets had been one of the worst teams in the majors during the early part of their existence, but Hodges brought instant respect and began to run the club like a business. "Gil was the boss and we knew it," said Gaspar. "We knew what we had to do, and he expected us to do it. If we didn't, he corrected us and showed us the right way. We all respected him greatly." The '68 Astros featured some young talent too, as they had Joe Morgan, Bob Watson, Rusty Staub, and Jimmy Wynn on the club.

Ryan faced off in this early-season matchup against Larry Dierker. They were both 21-year-old righties, and both clubs had high hopes for each young pitcher. The game was played in front of 15,290 in the Astrodome on a Sunday afternoon. Dierker started off impressively by retiring Bud Harrelson, Ken

Boswell, and Tommy Agee in order in the first. Ryan outdid his counterpart by striking out the side, getting Ron Davis, Joe Morgan, and Hal King in order.

The Mets got to Dierker in the second as Ron Swoboda led off with a walk and Art Shamsky drove him in with a double to right. The threat ended there, however, and the game was 1–0 going into the bottom of the second. Staub led off by fouling out to third, and then Ryan flashed that talent again, striking out Wynn and Norm Miller to make it five strikeouts in his first six batters.

The Mets made it 2–0 in the fourth, as Shamsky drove in another run on a groundout. As the game progressed, both pitchers continued to pitch well. Ryan's strikeout pace slowed, and he ended his day after 6⅔ innings when Hodges replaced him with Danny Frisella with two outs and Wynn on first. Ryan allowed just three hits and struck out eight on the day to pick up the first of 324 wins in his Hall of Fame career.

While Ryan impressed in his first major-league win, his season did not go quite as planned. He went just 6–9 in a year dominated by pitching and averaged five walks per nine innings. He did, however, strike out 133 batters in 134 innings.

Although he had a mediocre first season with the team, Mets fans and management knew the potential was there. Ryan just had to harness his ability, learn how to pitch, and cut down on his walks. The Mets worked with Ryan as he started 73 games in four seasons, but he never materialized into the pitcher they thought he could be. Ryan's record during that time was 29–37, and his walks per nine innings rate was moving in the wrong direction. The number increased each year, and in 1971, Ryan averaged seven walks per nine innings and had just a 10–14 record.

After seven years in the Mets organization, the front office wondered if Ryan would ever be a consistent winner in the majors. He continued to strike out batters at a high rate but didn't develop at all as a pitcher. He frequently showed flashes of his tremendous talent but could never gain consistency.

Ryan played a key role in the 1969 playoffs, when he hurled seven innings in relief to pick up a win against the Dodgers in the National League Championship Series and also pitched 2⅔ shutout innings to get the save in a 2–1 win against the Orioles in Game 3 of the World Series. Moreover, he struck out 15 batters in a game in 1970. His ability was apparent to his teammates, even if he never could harness that ability on a consistent basis early in his career.

"He had more physical talent than just about anybody," said Gaspar, a teammate of Ryan's with the Mets in '69 and '70. "He had that fastball and curveball, and you could just see the talent was there. I'd be lying if I said I knew he'd have the career he did, but the talent was there." Former All-Star pitcher Lary Sorensen agreed with Gaspar: "I'd give up a vital body part to go out and experience what it is like to have his stuff just for one night," said Sorensen.

> His stuff was amazing, and he learned how to really pitch later in his career, but he was always an incredibly hard worker. I pitched against him on a getaway day once when he was pitching for the Angels. He threw eight or nine innings in the game. After we showered and our bus was pulling away from the stadium, I looked out and saw Nolan running on the track in the outfield. That's when I gained even more respect for him.

Hard work aside, it took Ryan a while to develop into a reliable starter in the bigs. Ryan wasn't happy about his lack of development and his undefined role in the pitching staff as he bounced between the bullpen and rotation. He expressed his feelings to management and requested a trade. On December 10, 1971, Ryan was shipped to the Angels with three other players for Jim Fregosi in what seemed to be a fair trade at the time.

Fregosi, at the peak of his career, was a five-time All-Star for the Angels and finished in the top 25 in MVP voting in each of the previous eight seasons; however, Fregosi and Ryan's careers famously went in different directions from there. Angels manager Del Rice put Ryan in his starting rotation and committed to him as a full-time starter immediately. He started 39 games that year and did not come out of the bullpen once. Whether it was the change of scenery, the commitment from Rice, or just maturity, Ryan began a remarkable stretch of development. He went 19–16 in his first year in California and struck out 329 batters in 284 innings. Ryan led the AL in strikeouts in seven of the eight seasons he played for the Angels but still hovered around .500 as a pitcher. Incredibly, he averaged 302 strikeouts a season for the Angels and fired four no-hitters. He also had two 19-strikeout games for the club.

Rudy May, a 16-year major-league veteran who was on the same staff as Ryan in California, experienced Ryan's legendary competitiveness firsthand: "One summer day we were on the way to play the Rangers in Texas," said May.

> Our team bus broke down on the way to the game, and it was just hotter than anything. We were sweating and stuck, and Nolan was scheduled to pitch that day. Nolan was pretty mad and said on the bus, "Someone's gonna pay for this." He went out and struck out 15, and the game was over in less than two hours. Honest to God, Nolan had no idea where the ball was going once it left his hand, but he was just great.

However, Angels GM Buzzie Bavasi still didn't think Ryan would evolve much more as a winning pitcher, despite being in the league for 12 seasons. Ryan became a free agent, and the Angels let him sign with the Astros.

The latter part of his career is what made Ryan a legend. He went on to pitch 14 more seasons in the big leagues before retiring at the age of 46. At age 45, in 1992, Ryan was still throwing heat and averaged at least nine strikeouts per nine innings for the 17th time in his career. In 1991, he extended his record for career no-hitters by hurling his seventh against the Blue Jays. Ryan ended his career with an incredible 5,714 strikeouts, a total that still is almost 1,000 more than his closest competitor.

Ryan's impact on the majors could even be felt after he left the game, through the scores of big leaguers he influenced and inspired throughout his remarkable career: "Without a doubt Nolan Ryan was one of my favorites growing up," said Aaron Small, who pitched nine years in the majors. "We had one of those old video cameras you had to plug into the wall that looked like a full TV camera. We didn't have a VCR, so I filmed him pitching on our TV. I then had to play the tape back and watch it through the eyepiece to try to learn his mechanics."

Shawn Estes, who won 101 games in 13 major-league seasons, was another pitcher who was influenced by Ryan as a young fan: "Nolan was just pure dominance on the mound," said Estes. "He maintained it and sustained it well into his 40s. I really appreciated how hard he worked and even used his videos in my own workouts."

The Mets' trade of Nolan Ryan and the Angels' choice to let Ryan leave via free agency remain two of the most regrettable moves in franchise history; however, upon closer examination, at the time of the transactions, neither team could really be faulted for parting ways with Ryan. The Mets gave Ryan seven years to develop, and although Ryan's strikeout totals were otherworldly in California, his average season for the Angels was 17–15, just barely over .500.

Potential and development are funny things in baseball. People spent more than a decade wondering when Ryan would turn into the pitcher who'd put up a 25–8 season or have an ERA below 3.00. Those days never came. He won 20 games just twice in his 27-year career, and even in those years he had 16 losses in each. But when he stepped off the mound for the final time in 1993, his career was one that people marveled at.

Ryan was inducted into the Baseball Hall of Fame in his first year on the ballot, when 491 of the 497 voters chose him for enshrinement. His 98.79 percent of the vote was just short of the all-time record. The only person to receive a greater percentage was Seaver, who was named on 425 of 430 ballots in 1992.

"Nolan was great to watch," said Matt Galante, who was an assistant coach with the Astros during Ryan's tenure there. "He was one of the hardest workers we ever had. He prepared so well in the offseason that by the time he got to spring training, he was ready to go. He's the only one I've ever said this about, but in at least one-third of his starts he had no-hit stuff."

Galante continued, "His curve was just unbelievable, and he developed a changeup too. His curve is what made his fastball such a great pitch. He was such a competitor. When you watched him pitch you just knew you were watching a Hall of Famer."

On April 14, 1968, Ryan's game against the Astros gave a glimpse of what so many people thought they'd see on a consistent basis from the flame-thrower: 6⅔ innings, 8 strikeouts, and no runs. While he certainly enjoyed many days like that throughout his career, Ryan never did harness the potential to be a consistent winner in the major leagues.

· 4 ·

Incredible Feats and Unbreakable Records

HIPPO VAUGHN AND FRED TONEY:
THE "DOUBLE NO-HITTER"

May 2, 1917

Baseball is a game that reveres rare feats and unique occurrences. With more than 2,400 games played every season, the chances of something "one of a kind" happening would seem slim; however, baseball somehow finds a way to have statistical anomalies with regularity. Every so often, there will be an event that is so rare that it sends fans and historians scrambling to the record books to see if anything even compares. One such event occurred on May 2, 1917, when the Cubs took on the Giants. It's referred to as the "Double No-Hitter" and has happened just one time in more than 150 years of professional baseball.

On a Wednesday afternoon, with the 1917 season not even a month old, the Cubs and Reds hooked up for a game at Wrigley Field, which was then known as Weeghman Park (named for Cubs owner Charles Weeghman). Hippo Vaughn was the starting pitcher for the Cubs that day, and Fred Toney was on the hill for the Reds. Vaughn was a good pitcher for the Cubs, enjoying the best success of his career, having won 58 games in the previous three seasons. Toney would go on to win 24 games in 1917, his first of two 20-win seasons.

The Cubs and Reds were annually two of the lesser teams in the National League during that era, although the Cubs did have moderate success in 1913 and 1914. In early 1917, the Cubs and Reds got off to good starts and, with the Cardinals, were the only NL teams who had 10 wins to that point.

The Cubs were led by Deadball Era star Cy Williams, a former football teammate of Knute Rockne who was the first NL player to surpass 200 career homers, and Fred Merkle, who was at the tail end of a productive career and would always be remembered for his epic mistake as a New York Giant nine years earlier.

The Reds featured first baseman Hal Chase, the former New York Highlanders star who was playing in his second season in the NL after playing two seasons in the Federal League. The Federal League was a league in direct competition with American and National Leagues, and was eventually bought out by AL and NL owners. As part of the agreement, two FL owners were allowed to purchase one franchise each. The owner of the FL's Chicago Whales at the time was Weeghman, and he was able to buy the struggling Cubs franchise.

Play-by-play records from the game between the Reds and Cubs from this day are hard to come by, but the feats of Vaughn and Toney are well known. They were sharp from the start and both dominated opposing lineups. Vaughn struck out 10 Reds and, according to reports, allowed just one ball to leave the infield—a popup to short right by Greasy Neale. Toney matched Vaughn's excellence, as he allowed just one runner to reach second base through nine innings.

In front of an estimated crowd of about 3,500, neither Vaughn nor Toney allowed a hit through nine innings; however, in the top of the 10th, Larry Kopf hit a one-out single for the Reds for the first hit of the game. Chase then hit a fly ball to Williams in right field that was dropped for an error, allowing Kopf to go from first to third. Vaughn then had the task of facing a legendary role player who never quite reached the potential that was hoped for him as a pro baseball player. That player was the hero of the 1912 Olympic Games, Jim Thorpe, who was considered to be one of, if not the, greatest athletes of all time.

Thorpe was an All-American football player in 1911 and 1912, at Carlisle Indian Industrial School and placed first in eight of the 15 events in the 1912 Olympics in Sweden. His accomplishments were widely celebrated in the United States. Thorpe turned to pro baseball in 1912, when he signed with the New York Giants as a bench player. On April 23, 1917, the Reds purchased Thorpe from the Giants in hopes that the struggling team would draw more fans as a result and that by expanding his role Thorpe could blossom as a player.

In his three seasons with the Giants, Thorpe batted just .195 with one home run in 118 at-bats. But Thorpe would play 77 games for the Reds in 1917, where he hit .247 with eight triples and four home runs, respectable numbers in the Deadball Era.

So, with Thorpe at the plate and Chase and Kopf on second and third base, respectively, the game was on the line. Vaughn would explain what happened in an interview some years later.

He said that he pitched Thorpe inside, jamming the righty, who was swinging away. He hit a slow chopper toward the third-base line, and Vaughn broke off the mound to field it. As he went to make a play on the ball, Vaughn knew he didn't have a chance to get the speedy Thorpe at first. He had seen Kopf break for home out of the corner of his eye and realized his best chance was to try to nail him at the plate; however, Kopf froze for a second, possibly confusing catcher Art Wilson. Vaughn threw home, but Wilson dropped the throw, allowing Kopf to score. The play was ruled an RBI single for Thorpe.

Toney retired the Cubs in order in the bottom of the 10th to seal the win and finish the "no-hitter." Through the first half century of Major League Baseball, the "Double No-Hitter" was considered one of the greatest and most talked about games ever played. Vaughn played four more seasons for the Cubs and continued to be productive. He won 62 games between 1918 and 1920, before ending his final season with a record of 3–11. In the offseason between 1920 and 1921, Vaughn was stabbed in the stomach by his father-in-law concerning allegations that Vaughn had made about his wife in regard to his pending divorce. While it isn't documented if the stabbing played a role in Vaughn's ineffective 1921 season and retirement, the dramatic drop in performance at just 32 years old suggests it might have.

Toney would also go on to a strong finish in his career. Including the 1917 season, when he went 24–16, Toney accumulated a record of 104–74 in the final seven seasons of his career, pitching mostly for the New York Giants. Toney was on the MLB Hall of Fame ballot in 1949, but received just one of the 153 votes.

At the time, baseball credited a no-hitter to any pitcher who completed an official game or pitched nine full innings without giving up a hit. Even though Vaughn gave up two hits to the Reds in the 10th, he was still credited with a no-hitter because he didn't allow a hit in the first nine innings; however, in 1991, a committee headed by Commissioner Fay Vincent changed the rules regarding no-hitters. They decided, among other things, that any pitcher who had pitched nine no-hit innings but had given up a hit after that would not be credited with a no-hitter. They also decided that any previous no-hitters accredited after nine innings would be stricken from the record. Vaughn's game on May 2, 1917, obviously falls into that category and is no longer considered a no-hitter.

Of all the rare feats in baseball history, the "Double No-Hitter" is one that stands out from the rest. Typically, 2,430 games are played in a major-league season, which means 4,860 pitchers take the mound as starters throughout the year. On average, two of those 4,860 will toss no-hitters, which makes the feat rare enough. In more than 150 years of baseball, just one game featured two pitchers who did not allow a single hit or run through nine innings.

JOE SEWELL: BASEBALL'S UNBREAKABLE RECORD

July 28, 1932

One of the great debates among baseball fans is which records are most unbreakable. Invariably, Cy Young's 511 wins comes up, as does Joe DiMaggio's 56-game hitting streak and Barry Bonds's 73 homers in a season. Some fans who are deeper thinkers even bring up Johnny Vander Meer's back-to-back no-hitters (someone would have to throw three in a row to break that) or Orel Hershiser's 59 straight scoreless innings.

One name in the record books that should be included in that argument is Joe Sewell. Sewell's name doesn't stand among the great record-holders, like Babe Ruth, Cal Ripken, or Nolan Ryan, but his records are just as impressive. Sewell is known by baseball historians as the toughest batter to strike out in major-league history, averaging an incredible one strikeout for every 63 at-bats.

Sewell's contact numbers have never been approached by anyone, and it's highly unlikely anyone can come close. Most of the game's sluggers strike out more times in one season than Sewell struck out in his career, and even the best contact hitters surpass many of Sewell's season totals in just one full month of games. During his 14-year career, Sewell struck out just 114 times in 7,132 at-bats. In his last nine seasons, Sewell's strikeout totals never reached double digits, as he averaged just five strikeouts per season.

On July 28, 1932, Sewell's Yankees took on the Cleveland Indians in a battle of the top two teams in the American League at the time. Sewell was a main cog in the famed Yankees lineup, and on July 28 he was part of a Yankees lineup in which the top five hitters were all Hall of Famers. Earl Combs led off for the Yankees, followed by Sewell, Babe Ruth, Lou Gehrig, and Tony Lazzeri. On that date, they also had Hall of Famer Red Ruffing on the mound.

The Indians had a solid team but lacked the big names of the Yankees. They had their own Hall of Famer in Earl Averill, who was in the middle of a season in which he hit a career-high 32 home runs, but the rest of their lineup consisted of average players at best.

While the Yanks pounded the Indians 10–1, the significance of the game had more to do with Sewell's failure. Up to that point in the season, which was 96 games old, Sewell had yet to strike out in 311 plate appearances. He recorded 76 hits and 33 walks for a .370 on-base percentage and, with Ruth and Gehrig batting behind him, scored 55 runs. He finally struck out for the first time against the Indians on this day.

While it was a battle between the first- and second-place teams in the AL, the Indians didn't pose a real threat to the Yankees, as the Yankees had already opened an 8½-game lead on their way to winning the league by 19 games. They went on to sweep the Cubs in a World Series that featured Ruth's famous called shot. In fact, Sewell had grounded out to short in the at-bat prior to Ruth's tiebreaking historic homer.

In the game on July 28, the Yankees jumped out to a quick 3–0 lead in the first inning, and the game was over from there. They added two runs in the fourth and sixth innings to extend the lead to 7-0 as Ruffing cruised along with ease. The Indians tallied their lone run of the game when Averill hit a solo homer in the bottom of the sixth, but the Yankees answered with three runs in the next half inning to make it 10–1.

Ruffing slammed the door and ended with a complete game, his 13th of the season, to raise his record to 12–4. The powerful Yankees lineup was led by Ruth, who went 3-for-4 with seven RBIs and two home runs. Combs, Sewell, and Gehrig each had three-hit games as well to pace a 16-hit attack.

The real story of the game was Sewell's strikeout. Sewell would go 79 at-bats before he struck out again that season, and he struck out just one more time in September.

The Yankees finished the season on September 25, and Sewell's historic season ended with just three strikeouts in 576 plate appearances. It should also be noted that while Sewell wasn't a slugger on the level of some of the big home run hitters of the era, he also wasn't just a little slap hitter looking to make contact and place the ball through the infield. Sewell's best power year came in 1932, when he hit 11 homers, which in the '30s made him one of the top 20 home run hitters in the American League.

Sewell is a Hall of Famer who was a key element in perhaps the best lineup of all time. He was the Yankees third baseman and was counted on to get on base for Ruth and Gehrig while batting second in the feared lineup from 1931 to 1933.

Joe Sewell's name rarely comes up when mentioning the game's unbreakable records. He's never really mentioned as an immortal. But is it really possible for someone to break his record? For a player to do so, he'd have to play a full season and strike out just two times all year.

PAUL MOLITOR: APPRECIATING DiMAGGIO'S STREAK

August 26, 1987

One of baseball's most revered records, Joe DiMaggio's 56-game hitting streak, rarely receives the slightest of competition. Every so often, however, a player will creep past the halfway point, drawing some attention to the record. Nonetheless, most "serious" threats die soon after a player crosses the 30-game mark.

Through 2015, 26 players have amassed 30-game hitting streaks, but 23 of those streaks ended before they could surpass 35 games, which means they were still more than three weeks from beating DiMaggio. In 1987, two players had streaks that lasted more than 30 games, Benito Santiago, then a rookie catcher for the Padres, and Hall of Famer Paul Molitor. While Santiago's streak ended at 34, Molitor's continued to August 26, before finally ceasing at 39 games.

When any streak progresses past the 30-game mark, the whispers start about how long it can possibly go. There have been only six streaks of at least 40 games in MLB history, and just two of them happened after 1922, so even a 40-game hitting streak would create hysteria in the baseball world. As Molitor crept up the list, his streak drew national attention. He cracked the 35-game plateau on August 20, with a 3-for-5 effort against the Indians, and then moved up to ninth on the all-time list when he doubled in the fifth inning against the Royals' Danny Jackson in a 3–0 Brewers win.

With Molitor holding one of the 10 longest hitting streaks in MLB history, talk of him challenging DiMaggio started to gain momentum, even though he was still about three weeks from what would be the record. While the talk may have been premature, it wasn't totally incomprehensible.

Although plagued by injuries in the early part of his career, Molitor was considered one of the top hitters in the American League when healthy. He was a good contact hitter who never struck out more than 100 times a season, and his great speed gave him the ability to beat out infield hits.

"Molitor's approach was nearly slump-proof," said Tim Leary, a teammate of Molitor's in '85 and '86. "He never moved his hands until they went to the ball. They were so still and then exploded to the ball. He was an awesome teammate. What a quick bat."

Molitor also batted leadoff, which allowed him to get the maximum number of at-bats each game. He was protected in the lineup by fellow Hall of Famer Robin Yount and spent much of his time as the team's DH, avoiding the rigors of playing the field every day. It seemed if there could be a perfect challenger to DiMaggio's streak, it was Molitor.

Molitor's hitting streak began on July 16, 1987, which coincidentally was exactly 46 years to the day of DiMaggio's 56th straight game with a hit. His first hit was a double against the Angels' Kirk McCaskill, during his first game back from a stint on the disabled list. Molitor hit .415 in July, recording 27 hits in the 15 games he played. In more than half of those contests, Molitor recorded multihit games. By comparison, DiMaggio hit .379 in the first 15 games of his streak in 1941, with just four multihit games.

Molitor reached game number 25 with a 2-for-4 day against the Rangers on August 10, and at that time his streak started to gain more attention. He had a close call in game 28, as he was 0-for-3 after grounding out in the seventh on August 13. He needed at least two Brewers to reach base before the end of the game if he was to extend his record. Greg Brock and Rob Deer drew back-to-back walks in the eighth inning against Orioles starter Mike Boddicker.

Molitor got his final chance to extend the streak as he came up in the game against reliever Tom Niedenfuer. He kept the streak going in grand fashion as he belted a home run to make it 28 games in a row. It was one of seven homers he hit during his streak.

The Brewers returned home from an eight-game road trip for a nine-game homestand against the Royals, Indians, and Twins. If Molitor could hit safely in each of those games, his streak would be 44 games, tying Pete Rose for third all-time. He got a hit in each game against the Royals and singled in the sixth in the first game of the Indians series to bring it to 39 games, which was the seventh-longest streak of all time, just one behind Ty Cobb's streak of 40 from 1911.

Molitor looked to extend his streak to 40 games on August 26, in game two against the Indians. Despite the national attention, only 11,246 fans showed up for the Wednesday game as the Brewers were set to face rookie (and future World Series–winning Red Sox manager) John Farrell, who was making his second career start and had a grand total of 10 innings pitched in his career to that point.

The Indians were 48–79 at the time, which was the worst record in baseball. If any game would be considered the least threatening to Molitor's streak, it would be this one; however, as is often the case in baseball, you are reminded that anything can happen.

Teddy Higuera, the Brewers' ace at the time, got through the Indians in order in the first. Molitor led off the bottom of the first with a strikeout against the Indians' righty leading off the inning. Higuera and Farrell were making quick work of their opposition when Molitor came up in the third for his second chance in a 0–0 game. Molitor again came up empty against Farrell, grounding a shot right at shortstop Julio Franco for an inning-ending double play.

Farrell had set down 13 straight Brewers by the time Molitor got his third chance of the game. With the game still 0–0 in the sixth, Molitor again could not break through and, for the second at-bat in a row, grounded out to short. Farrell took a two-hitter into the eighth as the game remained 0–0. Molitor was due up fourth in the inning for what could have been his last chance to extend his streak. Dale Sveum hit a one-out single, and Castillo bunted him to second.

With two outs, Indians manager Doc Edwards bypassed conventional wisdom and chose not to intentionally walk Molitor. While it was true that Yount was batting behind Molitor, he was batting .314 on the year and .304 in the month of August, as opposed to Molitor's .364 on the year and .414 in August.

Molitor hit the ball hard, but like his previous two at-bats, it was right at a Cleveland infielder. Indians third baseman Brook Jacoby corralled the grounder and threw it to first, but the throw was bobbled by first baseman Pat Tabler, allowing Molitor to reach the bag. There wasn't much of a grey area in the play, and the official scorer had no choice but to score the play an error. Yount followed with a pop out to first to end the inning.

At the time, it looked like it could have been Molitor's last shot, but the game was still 0–0, and Higuera and Farrell were locked in a pitchers' duel. The Brewers would need to get three batters to reach base safely, and the game needed to remain tied to get Molitor one more chance in the 10th. Higuera did his part, as he retired the Indians in order in the ninth and 10th. The Brewers went down in order in the ninth, so the only way Molitor would be denied another chance would be if the Brewers won it in the 10th.

Closer Doug Jones relieved Farrell and hit the first batter he faced in the 10th. Ernest Riles grounded out for the first out as pinch-runner Mike Felder crossed over to second. Sveum drew an intentional walk to put runners at first and second to bring up pinch-hitter Rick Manning with Molitor on deck. Manning lined the game-winning single to left and was promptly booed loudly by his home Brewers fans as Molitor's streak died.

With the Brewers still fighting for the AL East crown and with every win vital, third-base coach Tony Muser had no choice but to send Felder home with the winning run. The win put the Brewers 10 games over .500 on the season as they chased the Tigers, Blue Jays, and Yankees in the AL East.

The end of Molitor's streak not only brought accolades to the Brewers' DH, but also reiterated just how difficult it would be for DiMaggio's streak to be broken. When his streak stood at 38 games, the understated Molitor said in a *Sports Illustrated* article that while it was nice the higher he went, "when you talk about the streak in comparison to what the record is, it's really not that significant." But Molitor's streak was significant in the grand scheme of baseball history. It was the fourth longest in American League history, behind DiMaggio's, George Sisler's (41 games in 1922), and Cobb's, and was the seventh longest overall.

Throughout the course of the 39-game streak, Molitor batted .415 with 27 extra-base hits and 22 strikeouts. DiMaggio hit .408 during his streak and struck out just five times in 247 plate appearances. The contemporary streak that was most similar to Molitor's was Pete Rose's 44-game hitting streak in

1978. During that streak, Rose batted .385 with 14 extra-base hits and also struck out just five times. In the 25 years after Molitor's streak, the only person who was able to top 35 games was Jimmy Rollins, who hit in 38 straight games during the 2005 and 2006 seasons.

Streaks aside, Molitor and Yount were two of the great hitters and athletes of their era and remain incredibly respected in Milwaukee and throughout baseball. "I purposely, consciously said to myself that these are special players, and I made sure I really enjoyed watching them play every day," said Don August, who played with them both for four years. "They showed us younger players how to play the game properly and how to be major leaguers. Robin Yount ran every single ball out and never argued with an umpire. They were just among the best ever."

Matt Walbeck, Molitor's teammate later in his career with the Twins, also discussed what it was like to play alongside the Hall of Famer: "It was just awe-inspiring," said Walbeck.

> Just to sit there and listen to him talk about hitting was incredible. He just prepared so well and worked so hard at it. He hit .341 at the age of 39 because of that hard work. He was also the best baserunner I ever saw. He took an extra base on you at the blink of an eye. Robbie Alomar was up there too, but Molitor was just the best.

Long hitting streaks are a part of baseball that really captures the imagination of the fans. Due to the magical number 56 and the popular conception that it is among the most unbreakable records in sports, anyone who even gets halfway to DiMaggio's streak starts to generate attention; however, it is the fan interest in seeing somebody challenge the streak that might make it one of the reasons it is so tough to break.

In an era when media coverage is more extensive than ever, the attention paid to any streak puts even more pressure on the player to perform each night. The media and fan attention is nothing like DiMaggio had to face, and one can only imagine what a true challenger to the 56-game hitting streak would encounter. In addition to the media presence, the specialization of relief pitchers will also make it extremely difficult to break.

"Now you have starters going five or six innings, and then you have relievers to work against," said Kelly Paris, who played five seasons in the majors during the peak of Molitor's career. "Not only do you have to be good, but you have to be lucky too. You can hit three rockets in a game, but if you hit them right at people, you're going 0-for-3. DiMaggio's record won't be broken."

Molitor came closer than anyone to breaking the record, but it was Rose who found out just what the pressure would be like. If it wasn't for an

RBI single by Rick Manning on August 26, 1987, Molitor would have had a chance to continue his streak and discover the type of pressure a 40-game hitting streak would encourage.

MARIANO RIVERA: 1,000 GAMES IN PINSTRIPES

May 25, 2011

Athletes who have long, productive careers usually find themselves attached to certain adjectives. They can be called enduring, consistent, or reliable. It may not happen often, but athletes come along who deserve more justice than to be described with just a one-word accolade. To describe Hank Aaron as "enduring" might be accurate, but there has to be a more fitting way to describe a career that encompasses greatness, consistency, dignity, and reliability. Perhaps such a word is so hard to come up with because that type of player is so rare. The player who is the best embodiment of the indescribable in the new millennium would have to be Yankees closer Mariano Rivera.

There are players like Miguel Cabrera and Mike Trout who put up insane numbers every year, and they have their star quality to be sure; however, debates about just how high up on the "immortal" list they deserve to be will remain unsettled. When you consider the amazing regular-season performances, the clutch postseason games, the dignified and professional way he went about his career, and the fact that he did not show the slightest signs of slowing even as he celebrated his 40th birthday, nobody measures up to the standards set by Rivera.

To top it all off, he basically did it with just one pitch.

"It's always talked about, and it'll be talked about on the day he is put into the Hall of Fame; he's a one-pitch wonder," said Aaron Small, who was Rivera's teammate in New York for two seasons. "He did it all with his cutter, it was amazing. He is talked about as the best reliever of all time, but it's even up for debate that you could put his name into the discussion as one of the best pitchers of all time."

Matt LaPorta, who played for the Indians from 2009 to 2012, agreed with Small's assessment: "It's just a tough pitch to hit; he just mastered it," said LaPorta, who actually beat Rivera with a two-run single in a 2011 game.

> You just never knew what it would do. Sometimes he threw it with the cutter spin, but it didn't break. You'd know it was a cutter, look for it to break, and it wouldn't. Then there were those times where it looked like it was hittable, and it would have that sharp, late cut. He basically said, "Here's what I got, take it or leave it."

On May 25, 2011, Rivera's career, which was already worlds ahead of every other closer in baseball history, reached a height that no other pitcher has approached in more than 100 years. Rivera pitched in his 1,000th game for the Yankees. It was the first time any pitcher had pitched in 1,000 games while playing the entirety of his career for one team.

Rivera began the 2011 season with 978 games pitched for the Yankees. He started 10 of them in 1995, but then became exclusively a reliever after that. He was a setup man for John Wetteland for the Yankees' 1996 World Series run and performed so well, the Yanks let the All-Star Wetteland walk after the year and converted Rivera to the closer's role. It would be one of the key moves in Joe Torre's early years as Yankees skipper and one that was surprisingly risky when looked back upon.

"When he pitched in '96 as a setup man, he threw a lot of innings, somewhere over 100 innings," said Jeff Montgomery, the Royals' All-Star closer at the time. "I was concerned when the Yankees let Wetteland walk. I didn't know if Rivera's arm would hold up as a closer, especially after having thrown so many innings as a middle reliever the year before." Those concerns were well founded, even if they never manifested during the next 16 years.

Every year, fans had an internal struggle with Rivera. They knew that one of those years he had to show signs of fading; baseball logic dictates that. Yankees fans were fearful that any year could be "that year." But that time simply never came for Rivera.

On Opening Day in 2011, Rivera came in to pick up the save in a 6–3 win over the Tigers. It took him 12 pitches to get through three batters, and the Tigers didn't stand a chance. Rivera didn't allow a run through his first nine appearances and was just about as flawless as could be.

Despite high expectations, the Yankees were just two games over .500 on May 17. Big-name players like Mark Teixeira, Robinson Canó, Derek Jeter, and Alex Rodriguez were either underachieving or playing inconsistent ball. Jorge Posada and Jeter, two staples from the late '90s run of Yankees dominance, showed obvious signs of aging in the early part of the season. The 39-year-old Posada's average was .179, and Jeter, who was set to turn 37 that June, hovered around .260, with little power.

Rivera showed no signs of aging and was pitching like he was in his mid-20s. He'd appeared in 20 games and had left his opponents runless in 18 games. Batters were hitting .197 against Rivera, and his ERA was 1.42. By comparison, Rivera actually had better stats as a 41-year-old than he did a decade earlier.

The night after Rivera was asked to pick up the save against the Tampa Bay Rays on May 17, 2011, he was called into duty again against the Orioles. As Rivera crossed into his 40s, his need to pitch on consecutive nights became more magnified. People assumed this was when he might start showing some cracks. Bartolo Colón was pitching a gem that night and had thrown just 87 pitches through eight innings as the Yanks took a 1–0 lead to the ninth. Rivera was warming up, but since he had pitched the night before and Colón's pitch count was low, fans figured manager Joe Girardi might give Colón a chance at the shutout. Nevertheless, because of recent struggles of the team, Girardi opted to go with the most consistent player on his roster to close out the game.

This didn't work. The Orioles got to Rivera for a run in the ninth to tie the game. It was far from a meltdown, as the Orioles scored when Adam Jones singled sharply, a weak grounder found its way through the right side, and Vladimir Guerrero followed with a sacrifice fly, but the result was surprising and left Girardi open to second-guessers. After the game, Girardi vehemently defended his decision. He argued that opting for Rivera is never a bad choice.

This appearance was Rivera's 999th in a Yankees uniform, and the loss kept them two games out of first place. After the back-to-back appearances, Girardi didn't need Rivera in a game for a full week. Normally, even if the Yankees didn't have any save situations for a few days, Rivera would come in to get some work. In the one save situation they did have during that time, Girardi let CC Sabathia close out a 4–1 complete-game win against the Blue Jays on his own.

The next day was May 25, and the Yankees took on the Blue Jays in the rubber game of the three-game set. The pitching matchup was Jo-Jo Reyes versus the Yanks' Freddy García. García had battled injuries in the previous four seasons and was averaging just six innings. It was highly unlikely that García would finish the game; logic dictated that Rivera would appear.

The Yankees were up 5–0 through three innings thanks to home runs by Teixeira and Andruw Jones, and García was off to a good start. The Jays finally broke through for a run against García in the sixth, but the Yankees answered with two in the bottom of the sixth on another home run by Jones. Girardi let García begin the seventh, but the first three batters for the Jays got hits, and with the score 7–3 Girardi turned to the Yankees bullpen.

David Robertson and Joba Chamberlain bridged the gap from Garcia to Rivera. Rivera gave up a hit to Eric Thames to start the inning but got two fly outs on the next two batters. J. P. Arencibia came on as a pinch-hitter, but the 25-year-old rookie didn't stand a chance against the 41-year-old closer. Rivera mowed down Arencibia on a three-pitch strikeout to end the game and preserve the 7–3 win.

Rivera's career was so remarkable that it's impossible to find any glaring flaws. There were games blown along the way, including big postseason and World Series games, but Rivera's cool professionalism always allowed him to bounce back quickly. In fact, by blowing such big games, Rivera was able to prove his greatness by the way he returned for his next appearance as if nothing happened. He still went out, threw his cut fastball just about every pitch, exuded little emotion, and got the job done.

Rivera's greatness can be summed up the way just about any baseball fan or player would speak of it. He is simply the best ever. Mark Dewey, who was a reliever in the '90s, when Rivera was getting started, confirmed his greatness: "Multitudes have eloquently and rightfully given high praises to Mariano Rivera as both a man of integrity and pitcher," said Dewey. "I can only add one small voice to the throng that recognize him as a faithful follower of the Lord Jesus Christ and acknowledge that he is the greatest closer in the history of our wonderful game."

If you choose to quantify Rivera's supremacy with yearly statistics, that's easy to do. He topped the 50-save mark twice and had 11 seasons with an ERA under 2.00. If you want to look at career numbers, he finished the most games in MLB history and is one of just two pitchers to top 500 saves. Rivera was an All-Star 13 times and was a five-time World Series champion. His excellence in the postseason is well documented, as he is the career leader with 42 postseason saves and earned both a World Series MVP and an American League Championship Series MVP.

Pitching so well in such high-pressure situations was something that rightfully boosted Rivera's career. Adam Melhuse, who is an advanced scout for the Cubs and played with the A's in the 2003 and 2006 postseasons, discussed the difference between the regular season and postseason from a player's perspective: "When they put the red, white, and blue banners up around the stadium, the aches and pains kind of go away and you just go on adrenaline," said Melhuse. "Everyone is hanging on every pitch. Sometimes the regular season gets mundane. There are 162 games, so sometimes players might say, 'What's one game out of a season? It doesn't mean too much.' But in the playoffs, every pitch, every play is magnified."

That's what makes Rivera's success in the postseason even more impressive. The accolades and amazing statistics could go on for pages in support of Rivera; however, the intangibles are what made his career truly special. One can't measure the impact Rivera has on teammates by just walking onto the field. It's often said that the best of the best, like Wayne Gretzky and Michael Jordan, made the players around them better. Rivera made everyone calmer through his consistency, demeanor, dominance, and actions as a teammate and a person.

"From the time I met him on day one of spring training in 2005, he went out of his way to make me comfortable," said Small.

> He held Bible studies at his home in Tampa during spring training and invited me from the start. Once a week he opened his home to players

for these studies, had a big spread of food, and even had people translate to Spanish so nobody felt left out. He is a great Christian man who always took care of the guys.

Montgomery, who was the only player to beat Rivera to 300 saves recorded with one ball club, talked about the role of the closer: "The biggest thing regardless of your role on a field is consistency," said Montgomery. "As a closer, every year I wanted my manager to know what he could expect for the full season. It's great when you could just eliminate all questions and concerns about a specific role. [Rivera] is just a special player."

Rivera finished the 2011 season with 44 saves and an ERA of 1.91 at the age of 41, and there were rumors in early 2012 that he could be wrapping up his career. But Rivera tore his ACL in the outfield at Kauffman Stadium in Kansas City during his pregame workout routine: "I didn't like that it was portrayed through the media that Rivera hurt himself goofing around," said Small. "He was out there working hard like he does before every game. He does his running and helps his team by shagging fly balls. It was just an unfortunate accident."

Rivera refused to let an injury dictate the way he left the game. He returned for his 19th year in 2013, and was as consistent as ever. He posted 44 more saves, had an ERA of 2.11, and finished his career with an MLB-record 652 saves.

On May 25, 2011, Rivera came onto the field as a New York Yankee for the 1,000th time. By then, 14 other pitchers had appeared in 1,000 games, but none for a single team. In the 125-year history of baseball, no player had even approached that mark with a serious threat. The record may seem like a simple statistic at first glance—the player just showed up 1,000 times and never played for anyone else—however, to do that for baseball's elite franchise, so many factors come into play that simple words don't describe.

GREG MADDUX: PROLONGED
EXCELLENCE ON THE PATH TO 350

May 10, 2008

For every generation of pitchers that reaches the 300-win plateau, speculation ensues about whether the 300-game winner is a dying breed. Changes in the game have made the exclusive club seemingly harder to gain entry to, but when comparing the careers of the pitchers who've reached 300 wins, there are a few common factors: Most were called up early and had immediate success, most enjoyed a sustained career peak during which they were annually around 20 wins, and all remained healthy throughout lengthy careers.

"When I umpired Greg Maddux's 300th win, I really believed I was looking at the last 300-game winner," said Ted Barrett, who worked home plate in the historic game. "The way they treat pitchers now, it's hard to see many more players accomplishing the feat. It was a pleasure to work the game."

Even if the pitchers in the club did all of that, most had to hang on past their prime and sputter toward their goal of 300 wins. The fact that Greg Maddux blew by 300 on his way to 355 makes his accomplishments even more impressive.

"Greg was a master craftsman," said Lary Sorensen, who won 93 games in 11 big-league seasons and has worked as a broadcaster for much of the past 25 years.

> He was so smart and pitched three pitches ahead of the batters. Maddux knew in his head the calculations as to how long a fly ball needed to be in the air in order for his outfielder to make a catch on normal effort. He could tell if an outfielder was trying to showboat or slide unnecessarily. He would get on his fielders if they left their feet if they didn't have to. That's how smart and intense he was.

The 350-win milestone is one that is reached with such rarity that it is often not even discussed among the magic numbers of baseball. Besides Maddux and Roger Clemens, only Warren Spahn has passed the 350 mark since 1920. Spahn played his entire career in an era of pitching dominance, with four-man rotations where pitchers routinely started 35–40 games and finished 20–25 of them complete.

"Greg made my job very easy because of his command and preparation," said Paul Bako, who caught Maddux's 250th and 300th wins, and served as a personal catcher to Maddux during his time in Atlanta. "When you combine his command with his preparation and just knowing when to throw what pitch, that's what made him so incredible."

Sorensen shared a story about just how "in charge" Maddux was when he was on the mound. The story was passed along through Leo Mazzone, who served as Maddux's pitching coach during his time in Atlanta: "J. R. Perdew was a pitching coach who worked with Leo Mazzone," said Sorensen.

> He tells a story that Mazzone told him. He said Mazzone went out to the mound once to talk strategy, and Maddux stopped him before he could talk. He told Mazzone, "I'll get the guy to a 2–2 count, throw him a changeup, and he'll pop it up right down the left-field line." Sure enough, Maddux got the guy to 2–2, threw him a change, and the guy

popped out down the left-field line, just a foot or two foul. That's how smart and in command he was.

Maddux pitched in the heart of the batter-dominated steroid era in a five-man rotation when complete games were a dying accomplishment. His high-water mark for complete games was 10, and he accomplished that feat just twice. On the night of May 10, 2008, Maddux was pitching for the Padres and took the mound against the Rockies in his fifth attempt at reaching the unfathomable goal of 350 wins.

The 42-year-old righty was off to a good start in 2008 and notched wins 348 and 349 in successive starts in early April. In those games, he pitched a combined 12 innings and allowed just five hits; however, hard luck in some games and subpar performances in others kept him away from 350. On the night of May 10, Maddux faced off against a Rockies team that was known for its hitting. With stars like Todd Helton and Matt Holliday in the lineup, and promising youngster Ubaldo Jiménez on the mound for Colorado, Maddux had a tough test in front of him.

But Maddux was efficient as usual and got off to a great start. He retired nine of the first 10 batters he faced, allowing just a harmless third-inning single to Clint Barmes. The Padres' offense sputtered as well and had been unable to mount anything against Jiménez.

In the bottom of the fourth, the Padres rallied as Tad Iguchi and Brian Giles led off with walks to bring Adrian Gonzalez to the plate. Gonzalez, who was just coming into his own as one of the top young stars in the National League, belted a three-run opposite-field homer to left to give Maddux a 3–0 lead to work with.

Maddux retired the Rockies in order in the top of the fifth on just nine pitches. Jiménez got the Padres out quickly in the bottom of the fifth, sending Maddux right back out for the sixth. Rockies leadoff hitter Willy Taveras, one of the fastest players in the game, attempted to get things started with a bunt hit. Maddux, a winner of 18 career Gold Gloves, threw the ball up the right-field line for an error, allowing Taveras to go all the way to third. He scored on a groundout by Omar Quintanilla to cut the score to 3–1. Maddux, however, didn't give the Rockies anything else, as he retired Helton and Holliday on weak grounders, using just five pitches.

The Padres had a very good bullpen at the time, anchored by All-Stars Heath Bell and Trevor Hoffman, so manager Bud Black chose to lift Maddux after six. Cla Meredith, Bell, and Hoffman combined to pitch the final three innings, with Bell allowing a single run in the eighth. With the tying run on first and one out in the ninth, Hoffman got Brad Hawpe to bounce into a game-ending double play to preserve the 3–2 win and catapult Maddux further into baseball immortality.

With the win, Maddux became the ninth pitcher to win 350 games in his career. Clemens achieved the feat the year before, and Spahn reached his 350th career win in 1963. The remainder of the 350-win club pitched most of their careers between 1885 and 1920.

Maddux used a formula of prolonged greatness to reach the elusive feat of 350 wins. He played on great teams for nearly his entire career and was remarkably consistent. While some great pitchers, like Bob Gibson, Sandy Koufax, and Pedro Martinez, had short peaks of dominance, Maddux was at the top of his game for 15 years. From 1988 to 2003, Maddux averaged a record of 18–9 with a 2.76 ERA during a time of incredible offensive statistics.

Maddux was able to stay dominant mostly because of the movement on his pitches and his impeccable control. He pitched so efficiently that he rarely had stressful starts and was able to keep his arm in tremendous shape for his entire career. Because he was known to be around the plate, batters often took an aggressive approach to him, and since he had such great movement on his pitches, batters rarely hit the ball solidly. Even though Maddux wasn't known as a strikeout pitcher, he still accumulated 3,371 strikeouts in his career, which was good for 10th all-time upon his retirement. He allowed only 1.8 walks per nine innings, leading the league in that category nine times.

On August 7, 2004, fans thought they were seeing the culmination of Maddux's greatness when he recorded his 300th career win over the San Francisco Giants. While he was still pitching effectively, he was 38 at the time, and 350 wins was such a mythical number that there wasn't much discussion of Maddux approaching it; however, like he had done for the previous 19 seasons of his career, Maddux persevered, worked efficiently, and continued to pitch winning baseball.

"Greg always stuck to the percentages," said Bako.

> As an example, if there were guys on first and third with less than two outs, Greg worked to get a ground ball double play every time. He knew how to work the batter to get that result. Sometimes the ball would go through, but he always seemed to get the result he was working for. He really studied video on every hitter, and it made him so prepared to deal with any situation.

Barrett discussed what it was like to umpire behind home plate for Maddux's starts and just how precise his control was.

"Early in the game, the catcher would set up right on the outside corner, and he'd hit the glove perfectly," started Barrett, who has umpired 20 seasons in Major League Baseball through 2015. "The catcher would then a move few inches further outside, and he'd hit the glove perfectly again. If it was a strike, he'd continue the process. If it was a ball, then he knew where the outside border of the strike zone was, and he would just pound that spot all game long."

In the games after his 350th win, Maddux continued to pitch well for the Padres. But a string of bad luck caused him to record eight no-decisions in his next 18 starts. In those 18 starts, he had a record of just 3–6 and was traded to the Dodgers to help them in their postseason push. He went 2–2 for the Dodgers in five starts, topping the Giants and Matt Cain on the second-to-last day of the season in what would be the last start of his career. He pitched six innings of two-hit ball and, of course, walked nobody.

Maddux made three relief appearances for the Dodgers in the postseason, as they lost in the National League Championship Series to the Phillies. In four innings, he didn't allow an earned run. His only walk was an intentional walk to Shane Victorino in the fifth inning of Game 5 of the NLCS. Maddux retired Cole Hamels on a groundout to end the fifth and would walk off the field for the last time as an active player.

Maddux, Clemens, Randy Johnson, and Tom Glavine were the 300-game winners of the steroid era. As their careers finished, talk began again of how the 300-game winner was a dying breed. No current pitchers were close to 300 wins as that quartet retired, and with baseball being such an unpredictable sport, it remained unclear whether any of the young pitching stars of the day would reach that goal.

On the night of May 10, 2008, Maddux was living proof that no matter what baseball pundits might speculate, pitching milestones that appear to be unreachable can be attained through prolonged excellence and a healthy arm.

· 5 ·

Tragedy, Trials, and Tribulations

RAY CHAPMAN: TRAGEDY IN THE BATTER'S BOX

August 16, 1920

As with any profession, the world of baseball is not immune to tragedy. Like any physical occupation, certain work hazards come with the territory. While there have been hundreds of tragedies surrounding the sport throughout the years, there still remains just one player who died of injuries sustained in a game: Ray Chapman.

It was August 16, 1920, and the Yankees were taking on the Indians at the famed Polo Grounds. The game was filled with baseball royalty; Babe Ruth led Miller Huggins's Yankees against the Indians, who featured Hall of Fame player-manager Tris Speaker. Ruth was in his first season in a Yankees uniform and was on his way to a record-setting 54 home runs that season. Along with the White Sox, the Yanks and Indians were the best teams in the American League in 1920.

Chapman was a scrappy shortstop who was widely respected through-out the league, even by the famously ornery Ty Cobb. He batted second in the powerful Indians lineup and was a table-setter with leadoff batter Charlie Jamieson. Jamieson and Chapman each batted over .300 in 1920, ahead of Speaker, who enjoyed one of the best seasons of his storied career.

The game pitted Yankees hurler Carl Mays against Cleveland's Stan Coveleski. Coveleski would win 24 games in 1920 and was at the peak of his Hall of Fame career. Mays, a known spitballer and accused head hunter, was in his first season with the Yanks after coming over in a trade with the Red Sox. Mays was the Yankees' top pitcher in 1920 and would go on to a 26–11 record.

Although known mostly for the fateful pitch that induced so much damage, Mays was not considered a fireballer by any means. In 312 innings, the submarine-style pitcher struck out just 92 batters in 1920. He averaged just 2.4 walks per nine innings and threw just two wild pitches all season.

The game itself was a typical close battle between the two teams. Cleveland had jumped to a 3–0 lead behind a great day from light-hitting catcher Steve O'Neill. O'Neill drove in two runs to that point, with a second-inning homer and an RBI single, and Coveleski added a sacrifice fly to support his effort against the Yankees lineup.

Chapman led off the fifth inning and was 0-for-1 with a sacrifice bunt (his 41st of the season). Mays got strike one on the righty, and the second pitch was a ball. On the pitch, Mays contended that he noticed Chapman shift his feet as if to attempt a bunt hit. Figuring he might try it again, Mays chose to come inside, a pitch that would be difficult to push down the first-base line. There are varying accounts of exactly what happened next.

Most stories concur that Chapman simply froze. The Polo Grounds was always known to have vicious shadows in the midafternoon, and on August 16 that was no different. Already a tough pitcher to pick up due to his sidearm delivery, the shadows made it even more difficult to see.

Also factored into the mix was Mays's reputation as a spitballer. While a modern-day spitballer like Gaylord Perry was known to sneak a little Vaseline onto the ball, in 1920 their methods were much different. Dirty and scuffed baseballs were kept in play, and a pitcher known to load the baseball would add even more grime and grease. Simply put, the baseballs in 1920 were not the pristine white pearls fans today are used to seeing.

So, Chapman was looking out at a submarine pitcher who was trying to come inside with what had to be a weathered and brown baseball while tracing it through the midday shadows of the Polo Grounds. With those factors, it's amazing this hadn't happened before or since.

The pitch cracked into the left side of Chapman's skull and rolled out toward Mays. Thinking it may have hit the bat, Mays flipped the ball to Wally Pipp at first, but all eyes quickly focused on Chapman, who had collapsed at home. Despite a reported 3½-inch depressed fracture in his skull, Chapman didn't lose consciousness and was helped by his teammates off the field. He collapsed again on his way off the field but was not immediately rushed to the hospital. After receiving treatment at the ballpark, Chapman was then transported to the hospital, where he died at 4:40 the following morning.

Dr. T. M. Merrigan performed a surgery on Chapman in which he removed part of the skull to alleviate some of the pressure. Reports showed that

Chapman not only had damage done to the left side of the brain, where he had been hit, but also to the right side. Allegedly, the jolt of the pitch knocked Chapman's brain into the right side of his skull, causing lacerations and blood clots.

The game continued after Chapman left, and the Yanks mounted a ninth-inning rally against Coveleski. Ping Bodie doubled home Ruth and Del Pratt, and Muddy Ruel would drive in Bodie with a single, but Coveleski would slam the door on the 4–3 win to boost Cleveland into first place with a half-game lead.

Obviously, the game result took a backseat to the Chapman incident and the subsequent ramifications. Mays was quickly vilified for his actions by fans, and word even circulated that he could face legal consequences for the accident. While players from both the Indians and Yankees flocked to the James F. McGowan Funeral Home in New York after learning of Chapman's death, Mays reported to the district attorney's Homicide Bureau. He would be exonerated of any wrongdoing after a short investigation.

Speaker, who was Chapman's teammate for nine seasons, was too distraught to leave his hotel room that day; however, in a statement, Speaker tried to help the bitterness subside: "It is the duty of all of us, of all the players, not only for the good of the game, but also out of respect to the poor fellow who was killed, to suppress all bitter feeling," said Speaker in a *New York Times* article about the incident.

The fallout from the event was widespread. Players on many teams, including Ty Cobb, called for the expulsion of Mays from Major League Baseball. Cobb and Mays had a beanball incident of their own during a prior season in which the stubborn players refused to give in to their opponents' styles.

Mays would play for nine more seasons and finished his career with 208 wins. He even received six votes in the 1958 Hall of Fame balloting. Rumors later followed him about an alleged fix on the 1921 and 1922 World Series, but investigations turned up nothing.

While Chapman's baseball family was clearly distraught, his family was stricken as well. His wife Katie was three months pregnant at the time. She would give birth to a baby girl named Rae but could not escape bouts of depression. Katie Chapman committed suicide in 1926. Sadly, Rae Chapman contracted the measles in 1928 and also passed away.

Mays went on to a 20-year career in baseball and retired as a scout in 1952. He died on April 4, 1971, at the age of 79. Mays went to the grave not only insisting that he did not intentionally hit Chapman, but also that if the pitch wouldn't have hit the crouched-over Chapman in the head, it would have been a strike.

J. R. RICHARD: A FLAMETHROWER EXTINGUISHED

July 3, 1980

On July 3, 1980, everything was great for J. R. Richard and his Houston Astros. Richard was virtually unhittable in the first half of the season and had just won his 10th game of the year. His ERA rested at 1.96 after he made his last start before the All-Star break, and he was averaging more than a strikeout per inning.

Richard had developed into one of the premier pitchers in the game as baseball was moving forward into the '80s. In fact, he was named the NL starting pitcher for the All-Star Game ahead of future Hall of Famers Tom Seaver, Steve Carlton, Phil Niekro, Don Sutton, Bert Blyleven, and Nolan Ryan. In addition, the Astros were in first place as the team sought its first playoff appearance since joining the league in 1962.

"I faced J. R. in the minors and later coached him," said Matt Galante, who was a longtime coach and manager with the Astros.

> When I faced him, he was so big that when he landed and his arm came through, it looked like he was about three feet away from you. The ball was right on you so fast. My claim to fame with him is that my last at-bat against him I got a hit. I managed to hit a ground ball, and the ball hit a baserunner and that was it.

Barry Bonnell, who came up with the Braves as a 23-year-old in 1977, faced Richard a number of times early in his career: "J. R. got me out like I wasn't there," said Bonnell.

> I was 0-for-15 in 18 appearances. I finally decided that I was better off not swinging at all, and he walked me once and hit me in the back once, the only way I ever reached first. I did hit a sac fly off of him for an RBI, but I don't even remember it. Probably had my eyes closed. He was the one pitcher in my experience that I found truly intimidating. His release point was very close; even his curveball was in the high 80s.

Richard was outright dominant during the four-year period between 1976 and 1979. He averaged 260 strikeouts and won a total of 74 games. In '78, Richard topped 300 strikeouts for the first time, becoming the first NL righty to accomplish that feat.

Nobody could have predicted how fast it would all come crashing down for Richard as July ended. On July 3, the first-place Astros were up against the Braves in a showdown at Atlanta–Fulton County Stadium. Houston featured one of the best pitching staff in the majors, led by Joe Niekro, Ryan, and Richard. Joe Morgan was the veteran leader on the squad, and players like José

Cruz and César Cedeño added excitement to the mix. With six players who had stolen more than 20 bases on the team and fireballers like Ryan and Richard, the Astros were playing some of the most exciting baseball in the majors.

Richard was the Opening Day starter for the Astros and picked up the win against the Dodgers, striking out 13 batters in eight innings. He didn't look back from there and had won five of his last six starts coming into the July 3 game. Richard came into the game with a 9–4 record and an ERA of 1.90. The Braves countered with Tommy Boggs, a journeyman who lost twice as many games as he won in his career.

Richard had his usual great stuff that day, and, surprisingly, Boggs matched him inning for inning as the game remained scoreless through five frames. Through the first five innings, Richard allowed just one hit, a harmless single to center by Chris Chambliss in the fourth, and struck out six batters.

The Astros finally broke up the scoreless tie when Denny Walling led off the top of the sixth with a home run. Morgan and Cruz followed with singles to knock Boggs out of the game. Rick Camp relieved Boggs but gave up singles to Cedeño and Andy Ashby to make the score 3–0.

Later in the game, the Astros were ahead 4–2, when manager Bill Virdon removed Richard and went to his bullpen, which was a very solid part of their team. Dave Smith came on and gave up a run in the seventh as the Braves inched closer. He kept out of more serious trouble, and the game stayed 4–3 into the ninth. The Astros added an insurance run in the ninth when Enos Cabell scored on an error by Larvell Blanks to make the final score 5–3.

Richard's final line was impressive: 6 innings pitched, 3 hits, 2 runs, 1 walk, and 8 strikeouts. He picked up the win as Smith, Joe Sambito, and Frank LaCorte pitched well in the final three innings.

Shockingly, this would be the final win in the storied career of J. R. Richard. He'd been complaining of shoulder and arm soreness throughout the season, but initial tests failed to show anything structurally wrong. He started the All-Star Game, throwing two scoreless innings in which he struck out Hall of Famers Reggie Jackson and Carlton Fisk.

Richard made his next scheduled start on July 14 against the Braves and once again was pitching well. In the first three innings he allowed just one hit and had four strikeouts. He even hit a double leading off the bottom of the third for Houston. Richard went out to the mound for the fourth inning and walked Dale Murphy, who was leading off. He got Chambliss to ground into a fielder's choice in what seemed to be a harmless play.

However, Richard called time and asked for the Astros' medical staff. He not only was having problems with his shoulder and arm, but was also complaining of blurry vision and an inability to see the catcher. He later said he threw a pitch and felt like his arm went dead.

Richard was placed on the disabled list and went through a battery of tests. In short, the doctors felt that when he pitched, his collarbone and first rib were pinching his subclavian artery, causing circulation problems and a blockage in an artery of his right arm. But they concluded that surgery was not needed.

Richard tried to make a quick comeback and was even able to go through pregame warm-ups just two weeks later; however, on July 30, 1980, he suffered three separate strokes while warming up before a game with the Phillies.

It was not only shocking to learn that the 30-year-old, 6'8" man was felled by a stroke that afternoon, but the insensitivity that the Astros organization had shown Richard in the previous two weeks was also concerning.

Although he was dominant on the mound for years, many were suspicious of Richard's work ethic and drive. Nagging injuries were always met with a sense of disbelief from the media and fans, who had tabbed Richard as lazy and were quick to point out his well-known drug use. Local sports reporters had to take to the air after Richard's stroke to publicly apologize for doubting that there was anything wrong. Even Virdon said in a TV interview that "there's no chance that he can hurt himself seriously, and he's agreed to pitch, so he's gonna pitch."

Richard eventually won a $1.2 million lawsuit against the Houston Astros for their misdiagnosis.

Luckily, Richard was able to recover enough to attempt a comeback just a year later. He worked out with the Astros throughout the season and on September 1 was placed on the extended 40-man roster. Virdon, however, didn't feel that Richard was 100 percent and never inserted him into a game. He tried to work his way back to the majors, but after two seasons in the minor leagues, Richard's second chance never materialized.

Bonnell witnessed Richard trying to make his comeback in spring training: "After his stroke the closest I came to facing him again was the on-deck circle in spring training," started Bonnell.

> He had walked everybody before me, and most of his pitches hit the screen halfway up. Jerry Royster stood in the far back corner of the box and still almost had his head taken off. J. R. still threw in the high 90s but had no control at all. I was so glad they took him out before I came to the plate.

Galante was there as Richard tried to make his comeback as well: "I was managing in AA when he tried to make his comeback," said Galante. "Bill Virdon asked me to take him to a separate field and hit him some comebackers. He was fine on the low ones, but when the ball came up he just couldn't react to it. I said to Bill, 'He just doesn't have it anymore.'"

Richard's fall from grace didn't stop there. A series of bad investments and divorces left him broke and homeless. A little more than a decade after he stopped pitching professionally, Richard found himself living under a bridge on Highway 59 in Houston, just eight miles from the Astrodome.

Eventually, former teammates Bob Watson and Jimmy Wynn learned about Richard's plight and assisted in getting him back on his feet. He has since become involved as a preacher and has been successful in putting his medical and drug problems behind him.

Richard made a name for himself as a schoolboy in Texas, when he didn't lose a single game during his high school career. He was the number-two pick overall in the 1969 MLB Draft, behind Jeff Burroughs. Just eight picks later, a player by the name of Charlie Spikes was drafted by the Yankees. That would be the same Charlie Spikes who made the final out of the Astros–Braves game on July 3, 1980, in J. R. Richard's last win as a Major League Baseball player.

THURMAN MUNSON AND BOBBY MURCER: HONORING THE CAPTAIN

August 6, 1979

In life, times of the deepest sorrow often bring people closer. As baseball reflects life, there are many instances of teammates, family, and fans rallying to mourn and honor in tragic circumstances. One of the great examples of tremendous honor through incredible sadness came on the night of August 6, 1979, when the Yankees took on the Baltimore Orioles just hours after they flew to Ohio to bury Thurman Munson, who'd died in a plane crash just four days earlier.

Munson was the backbone of the Yankees' rise back to elite status in the American League. The gritty catcher won the 1970 AL Rookie of the Year Award and was also the 1975 MVP. He was a seven-time All-Star in his 11-year career and was one of the great leaders in the game.

"Thurman was great, I loved him," said Rudy May, who was Munson's batterymate with the Yankees from 1974 to 1976. "He was one of the leaders who was just 'all win.' He was the core of our team and really pushed the Yankees back into that winning attitude."

Matt Galante, a baseball lifer who spent more than four decades in the sport, was a minor-league teammate of Munson's: "I was with Reading in AA when Munson joined the team," said Galante. "I didn't know who he was, I just saw a new guy in the lobby with a baseball bag. I introduced myself and he said, 'Hi, I'm Thurman, and I'm going to hit .300 in this league.' Well, he did, he went out and hit .301."

In addition to his hitting prowess, Munson was also stellar defensively: "He was very smart as a catcher and had great instincts," said Galante, who was a second baseman in the minors. "One day I went to him and asked if he wanted to set up some kind of pickoff play. He said to me, 'If you want a pickoff play, just get to the bag and I'll get it there.' We may not have gotten guys picked off all the time, but we got some and kept everyone close."

When Munson started as a Yankee in 1969, the team was typically a .500 squad as the stars of the last great run retired. Munson's career began on August 8, 1969. Ten months prior, Mickey Mantle had played his last game in pinstripes, and clearly this was going to be a new and difficult era of baseball in the Bronx. After nearly a decade of mediocre baseball, the Yanks had a revival toward the end of the '70s and found themselves back on top with back-to-back World Series titles over the Dodgers in 1977 and 1978. Much of that had to do with Munson.

In 1979, the Yanks didn't seem themselves and spent much of the early part of the season lingering five or six games out of first place in the AL East. Despite an early-season slump, Munson's average hovered around .300 for most of the campaign.

Munson played the final game of his career on August 1, 1979, as the team's starting first baseman and third hitter. He walked his first at-bat and struck out in his next. After his strikeout, Billy Martin lifted Munson for Jim Spencer with the Yanks ahead of the White Sox 3–0. The Yankees went on to win 9–1 but were still 15 games out of first place. As Munson walked off the field after striking out against Ken Kravec, it would be the last time anyone would see him as an active player in a Yankees uniform.

The Yanks had a day off after completing the three-game sweep of Chicago, and the team flew home to get ready for a showdown with the powerful Orioles. Munson instead flew home to Ohio to spend time with his family. He had been taking flying lessons for two years so he could fly home to be with his family on off days.

What happened on August 2, 1979, is recognized as one of the most tragic events in baseball history. While practicing takeoffs and landings, Munson's Cessna clipped a tree, which sent the plane crashing toward the runway. The plane skidded across the ground and crashed into a tree stump, bursting into flames. All three people on board survived the initial crash, including Munson. His passengers were able to escape, but Munson was pinned in the wreckage. Despite furiously trying to get Munson out of the plane, it became apparent that there was nothing his friends could do to get him out. Munson's two passengers had no choice but to leave Munson behind. It is believed that asphyxiation from toxic fumes and smoke inhalation killed him.

Despite the tragedy, the series with Baltimore went on. The Yanks lost the first two games by one run each but bounced back to take game three 3–2, behind a great effort on the mound from Tommy John and a home run by Graig Nettles. The game on August 6 would be the most difficult.

Munson's family planned the funeral services for the morning of August 6. The Yankees were scheduled to play a night game in front of a national TV audience. With nobody really sure what to do about the situation, George Steinbrenner took control. He said that the first priority of the Yankees was to honor Munson and show respect to his family, so he decided the team would fly to Ohio to attend the service. If they made it back in time for the game, they'd play. If not, that was just too bad.

At the service, Bobby Murcer was one of the eulogists. He was Munson's teammate from 1969 to 1974, and again in 1979, and was one of his closest friends. Murcer had just been reacquired to bolster the Yankees lineup on June 24, but was hitting .220. After an emotionally draining day in which he served as a pallbearer and read a eulogy, it would have been understandable if Murcer did not play that night against Baltimore. Martin approached Murcer on the plane about sitting out, but Murcer wanted to honor Munson by playing.

Barry Foote played with Murcer in both Chicago and New York, and reflected on the type of person he was: "Bobby was just a great guy," said Foote. "Like most midwesterners, he was just a good guy, very likable. He was a consummate professional who did what was asked of him. Even towards the end of his career, he was asked to become primarily a pinch-hitter, so he went out and became a very good pinch-hitter."

The Yankees made it back in time for their game against Baltimore and honored their captain with a brief but stirring pregame service. The starters took their positions but left the catcher position vacant. Cardinal Terence Cooke read a prayer, the stadium observed a moment of silence, and Robert Merrill sang "America the Beautiful." After the brief ceremony was over, the crowd of more than 36,000 gave an eight-minute standing ovation in honor of their fallen star. Eventually, public address announcer Bob Shepherd announced, "And now it is time to play ball. Thank you, ladies and gentlemen for your cooperation." Brad Gulden then trotted out of the dugout as the Yankees' starting catcher.

The game featured two ace starting pitchers as Ron Guidry took the mound for the Yanks against Dennis Martinez. Guidry retired the side in order in the first, and Willie Randolph led off the home half of the inning with a single. Martinez struck out Murcer, Chris Chambliss, and Reggie Jackson to end the frame. Lee May gave the Orioles the lead in the top of the second with a solo homer off Guidry, and Martinez would settle into a groove against the understandably drained Yanks.

Rich Dauer hit a fifth-inning sacrifice fly, and Ken Singleton hit a two-run homer in the sixth to make it 4–0. Martinez was cruising into the seventh and started the inning by striking out Bobby Brown and getting Gulden on a fly out to left. Bucky Dent drew what seemed like a harmless two-out walk to bring up Randolph. The young second baseman doubled to left to bring the quiet stadium crowd to its feet.

The next batter in the lineup was Murcer. In his previous three at-bats, Murcer struck out, lined out to short, and flew out to right. His struggles at the plate were still apparent. Sensing a moment, however, the Yankee Stadium crowd became as lively as it had been all night. In the best way to honor his fallen friend, who was one of the most clutch players on the team, Murcer came through with a magic moment of his own. He drove a pitch into the seats to bring the Yankees to within one run of the Orioles. Chambliss followed with a hit to chase Martinez from the game and Jackson followed by reaching on an error; however, Nettles struck out to end the seventh with the Yankees still down 4–3.

The game eventually went to the bottom of the ninth, with the Yanks down 4–3 and Dent, Randolph, and Murcer due up.

Despite the fact that Don Stanhouse, the Orioles' leader in saves in 1979, with 21, was available in the bullpen, Earl Weaver chose to stick with reliever Tippy Martinez for the ninth. Martin's genius as a manager was seen in the way that he handled the ninth. Dent led off with a walk, and Martin chose to go by the book and call for a sacrifice bunt with Randolph. Typical strategy calls for the home team to play for a tie in the bottom of the ninth or in extra innings, so that's what Martin did. Randolph dropped a perfect bunt, and Martinez threw it away, putting runners on second and third with no outs.

Murcer was on deck for the Yanks, and there was some question as to whether he would bat. Murcer had struggled overall for the past month and was not hitting lefties well. A tough lefty like Martinez had a huge advantage over Murcer in that spot. Martin could have called for a righty bat off the bench with the game on the line, but sensing the moment, he stuck with Murcer instead.

The move paid off, as Murcer hit a two-strike, opposite-field double down the line to plate both Dent and Randolph to give the Yanks the 5–4 win.

Guidry pitched a complete game with nine strikeouts to move to 10–7 on the year. Randolph was 2-for-4 with two runs scored as the team's leadoff hitter that night; however, the real star was Murcer. Just hours after carrying a casket holding his best friend's body, Murcer went 2-for-5 and drove in all five Yankees runs.

As Murcer came off the field after delivering the walk-off hit, his teammates ran out to meet him. While he didn't exactly collapse into their arms, it seemed as though the emotions of the week hit the left fielder all at once. His body language showed exhaustion and elation at the same time, while his face showed the excitement of the win and the pride in honoring Munson.

The Yankees would play close to .500 ball the rest of the season and finish 13½ games out of first place. The Orioles won the AL East in '79 and topped the Angels in the American League Championship Series, but fell to the Pirates 4–3 in the World Series.

Despite the legacy and history the Yanks have built in the years after Munson's tragic death, it seems the healing process still continues to this day. Because the anniversary of Munson's passing occurs in the middle of each baseball season, the stories are told and highlights are shown every year on Yankees broadcasts around August 2. Munson's number 15 was retired immediately by Steinbrenner and hangs beyond the outfield wall as a permanent reminder of their Yankees captain.

Perhaps the greatest tribute of all came on August 6, 1979. Despite playing subpar ball, the Yankees gutted out a 5–4 comeback win against a top American League foe behind clutch hitting from his former teammates, and especially from his best friend, Bobby Murcer.

TONY CONIGLIARO: A BOSTON MIRACLE, A BOSTON TRAGEDY

April 8, 1969

A baseball player has less than half of a second to react to a pitched ball. In that time, a batter needs to be able to recognize what type of pitch it is, where the pitch will be when it crosses the plate, and whether to swing. He also has less than half of a second to know whether to bail out of the way of an inside pitch. It's a losing battle for most hitters, as pitchers come out on top more than 70 percent of the time. For the Red Sox' Tony Conigliaro, the losing battle cost him much more than an out at the plate.

On August 18, 1967, Conigliaro dug in against Angels pitcher Jack Hamilton in the fourth inning of a scoreless game at Fenway Park. Hamilton, who had been accused of throwing a spitball in the past, came in high and tight to Conigliaro. The half of a second would not be enough time for Conigliaro to react, and Hamilton's fastball hit Conigliaro flush in the eye, fracturing his cheekbone and doing extensive damage to the left side of his face and eye.

Along with the beaning of Ray Chapman, who was killed when another spitballer, Carl Mays, hit him in the head with a pitch, Conigliaro's beaning would go down as one of the more infamous and graphic hit-by-pitches in major-league history.

Don Slaught, a 16-year major-league veteran, was another player who was hit in the face with a pitch. While the pitch that struck Conigliaro got him square in the eye, the one that hit Slaught got him less than an inch lower. That half inch made a ton of difference in the amount of damage done.

"It was 1986 in Boston [against Oil Can Boyd]; the pitch just came up and I couldn't see it to react," said Slaught. "Because of that, the Red Sox stopped letting people sit in the center-field stands. I just lost sight of the pitch in the crowd, and I couldn't react. My nose was gone, my cheek was gone, and to this day my eye sits on a piece of plastic."

While the damage done to Slaught was gruesome and extensive for sure, Conigliaro's injury was tragic in more ways than one. He was one of the most promising young sluggers in the game when he was hit by the pitch. He hit 24 homers as a teenager in 1964, and led the league with 32 homers the next year. Conigliaro would go on to become the second-youngest player to hit 100 career home runs, just missing out on topping Mel Ott, who was two months younger than Conigliaro when he reached that mark.

Adding to the graphic nature of the story was a *Sports Illustrated* cover that ran on June 22, 1970. The cover featured a close-up of Conigliaro's face with his eye swollen shut and dark purple from the injury. The cover is one of the most famous in *Sports Illustrated*'s history, as the photo of the young Conigliaro captured both the promise and tragedy of the beaning. If you cover half of the photo with your hand, you can see a young slugger with all the potential and good looks in the world wearing his Red Sox cap proudly. Cover the other side of his face and the severity of the injury hits you hard.

Conigliaro attempted a comeback in 1968, but had to cut his efforts short when vision problems in his left eye arose again. Although it was a setback, Conigliaro still worked in the offseason with a focus on Opening Day of the 1969 season for his return. Although he clearly wasn't back to his old self in spring training of '69, manager Dick Williams felt he was well enough to start in right field and bat fifth for the Sox on April 8, 1969, the team's Opening Day.

The Red Sox were a solid team during the time Conigliaro was away, and they hoped the return of their slugger would help them catch the Tigers, who had been the AL East's best team.

Opening Day in 1969 took place at Memorial Stadium in Baltimore and featured a pitching matchup of Jim Lonborg for the Sox and Dave McNally for Baltimore. Despite the fact that two All-Stars were on the hill, the offenses, which featured Hall of Famers Carl Yastrzemski, Brooks Robinson, and Frank Robinson, would win the day.

The Red Sox got started quickly as Reggie Smith led off the season with a walk and Mike Andrews singled to left. Yastrzemski doubled home Smith, and the Sox had a 1–0 lead with runners on second and third with no outs. Cleanup hitter Ken Harrelson fouled out to bring Conigliaro to the plate for the first time in 599 days. Even though McNally struck out Conigliaro, it was a major victory for the 24-year-old right fielder.

Just one year earlier, when he had to cut his 1968 spring training short due to poor vision, Conigliaro was told that the condition of his left eye was deteriorating. He was told by Dr. Charles Regan that the vision in his left eye was 20/300, which is just about blind. Conigliaro himself admitted that he couldn't even read or go to the movies; however, in what he classified as a miracle, his eyesight restored to 20/20 throughout time, and strikeout or not, Conigliaro made it back from the impossible.

After Conigliaro's strikeout, George Scott popped out to end the threat. The game stayed 1–0 until the third, when the Sox added a run on a single by Harrelson. Conigliaro was up next, and he worked out a walk. But the Sox couldn't continue the rally, and the score stood at 2–0. Light-hitting Mark Belanger got the O's on the board in the bottom of the frame with a solo homer, and the game stayed that way until the bottom of the eighth. Along the way, Conigliaro had his first contact since returning, as he singled to center in the fifth and flew out to left in the seventh.

The Orioles tied the game in the eighth on a Don Buford sac fly, and both teams mounted rallies in the ninth. In the top of the inning, pitcher Lee Strange walked and advanced to third with one out on consecutive wild pitches. But two infield popups doomed the rally for Boston. The Orioles loaded the bases with one out in the bottom of the ninth, forcing Williams to call on Sparky Lyle to get out of the jam. He struck out Belanger, and on the pitch catcher Russ Gibson picked Marv Rettenmund off third for a double play.

Harrelson led off the 10th for the Red Sox by reaching on a rare error by Brooks Robinson to bring up Conigliaro. Williams could have chosen to bunt at the time, as the Sox had two experienced hitters in Scott and Rico Petrocelli up next; however, the Hall of Fame manager chose to let Conigliaro hit. It ended up being the right call, as Conigliaro belted a long homer to left-center field to give the Sox a 4–2 lead. While it was a self-described miracle that Conigliaro was even playing that day, he now found himself set to be the hero of the game.

However, Lyle couldn't hold the Orioles down in the bottom of the inning. He walked Buford with one out but got Paul Blair on a groundout. Lyle had to get past Frank Robinson to end the game, but the task proved too tall, as Robinson belted a homer of his own to tie the game once again.

Conigliaro found himself in a key spot again in the 12th, as he was due up first after a scoreless 11th. He worked out his second walk of the day and advanced to second on a single by Scott. Petrocelli followed with a walk to load the bases, and Conigliaro would come in to score on a sacrifice fly by pinch-hitter Dalton Jones.

Red Sox reliever Juan Pizarro was asked to close out the game for the Red Sox, and he had to face both Robinson and Rettenmund in the 12th. He was able to get through them unscathed to pick up the save in the 5–4 win.

Conigliaro was back with the Red Sox in a big way. He finished the day 2-for-4 and had a hand in four of the five Red Sox runs, scoring two and driving in two. Conigliaro had a couple of other hurdles that he would face early in the 1969 season.

Three days later, the Sox went to extra innings again, this time against the Indians in Cleveland. In the 12th inning of that game, Indians manager Alvin Dark pinch-hit for pitcher Chuck Hinton. When they couldn't score in a bases-loaded situation, Dark called for his fourth relief pitcher: Jack Hamilton.

Conigliaro was due to face Hamilton as the second batter in order that inning, and it would be the first time the two had faced one another since that fateful day two years before. Harrelson led off the inning with a walk, and in the same situation that had faced Williams just three days earlier, the Red Sox manager changed his strategy. He called for the bunt, and Conigliaro executed it perfectly. But the Sox couldn't score, and Conigliaro faced Hamilton again in the 15th. This time he lined out to left. The Sox, however, would go on to win the game in the 16th inning.

Conigliaro harbored no ill feelings toward Hamilton and acknowledged that it was part of the game. Hamilton, however, took the incident quite hard. He'd spoken openly of retiring immediately after the incident and said he would have done so if Conigliaro had been blinded. The once-promising Hamilton was relegated to relief duties after he became reluctant to pitch inside after the event. In 1968, Hamilton pitched just 38 innings as a reliever with the Angels and then split '69 between the White Sox and Indians. After logging a 6.49 ERA and an 0–5 record in '69, he retired from baseball.

Meanwhile, Conigliaro continued his miraculous journey back to stardom in 1969 and 1970, playing alongside his brother Billy in the Red Sox outfield. In those two seasons, he belted 56 home runs and drove in 198 runs. He played in 287 games during that time and showed no ill effects of his previous injury. He was hit by a pitch 12 times and never once let it affect his approach at the plate.

After the 1970 season, Conigliaro was traded by the Red Sox to the Angels. He struggled to find his footing with his new team and suffered a relapse of the symptoms he struggled with during his 1968 season away from the game. Conigliaro's eyesight had deteriorated again, and he announced that he was retiring from baseball. Amazingly, while playing golf with his brother years later, Conigliaro noticed that his depth perception had returned and the symptoms he lived with for so long had disappeared once again. Damage to his eye that showed up on previous examinations was inexplicably gone.

Conigliaro tried one more time to make it as a major leaguer in 1975, and did well enough in the Red Sox spring training to earn a spot on the team. He went 1-for-4 as the cleanup batter on Opening Day and hit a home run off the Orioles' Mike Cuellar three days later.

Fred Lynn, a member of the Red Sox Hall of Fame, was a rookie on the 1975 Sox team and remembers Conigliaro's final comeback attempt well: "In spring training in '75 we were both outfielders so we were in the same groups working out," said Lynn. "I remember that Opening Day, the place was just electric. When they announced Tony's name the place just went bonkers. They loved him there."

However, it was clear that the three and a half years away from the game were too much to overcome, and he retired after hitting just .123 in 57 at-bats. His final home run came off of Vida Blue in a May 20, 7–0 win over the A's. "I don't know if he saw the writing on the wall or not, but Conigliaro finally called it a career," said Lynn. "He went out gracefully and on his own terms."

The roller coaster of Tony Conigliaro's life continued after baseball. He became a sportscaster in San Francisco in the early '80s, but hoped to end up back in Boston at some point. While he was being driven to the airport by his brother Billy on January 3, 1982, for an interview in Boston, Conigliaro suffered a heart attack. A subsequent stroke knocked Conigliaro into a coma from which he would never emerge. He remained in that state for eight years before finally passing away in February 1990, at the age of 45.

The story of Tony Conigliaro is one of the great "what might have been" tales in the history of baseball. The early home run pace that he set was matched by few in the game's history, even as home runs became more plentiful through the steroid era of the '90s. He suffered tremendous setbacks along the way and dealt with things few athletes ever had to deal with. After he was hit by that pitch in 1967, he rose to the occasion many times, despite being told it was impossible. Fans first saw that the word *impossible* meant nothing to Conigliaro on April 8, 1969, when he stepped back up to the plate on Opening Day and willed the Red Sox to a win just 599 days after nearly losing his eye and his life.

DARRYL KILE: A TALE OF TWO LEGACIES

September 8, 1993

Although millions of kids grow up with the dream of playing Major League Baseball, only a small fraction ever realize the chance to one day call themselves a pro. Of the thousands who've played the game professionally in the past 100 years, even fewer can say they left some sort of true legacy. Many players come up, toil in the bigs for a few years, and leave the game as afterthoughts.

All-Stars and Hall of Famers leave an obvious legacy, as they are heroes to millions of fans and bridge generations as the game moves forward. There is another group of players who leave their own mark on the game based on some unique situation or performance. As Darryl Kile's career progressed, it looked like his legacy was determined on September 8, 1993, when he no-hit the Mets in a masterful performance; however, nine years later, Kile's place in baseball history turned out to be a tragic one when he died of a heart attack before a game between the Cardinals and Cubs on June 22, 2002.

Nine years before the tragic turn of events in Chicago, Kile was a 23-year-old right-hander coming into his own in Houston. He was only a 30th-round selection of the Astros in the 1987 MLB Draft but immediately had success in the minors. He went 18–10 in his first two years in the minors and was extremely difficult to hit, allowing just 155 hits in 210 innings. He gained a promotion to AAA in 1990, and despite falling to 5–10, he earned a spot on the Astros' staff in 1991, as the team's second pitcher. After going 12–22 in his first two seasons, Kile blossomed in 1993.

Coming into his start on September 8, Kile was 14–6 with a 3.33 ERA and was one of the top young pitchers in the National League. The 6'5" righty had a knee-buckling curveball that froze batters as the pitch broke well out of the strike zone. The Astros were taking on the Mets as the 1993 season was in its final weeks. The Mets were one year removed from their "Worst Team Money Can Buy" season of '92 and again fell well below expectations in '93. By this point in the season, the Mets were on their third manager in two years and, despite another season with a high payroll, had been eliminated long before this game.

Kile was dominant right from the start as he retired the Mets in order in the first two innings on just 17 total pitches. The Astros got Kile a lead in the bottom of the second off Mets starter Frank Tanana, who was pitching in one of the final games of his 21-year career. Ken Caminiti belted a one-out solo home run to get the Astros on the scoreboard. After Kile got through Butch Huskey, Todd Hundley, and Tanana on five pitches in the top of the third inning, they again got to Tanana in the bottom of the frame. With two outs, Casey Candaele singled home Andújar Cedeño, and Jeff Bagwell doubled home Candaele to give Kile a 3–0 lead.

The top of the fourth provided Kile with the only bump in the road he would face all night. The inning started off well enough when Kile struck out Ryan Thompson, but he walked the next batter, Jeff McKnight. Eddie Murray flew out to deep left for the second out, bringing up Joe Orsulak, who would be part of a wild play. Kile got ahead of Orsulak 0–2 and tried to get him to chase an inside curve; however, the curve broke low toward Orsulak's feet, causing the left fielder to jump out of the way. The ball eluded catcher Scott Servais and went to the backstop. Servais thought the ball hit Orsulak and didn't give chase as the ball ricocheted toward the first-base line. Mc-Knight easily made it to second, and when he noticed Servais still at home, he took off for third. Bagwell finally ran the ball down and made an ill-advised throw to third. The ball got past Caminiti, allowing McKnight to score. Kile then got Orsulak to fly out to left.

Cedeño led off the fifth with a home run to make the score 4–1. Kile then got back to pure domination when he took his spot on the mound in the sixth. He retired the Mets in order in the sixth and seventh, this time on a combined 12 pitches.

Kile was helped by two tremendous defensive plays to keep his no-hitter alive. Murray was retired when Caminiti made a diving stop on a grounder down the third-base line, scrambled to his feet, and nabbed Murray by a step. As close as Murray's play was, Orsulak was retired on one even closer. He hit a grounder in the hole between short and third that was backhanded on a sparkling play by Cedeño. He turned and fired to first, a half step ahead of Orsulak for the 21st out of the game. The play was so close that Orsulak argued vehemently and was finally ejected by first-base umpire Mark Hirschbeck.

The Astros went down in order against reliever Josías Manzanillo, bringing Kile out for the eighth. At this point in the game, Kile had thrown just 63 pitches in an utterly dominant performance. Kile didn't need any sparkling defensive plays in the eighth to get through the Mets, as he struck out Jeromy Burnitz and Huskey around a Jeff Kent lineout.

Not that Kile needed it, but the Astros got him three insurance runs in the eighth on a single by Luis Gonzalez and a Mets error. With a 7–1 lead, Kile was on the verge of throwing the first Astros no-hitter since Mike Scott's gem on September 25, 1986, to clinch the NL West. Hundley led off the ninth with an easy groundout to short for the first out, and Tito Navarro, who played just 12 major-league games, struck out looking for out number two. With just one out to go, Kile had to get through another pinch-hitter, Chico Walker. Walker had been a solid role player in his career, but like everybody else, he was no match for Kile on this day. On a 1–2 count, Kile went to his trademark curve, and Walker waved wildly at it for strike three, setting off a celebration on the Astrodome mound.

After Servais corralled the final strike, he thrust his right hand into the air and sprinted out to congratulate Kile, his minor-league batterymate in Tucson during the 1990 season. With both arms raised, Kile embraced Servais before being mobbed by the rest of his teammates. Even as far as no-hitters are concerned, Kile's performance was incredibly dominant. He faced just 28 batters, allowing only McKnight to reach base on a four-pitch walk. Kile threw a grand total of 83 pitches in nine innings, 59 of them for strikes. According to baseball historian Bill James's "games score" statistic, Kile's performance at the time was the fourth-best performance in the pitching-rich history of the Astros.

In the years after Kile's no-hitter, he put together a very good career for the Astros, Rockies, and Cardinals. He won 133 games in 12 seasons and was a three-time All-Star. Kile placed fifth in the Cy Young voting in 1997 and 2000, and also received MVP votes in each of those years. As his career progressed, Kile looked like he would end up with a solid career, as he was a reliable innings-eater who was enjoying a nice peak through the age of 33. It seemed as if his 1993 no-hitter would be the legacy for which he would be remembered, but unfortunately, any time Kile's name was mentioned after June 22, 2002, one's thoughts immediately turned to the shocking event that staggered the baseball world.

As the Cardinals were preparing to take on the Cubs at Wrigley Field, Cardinals personnel realized that Kile had not reported to the facility with the other players. Because Kile wasn't known for unreliable or flighty behavior, the Cardinals contacted their hotel to send someone to check on Kile's room. After nobody responded to knocks or calls, the hotel staff entered and found Kile unresponsive on his bed after an apparent heart attack that had happened sometime the previous night. Kile had showed no signs of heart problems and passed his spring physical, which included an EKG. It was later revealed that Kile had two coronary arteries that were 90 percent blocked, an enlarged heart, and a familial history of heart problems; his father died from a heart attack at age 44.

After Kile's no-hitter, *Sports Illustrated* did a feature story on the tremendous performance. In the article, Servais talks about reminiscing about the game with his good friend Kile at 55 years of age during a round of golf. Kile mentions being emotionally moved when he saw Servais running to the mound and how he immediately thought of his dad. The article ends with Kile saying that he was sure his father was watching him and his performance that day. Although they didn't know it at the time, the comments by Servais and Kile were foreboding and a staunch reminder of the frailty of life. Kile's legacy to the common fan may be of the tragic events of June 22, but to teammates, it is that of the perfect teammate, family man, and friend.

· 6 ·

Passing Down Tradition
and Influencing the Pros

One of the great things about baseball is that there are so many nuances that even at the highest level of play, the game can really never be perfected. Even the greatest players in the game benefit incredibly from guidance and mentoring of those who came before them. The mentoring doesn't always have to do with fundamentals or technique, either. Players pass along the game's history, the respect that professionals have for the sport, and the way a player should carry himself as a big leaguer. It all comes with being a competitor at the game's highest level and having the proper humility when considering your place in history. No matter if a player is a Hall of Famer or someone who played a handful of games in the bigs, they all have influences who helped them or gave them the confidence to play in the major leagues.

Take a player like Ernie Banks. One of the greatest and most enthusiastic players to ever play the game, it's funny to think Banks needed any help along the way. It's conceivable that someone with Banks's ability could just roll out of bed and walk into professional baseball based on his God-given ability; however, one look at his Hall of Fame induction speech shows this was not the case.

Banks said in his 1977 induction speech, "If it had not been for the people who believed in me and gave me the encouragement, there would be no games and I would not be here today." Banks then went on to list Monte Irvin, Cool Papa Bell, and Bob Kennedy as people who taught him how to play the game. In Willie Mays's Hall of Fame speech, he mentioned that he tried to send himself down to the minors as a rookie but needed the encouragement of Leo Durocher to set him on the path.

Joe Morgan thanked Nellie Fox and Bob Lillis, Ted Williams expressed how impactful the support of the legendary Eddie Collins was to him as a young player, Tony Gwynn talked about the Padres sharing their spring training facilities with the Angels and sneaking around to eavesdrop on Rod Carew instructing younger players, and Mickey Mantle said the two people responsible for his Hall of Fame status were his father and Casey Stengel.

The point is that no matter how much talent a player is blessed with, he still benefits from that kind of guidance. It's not just mentoring and teaching someone the rules or tricks of the trade. There is a different kind of bond in teaching the sport of baseball. It's that connection of generations and the respect for the people who came before you. It's what makes the game special to players at all levels. In this chapter, former major leaguers from six decades discuss those who helped them on the path to playing successfully at the sport's highest level.

I learned how to play baseball the right way from Rod Dedeaux [the legendary manager for USC]. Coach always challenged us to play the "perfect game." He had a fine system in place and kept a little book in the dugout to track fines. Your first fine of the game was one dollar, and every fine after was fifty cents. One example of how this worked came one game with Gary Carter's brother Gordie. He was a big cleanup hitter who never bunted. But he came up with first and second with no outs, and coach wanted him to bunt. He fouled off two pitches and looked bad. The pitcher hung a slider though, and Gordie crushed it for a three-run homer. As everyone was jumping up and down celebrating, coach was walking over to his book in the dugout to write down the fine. The outcome of the at-bat didn't matter; he didn't get the bunt down like he was asked.

One time we got pretty close to a perfect game, and we were out on defense. A tough grounder got hit to Roy Smalley at shortstop. The ball took a bad bounce and just ate him up bad. I was out in the outfield and looked over into the dugout. I saw coach walking over to mark down the fine in his book. I was thinking to myself, "Man, that was a physical error, what's he getting fined for?" I walked in to coach and asked why Smalley got fined for missing a ball on a bad hop. He said, "If he would have taken that extra step like we practiced, he wouldn't have gotten that bad hop and would have made that play." We won three national championships during my time at USC and never had one perfect game.—Eight-time All-Star Fred Lynn, on Hall of Fame USC coach Rod Dedeaux, whom he credits as the greatest influence of his baseball career

I was very fortunate when I came up. Tony Oliva and Harmon Killebrew took me under their wings. Tony became my roommate, and together we won 10 batting titles. We talked hitting almost every chance we had. From Harmon I learned to respect the game and the people who played it. Nobody treated the fans better than Harmon. Have you ever seen his autograph? It's a thing of beauty. He said we owed a legible autograph to those who want it. To this day, I still hear his voice every time I sign for people.—Hall of Famer Rod Carew, on the early influences of his career

Reggie Jackson was very warm and friendly to me. Coming to that team, there were so many great veterans like Reggie, Dave Winfield, Tommy John, Goose Gossage, and Rudy May. Finally making it to the big leagues was such a big deal. I think a lot of times veterans are hard on rookies; they make you earn their respect. But this wasn't the case here. They were very welcoming right from the start.—Andy McGaffigan, who made his major-league debut with the Yankees as a 24-year-old in 1981

I was a teammate of Stephen Strasburg in AAA and was able to talk to him about dealing with the media when he made the majors. Everyone knew he'd be a big media draw, so I told him he needed to set a precedent right away. Tell them you won't be talking on days you're pitching; set boundaries. With a player of Stephen's magnitude, the media will try to monopolize his time. You have to do what's best for your own job.—Kevin Mench, on the advice he gave All-Star pitcher Stephen Strasburg just before he burst onto the scene as one of the most-hyped rookies of the decade

We were a young team, one of the youngest in the league. But we had guys like Ed Charles, Donn Clendenon, and Al Weis who were leaders. To this day, we all still get along great. When you get it right in New York, it's really special.—Rod Gaspar, outfielder for the 1969 New York Mets World Series champions

Buddy Bell and Terry Francona were very popular veterans when I came up with the Reds. You learn a lot of things from veterans like them. They pass the game down to you and then you do the best you can to pass it down to the next generation. A lot of younger players have credited me with being influential to them. That's really a great feeling.—Jeff Montgomery, member of the Kansas City Royals Hall of Fame and the team's all-time saves leader

I was drafted in the first round out of high school and sent right to the minors. I was totally overmatched and not ready for the minors at 18 years old, though. I spun my wheels for three years and just wasn't polished at all. I went to the Instructional League in 1994, and worked with pitching coach Ron Romanick and sports psychologist Gary Mack. Their help turned my whole career around.

The night before I was going to leave for the winter after the '95 season, I got a call that I was going up to the majors. I worked my way up from low A to the Texas League championship then to the majors in one season. Dusty Baker and Dick Pole, my pitching coach, were great influences when

I first got to the majors. I might not have been quite ready for the majors when I first got there, but having those two in my corner really helped a lot.—Shawn Estes, who was the 11th overall pick and third-highest picked high school pitcher in the 1991 MLB Draft, on making the adjustment to professional ball. He was the highest-ranked high school pitcher to make the major leagues from the '91 draft.

My very first call-up came with the Dodgers. F. P. Santangelo was on the team and was great with me. He was a role player, so he sat with me during games and we kind of played manager as the games went on. We just would sit there and map out the game, and I learned a lot. I went on to Oakland, and guys like Eric Chavez, Marco Scutaro, and Mark Kotsay were really awesome as teammates. I watched them and learned what it was like to be an everyday player, just the way they went about their business. I thought, "If I was an everyday player, that's who I would model myself after." When I got to Colorado, I got to play with Todd Helton and Larry Walker. Larry was just a special talent, and Todd was equally as good. The way they went about their business was different. Todd was very business-like, and everything just came easy to Larry. It was really special to be their teammate looking back.—Adam Melhuse, who played for eight seasons in the majors and is now an advanced scout for the Chicago Cubs, looking back on the influential teammates he played with during his career

I saw that Frank Robinson was in our organization, and I said to myself, "I have to do everything I can to try to get close to him so I can learn the game." It took me about three years, but I finally did and I was able to learn from him.—Benny Ayala, who played in the Orioles from 1979 to 1984

Sal Bando, who was one of the first free agents in the game, was a very influential player to me. I was young and dumb, and thought I knew everything. Having been there before and having been a World Series winner, he just knew what to do. He taught us the nuances of baseball. Larry Hisle was great too. He taught me about setting up a pitcher. He'd make a pitcher think he could jam him early in the game and then come up in clutch spot later on. The pitcher would try to come in again, but then Larry would turn on it and rip a double down the line.—Lary Sorensen, on the veteran leaders of the Brewers clubs of the late '70s who influenced young stars like Paul Molitor, Robin Yount, and Sorensen

Two people really stood out as influences in my career. Luis Gonzalez was my teammate for a year in Detroit and showed me naturally how to have fun and be professional. That was my first year in the majors. My manager that year, Buddy Bell, was great as well. He's just a tremendous baseball guy. I always wished Buddy was given one of those teams loaded with talent to see what he could do. I feel like he could have done great with a team that had the talent to win it.—Paul Bako, on the influential people with the Tigers team he broke in with in 1998

In 2005 and 2006, Yogi Berra was around the ballpark more than people realize. After batting practice, Yogi would pull up a chair and sit at my locker, and we'd just talk about life and the game. He was really amazing to be around.—Aaron Small, who went 10–3 in 26 starts in two seasons for the Yankees

When I first got to the Orioles, Mike Boddicker and Scott McGregor were still there, and they led by example. I learned a lot just by watching how they went about their business on a daily basis. They weren't hard throwers and I couldn't break a pane of glass, but they got people out consistently. So I watched how they set hitters up and tried to learn the finer points of pitching.—Orioles pitcher Jeff Ballard, who went 18–8 in 1989, to lead a resurgent Orioles team to a 33-game improvement between 1988 and 1989

I was one of the first new guys to break that lineup with George Brett, Hal McRae, Willie Wilson, Frank White, and all of those guys. They were all leaders, but Hal McRae was really respected in the locker room and helped me as much as anyone. Guys used to sit around after the game and talk baseball with guys like Brett and McRae. That's changed today. One game I made the mistake of sitting in the back of the bus as a rookie. Hal McRae made fun of the cheap suit I was wearing—my shoes, my socks, my jacket, everything. But then he gave me his credit card and said, go buy yourself some nice clothes and put it on my bill. I never paid for meals, the big-league guys paid.—Don Slaught, who caught 16 years in the majors, on joining the Royals at the age of 23

I knew how to throw, but I didn't know how to pitch. My first pitching coach was Marv Grissom [who pitched in the majors from 1946 to 1959]. I was warming up in the pen in 1965, and he said, "Lemme see your curve." I threw it and he snickered and said I needed work. Teammates like Dean Chance, Pat Dobson, Sparky Lyle, and Dick Tidrow helped me along the way. I could throw hard as a high school player and on the sandlot, so I never worried about the curve. I just threw hard, and that's what got me there. I learned the curve as a big leaguer.—16-year veteran Rudy May, on learning the curveball, which he developed into one of the best in the game during his time in the majors

Gil Hodges was a terrific manager. He was just a good guy, almost too good at times. He wasn't Earl Weaver, where he'd yell and scream at everyone. He was just the opposite. He was a good Christian man who knew the game and had the respect of everyone.—Fred Valentine, on Gil Hodges, who was Valentine's manager with the Washington Senators in the 1960s

I came up to a team of veterans. Bob Bailey was someone who I always used to talk hitting with. John Boccabella was a fine man. He was the starting catcher when I came up, and it was pretty understood that I was going to be taking over his job. But he went out of his way to help me, and I always appreciated that.—Barry Foote, on the veterans who helped him when he was called up to the Expos as a 21-year-old in 1973

A-Rod took me under his wing when I came up with the Rangers. I was 24 and came up onto a team with Kenny Rogers, Pudge Rodríguez, Carl Everett, Juan Gonzalez, and Rafael Palmeiro. Orel Hershiser was our pitching coach. There were all these great veterans, but A-Rod really took an interest. He had a little group of guys, and I was one of the guys fortunate enough to hang out with him during the season and offseason too. He really helped me get started out in the majors.—Kevin Mench, on coming up and forging a relationship with Alex Rodriguez as a rookie in 2002

I came up onto a team that already had Dave Winfield and Kirby Puckett, with Tom Kelly as manager. It was awe-inspiring knowing you're on the same team as Hall of Famers like that. Tom Kelly influenced my own managerial style. I remember one game we lost on a dropped popup. He took us out after the game and hit us popups. The fans weren't even out of their seats yet. It was embarrassing, but he wouldn't settle for us losing a game like that.—Matt Walbeck, who caught 11 years in the majors and went on to win the 2007 Minor League Manager of the Year Award at all levels of play, on the early influences on his career

I was pretty fortunate when I was working my way through the Tigers system, and I had a lot of pitching coaches along the way that made a difference in my career. I was able to get something from each one and add it to what I do. I had a Gulf Coast League coach who dropped me to a three-quarters arm slot, and all of a sudden I had a nasty sinker. An A ball coach taught me the importance of pitching inside and working quickly. In AA I learned how to change speeds, and in AAA I put it all together. One of the coolest things was in Baltimore when I would throw my side. B. J. Surhoff at times would come and stand in and then sit around and talk to me afterwards about pitching and what hitters are looking for.—Dave Borkowski, who pitched 181 games in the majors in seven big-league seasons, on his progression through the minors and what he learned along the way

The most influential managers and coaches I ever played for were Jim Leyland and Carlos Tosca. Leyland's tough love made me a hard man and taught me the game. Tosca had faith in me, and that faith gave me an enormous amount of confidence in my ability at the time when nobody else believed in me. As a result of playing for both of these men, I was able to carve out a decent career for myself.—Gregg Zaun, who played in more than 1,200 games in 16 seasons and was a member of the 1997 World Series champion Florida Marlins

With the Yankees, time with Don Zimmer was priceless to me. He passed on his knowledge, and hearing his experience and stories were second to none. I really paid close attention to Chris Chambliss, Willie Randolph, and Mel Stottlemyre. Hearing their perspectives on the game was fascinating. One unique thing about the Yankees in 1997 is they all were great teammates. I knew my place on the team and expected to be treated like the guy on the AAA shuttle to be seen but not heard. There were free agent stars on that team, Boggs, Gooden, Strawberry, Fielder, Cone, etc., but all were extremely friendly and professional.—Scott Pose, member of the 1997 Yankees, on his time in the Bronx

I had a number of managers and coaches who influenced me along the way. Buddy Bell was the manager when I got to Colorado. I was so green, I didn't know which way was up or down at the time. I was just trying to survive. Looking back, I wish I could have played better for him. Later in your career you figure things out and you're able to look back, and I realized what a great guy he was. Dave Hudgens was great as a hitting coach. I wasn't a big-name player and he wasn't a big-name coach, so we had that connection. He wasn't a "my way or the highway" kind of guy. He taught everyone differently, it wasn't just one way. In the game, and in life, you come across so many people who are like that, so I thought Dave's approach was great. My favorite though was Ron Washington. He was the third-base coach with the A's and then my manager when I was in Texas. He knew the game but wasn't a big Xs and Os guy. He was more about managing personalities. He was just so upbeat and positive, and I loved being around him. He'd jump on you when you needed it, but he stayed positive.—Adam Melhuse, on the influential managers and coaches he had during his career

Tony Gwynn really helped me out as a young player. I was traded to the Padres when I was 23, and he opened his arms to me and my family. I was scared to move across the country to a new team at first, but he and his wife helped us transition. Playing next to him in the outfield and watching him hit was amazing. He had thin fingers and his hands weren't too strong, so he used a small bat. But the way he would wield it was something to see. He studied video and was like a professor when it came to hitting. He was so ahead of his time.—Stanley Jefferson, who played next to Gwynn in the Padres outfield in 1987 and 1988

Regardless of how long a list I compiled, I'm sure I'd miss somebody, so I'll name just a few. All four big-league managers I had the opportunity to play for each impacted my career: Roger Craig, Jeff Torborg, Jim Leyland, and

Dusty Baker. I had excellent pitching coaches as well—Mel Stottlemyre, Ray Miller, and Dick Pole. From a player standpoint, Jeff Brantley was a big help when I first got called up with the Giants. I referred to him as my "Shell answer man." Some of my closest friends in the game were influential in a number of ways, guys like Mark Leonard and Bryan Hickerson. I'd be remiss to leave out the men who were vitally important to helping me at the minor-league level. Included among them are managers Billy Evers, Duane Espy, and Clint Hurdle, and pitching coaches Todd Oakes and Bob Apodaca.—Mark Dewey, who pitched 206 big-league games in his career, on the influential managers and teammates he had during his career

I was pitching for the University of Michigan, and Ray Fisher [Michigan's head baseball coach from 1921 to 1958] used to still come around the team when I was there. Now here's a guy who pitched in the majors in the 1910s. He lost Game 3 in the 1919 World Series as a member of the Reds during the Black Sox scandal. He taught me how important movement was on my pitches and used to show me different ways to hold the ball to get different kinds of speed and movement on my pitches. . . . I now do play-by-play for the Winston-Salem Dash in the Carolina League. Every so often I'll be down on the field watching the pitchers throw, and I offer some advice. The coaches will say, "See that guy over there? He was a major-league All-Star; he knows a thing or two. Take the time to listen when he talks."—Former All-Star Lary Sorensen, on how 100 years of baseball has been passed down from Ray Fisher, to himself, and on to professional players today

Ted Williams follows through on his swing in a game at Fenway Park during a game in 1954. Williams batted .345 in 1954 and led the league in walks (136), slugging percentage (.635), on-base percentage (.513), and OPS (1.148). Williams missed the first six weeks of the season with a broken collarbone and played in just 43 combined games in 1952 and 1953 due to service in the Korean War.

Courtesy of the Boston Public Library, Leslie Jones Collection

New York Giants Hall of Fame pitcher Carl Hubbell rests his head on the dugout railing at Braves Field in Boston in 1937. That season, Hubbell went 22–8 with a 3.20 ERA. The 34-year-old Hubbell finished third in the MVP voting that season behind Joe Medwick and Gabby Hartnett. It was also the only season Hubbell led the league in strikeouts. He struck out 159 in 304 innings pitched.

Courtesy of the Boston Public Library, Leslie Jones Collection

Hall of Famers Jimmie Foxx (left) and Joe DiMaggio talk before a game at Fenway Park in 1937. Foxx, who was in his second season in Boston after spending the first eleven years of his career with the Philadelphia A's, was 4th in the AL with 36 home runs and 6th with 127 RBIs. DiMaggio was just 22 years old at the time and in his second big-league season. He finished second in the MVP voting behind Charlie Gehringer after batting .346 with 46 home runs, 167 RBIs, and 151 runs scored.

Courtesy of the Boston Public Library, Leslie Jones Collection

Babe Ruth leans on the dugout in Fenway Park in a photo taken in 1933. Ruth, who was 38 years old and in his second-to-last season with the Yankees when this photo was taken, hit .301 with 34 home runs and 104 RBIs that year. Ruth also played in the inaugural Major League Baseball All-Star Game in 1933 where he hit the first ever home run in the game.

Legendary A's manager Connie Mack talks with outfielder Wally Moses during a game in 1937. Mack was in his 40th year as the A's manager in 1937 and would go on to manage the club until 1950, which gave him 53 years in that capacity. Moses made his only career All-Star Game in 1937 when he hit .320 with 25 home runs.
Courtesy of the Boston Public Library, Leslie Jones Collection

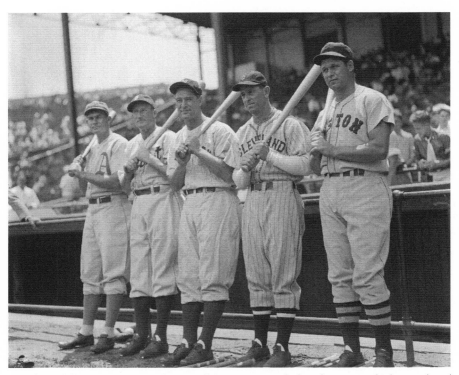

Members of the 1936 American League All-Star team pose before the game, which was played at Braves Field in Boston. The game was the fourth edition of the MLB All-Star Game and was won by the National League, 4–3. It was the NL's first All-Star Game win. In the game, Joe DiMaggio became the first rookie to start an All-Star Game, going 0-for-5 while batting third. Pictured left to right are Pinky Higgins, Goose Goslin, Lou Gehrig, Earl Averill, and Jimmie Foxx.

Satchel Paige (left) talks with manager Lou Boudreau. Paige became the oldest rookie to play in the majors when he went 6–1 with a 2.48 era in 72²/₃ innings at the age of 42 in 1948. He became the first black pitcher in the American League and the seventh black player overall. Paige played two seasons for Boudreau in Cleveland, including the 1949 season in which they won the World Series. Prior to being signed by Bill Veeck, Paige had a legendary career in the Negro Leagues.
Photo courtesy of the Boston Public Library, Leslie Jones Collection; Leslie Jones photographer

Baseball immortals Honus Wagner (left) and Pie Traynor pose before a game at Braves Field in Boston in 1938. Traynor managed the Pirates from 1934 to 1939, compiling a record of 457–406. Wagner served as the team's hitting coach from 1933 to 1952 after a career that spanned 21 years between 1897 and 1917. Wagner, who was 64 when this picture was taken, compiled 3,420 hits in his career and was tied for second with Babe Ruth in the voting for the initial Hall of Fame induction class in 1936. Traynor became the first third baseman selected to the Hall of Fame in 1948 after a 17-year career played entirely in Pittsburgh.

Courtesy of the Boston Public Library, Leslie Jones Collection

Boston Bees manager Casey Stengel (left) with pitcher Jim Turner before a game in 1938. Stengel, who was 47 when pictured, went 373–491 as manager of the Bees and Braves from 1938 to 1943. Because of a poor managerial record with Boston and the Brooklyn Dodgers previously, Stengel was out of Major League Baseball for six years, managing in the American Association and Pacific Coast League. He returned to manage the Yankees in 1949 and went 1,149–696 with 10 pennants and seven World Series titles over 12 years. He retired from managing in 1965 at the age of 74 after a four-year stint as Mets manager.

Courtesy of the Boston Public Library, Leslie Jones Collection

Derek Jeter makes a play in the hole in the 2012 American League Division Series against the Orioles. Jeter batted .308 (200–650) in 158 postseason games. The 2012 ALDS would be the final postseason series that the Yankees won during Jeter's career.

Los Angeles Angels center fielder Mike Trout catches a fly ball by Baltimore Orioles' J.J. Hardy during the first inning of a baseball game on Wednesday, June 27, 2012, in Baltimore. Trout established himself as the top young superstar in the game after finishing second in the American League MVP voting in each of his first two seasons before winning the award unanimously in 2014.

Bryce Harper has led a Washington baseball resurgence as one of the top young superstars in the game. Prior to Harper's arrival in 2012, the Nationals had not registered a winning season since moving to the nation's capital. During Harper's first three seasons, the Nationals averaged 93 wins a year and made two postseason appearances. He broke out in 2015 at the age of 22 to realize his potential as one of the elite players in the sport.

Photos by Keith Allison, keithallisonphoto.com

The 2015 Major League Baseball Hall of Fame Class pose for photos after the press conference announcing their induction. Pictured, left to right, are John Smoltz, Randy Johnson, Craig Biggio, and Pedro Martinez. Smoltz, Johnson, and Martinez were elected in their first year of eligibility. Johnson garnered 97.27 percent of the vote, the eighth-highest percentage at the time of his election. The year 2015 marked the first time since 1955 that the Baseball Writers Association of America voted as many as four players into one class.

Photo by Arturo Pardavila

Five Hall of Famers take in the ceremonies as the Yankees honored Willie Randolph with a plaque in Monument Park as part of their 2015 Old Timers Day. Seated, left to right, are Rickey Henderson, Wade Boggs, Goose Gossage, Reggie Jackson, and Joe Torre.

Photo by Arturo Pardavila

Jackie Robinson signs autographs for young fans at Braves Field in Boston.
Courtesy of the Boston Public Library, Leslie Jones Collection

· 7 ·

The Immortals

MURDERERS' ROW: A PITCHER'S WORST NIGHTMARE

April 12, 1927

The term *Murderers' Row* may have been in place before April 12, 1927, but the mystique surrounding that epic season started that day.

One of the great things about sports, and baseball in particular, is that it's a forum for memorable nicknames. The list stretches back as far as the game itself. From Cap Anson to A-Rod, thousands of players have been given monikers that have followed them just as much as their on-field accomplishments.

While individual nicknames are easy to come by, nicknames for entire teams are a lot less common. When you think of team nicknames, none strikes more fear than "Murderers' Row." While the nickname has been attached to a few different Yankees lineups, it is widely associated with the 1927 World Series championship team. They took the field for the first time on April 12, 1927, against the Philadelphia Athletics.

Surprisingly, the term *Murderers' Row* was first used in reference to the Yankees when Lou Gehrig was a 15-year-old schoolboy in Manhattan and Babe Ruth played for the Red Sox. The nickname was first used for the 1918 Yankees lineup, which consisted of Frank Gilhooley, Roger Peckinpaugh, Home Run Baker, Del Pratt, Wally Pipp, and Ping Bodie—all good players in their own right, but only Baker is a Hall of Famer.

The name was more fitting for the 1927 version of the Yankees, to say the least.

The lineup featured four Hall of Famers (Earl Combs, Babe Ruth, Lou Gehrig, and Tony Lazzeri), along with such stars as Mark Koenig, Joe Dugan, and Bob Meusel. This lineup was so far ahead of everyone statistically that it's hard to find a modern-day equivalent.

The Yanks hit 158 homers on the season, 102 homers more than the Athletics, who finished second. They outhomered the White Sox, Red Sox, Indians, and Senators combined. They averaged 6.3 runs a game and hit .307 as a team. Their accomplishments could go on for pages, and each would be more impressive than the next.

In 1926, the Yankees actually featured the same lineup and were almost as dominant; however, after falling to the Cardinals four games to three in the 1926 World Series, they would approach the '27 season with a vengeance.

The season opened on a Tuesday night in front of approximately 60,000 people at Yankee Stadium. The Yanks would take on the Philadelphia Athletics, who had finished in third place in the American League in 1926. It was a game that featured 11 Hall of Famers. In addition to the four Murderers' Row Hall of Famers, the Athletics fielded a team with Ty Cobb, Al Simmons, Eddie Collins, and Mickey Cochrane, all baseball royalty in their own right. Former St. Louis Browns legend Zach Wheat, in his final major-league season, also made a pinch-hitting appearance. Both starting pitchers were also Hall of Famers, as Waite Hoyt faced off against Lefty Grove. As if those names weren't enough, the managers in the game were Miller Huggins and Connie Mack, both Hall of Famers as well.

If there wasn't even one pitch thrown in the game, the magnitude of the cast alone was historic. Grove and Hoyt each toed the rubber that day to navigate through the Hall of Famers as best they could.

Hoyt and Grove hooked up in an early pitchers' duel, as neither allowed a run through four innings. Hoyt posted another scoreless inning in the top of the fifth before Murderers' Row broke through for four runs in the bottom of the fifth. After the Athletics crept back with two runs in the top of the sixth, the Yanks answered with four more in the bottom of the frame. In just a matter of two innings, that pitchers' duel turned into an 8–2 Yankees lead. The Athletics tacked on a run in the eighth, but that would be all as Hoyt picked up the complete-game win.

The only Yankees who registered multihit games were Dugan and Koenig, who combined for five of the Yanks' nine hits. Gehrig was 1-for-4 with a double and two RBIs, and Combs reached base with a double and a walk while scoring two runs. Ruth would blast 60 homers in '27 and hit .356 on the year, but he was 0-for-3 on Opening Day.

No homers were hit for either team this day, but the Yankees had four extra-base hits, which was a high for the era. Grove allowed nine hits on April 12, a total he'd only be touched for four more times in 51 appearances for the rest of the year.

The Yankees would go wire to wire in first place in 1927, and win a record 110 games. The Athletics finished second but were 18½ games back when the season was done. After ripping through the regular season, they dismissed the Pirates in a four-game sweep to win the World Series.

As for Murderers' Row, they had a season you'd expect. Ruth out-homered every team in the AL that season, while also knocking in 164 runs. Gehrig had arguably his best season, as he blasted 47 homers on a .373 average with an incredible 175 RBI. He was named the AL MVP that year.

Lazzeri was third in the AL in homers in 1927, with 18, and drove in 102 runs in his second season in the majors. Lost in the shuffle of big names was Combs. He led the AL in hits with 231. His total topped the likes of Hall of Famers George Sisler, Goose Goslin, Rogers Hornsby, and Pie Traynor. He also led the majors with 23 triples.

The further you analyze the 1927 Yankees season, the more awe-inspiring it seems. It gets to a point where words do not do justice to the individual and team accomplishments. No words are more fitting than "Murderers' Row."

On April 12, 1927, in Yankee Stadium, Lefty Grove, Ty Cobb, Al Simmons, and Connie Mack, along with 60,000 fans, got a firsthand dose of what the rest of the baseball world would encounter in the next 153 games.

SMOKY JOE WOOD: ROBBED OF IMMORTALITY

September 6, 1912

The legends of Major League Baseball from the 1910s are just about bigger than the game itself. Players like Christy Mathewson, Ty Cobb, Cy Young, and Tris Speaker still have legendary accomplishments that dot the record books.

On September 6, 1912, two pitchers who were establishing themselves as superstars of the game crossed paths in what is considered to be one of the best regular-season games of the decade. The legacies of the two legends who met on that day went in different directions not long after. Those two pitchers were Walter Johnson and Smoky Joe Wood. Johnson went on to become one of the true immortals of the game, while Wood became one of the earliest cases of "what could have been" after an injury curtailed a dominant pitching career.

Wood got his start as an 18-year-old for the Red Sox when he appeared in six games as a hard-throwing but erratic youngster. He started just two games but hurled a shutout in one of those starts. Johnson debuted a year earlier as a 19-year-old and went just 5–9, but with a 1.88 ERA. Wood went into the 1912 season with a career record of 47–38 and was coming off a 23–17 season in 1911. Johnson, who was two years older than Wood, was 82–78 through 1911 and had back-to-back 25-win seasons in '10 and '11.

In 1912, Wood and Johnson were the two most dominant pitchers in the American League. By the time the season was done, they stood first and second on the AL pitching leaderboard in ERA, strikeouts, wins, WAR, WHIP, complete games, and shutouts. Earlier in the season, Johnson won 16 straight decisions to set an AL record, and on September 6, Wood was on a 13-game winning streak of his own. Coming into September, the Red Sox had the best record in baseball and were led by a trio of 20-game winners in Wood, Buck O'Brien, and Hugh Bedient. The Senators had a rare strong season behind Johnson and Bob Groom, who combined to win 57 games that year.

Two of the biggest stories in the AL in 1912 were the pitching performances of Johnson and Wood. While Johnson was the premier pitcher of the time, Wood was making a run at that title. He was gaining headlines as his Red Sox were running away with the AL pennant, and Wood's 13 straight wins were putting him in the same discussion as Johnson. Fenway Park was in its first year of existence, and the Red Sox were treating the home fans to a great season. During the final month of the season, the Sox had just two home series scheduled, a late September series against the Yankees and a four-game set against Johnson and the Senators starting September 4.

Coming into the series, Wood's winning streak was making headlines. An early look at the pitching schedules saw that Johnson was slated to start the Friday game against the Red Sox, while Wood was scheduled for Saturday; however, fans, writers, and even the Senators themselves started a movement to try to coerce Boston manager Jake Stahl to move Wood up one day to create the dream pitching matchup. Stahl agreed and the showdown between Wood and Johnson was set for Friday night, September 6.

Newspapers began previewing the faceoff and hyped the game as the premier pitching matchup of the early twentieth century. The game was showcased more as a heavyweight boxing match between Wood and Johnson than a baseball game between the Red Sox and Senators. The buildup worked, as an estimated 30,000 fans showed up for the game, well more than the capacity of Fenway Park.

Red Sox management accommodated the overflow of fans by setting up standing-room sections on the field. They roped off areas in foul territory down each foul line and even along the outfield wall. Because of the overflow of fans, the teams weren't even allowed to use their own dugouts and had to set up folding chairs in foul territory for the game.

As expected, the pitching duel lived up to the hype. The Red Sox had the game's first threat as they put together two singles in the second. But Johnson got out of the inning without harm. The Senators loaded the bases in the third, but Wood struck out outfielder Danny Moeller to keep the game tied. The game remained scoreless into the bottom of the sixth, when the Red Sox struck for a quick run. Johnson got through the first two batters easily, but Tris Speaker connected on a pitch and drove it into left field for a ground-rule double. Duffy Lewis followed with a double of his own to drive home Speaker for a 1–0 lead. Wood made the lead stand up, pitching out of trouble in the eighth and ninth to win the classic showdown 1–0.

The *Boston Globe* headline for the game read, "Wood Beats Johnson in Baseball Classic," as writers recognized the importance of the incredible showdown. The *Globe* ran an extensive breakdown and analysis of the game, treating it as if it was a World Series game. The paper ran two large pictures of Speaker and Lewis under the headline, "Here Is the Pair Who Turned the Trick in the Sixth with Their War Clubs." Wood finished the game with nine strikeouts, and his shutout was one of 10 he recorded on the season.

Smoky Joe Wood went on to one of the greatest pitching seasons in major-league history, going 34–5 with a 1.91 ERA in 1912. He started 38 games and completed 35 of them, pitching 344 innings along the way. His excellence didn't stop with the end of the regular season, as he led the Red Sox to a World Series title in an epic eight-game showdown with Christy Mathewson and the New York Giants. The Sox topped the Giants four games to three, with game two going into the record books as a 6–6 tie.

At the age of 22, Wood had a career record of 81–43 and appeared on track for a phenomenal career; however, in 1913, he fell while trying to field a bunt and broke the thumb on his pitching hand. While he did return to pitch effectively, Wood experienced great pain while pitching and was limited in the amount of time he could spend on the mound. Between 1913 and 1915, he failed to start more than 18 games in any season and averaged just 138 innings a season. By comparison, Wood pitched 344 innings in 1912.

After missing the entire 1916 season, Wood was sold to the Cleveland Indians for $15,000 and converted into a center fielder. He enjoyed a successful five-year run in Cleveland after making the transition. He hit .298 during that time, with a respectable 18 homers and 275 RBIs during the Deadball Era. He had his most productive season in 1922, when he played in 142 games and hit .297 with eight homers and 92 RBIs. His RBI total was good for ninth in the AL and was just seven fewer than Babe Ruth had that year.

After the 1912 season, Wood was on top of the baseball world. He outpitched Walter Johnson in one of the greatest pitching showdowns of the Deadball Era and beat Christy Mathewson to give the Red Sox their second World Series title. In an era that featured Mathewson, Johnson, Eddie Plank, and Ed Walsh, Wood was the top pitcher in the game.

On September 6, 1912, when Wood's path crossed Johnson's, Wood came out on top. He looked ready to be the top hurler of his time, but his unfortunate thumb injury sent his career backward, while Johnson and Mathewson went down as immortals. For one year, however, Wood was at the pinnacle of the sport. From 1913 onward, people were left to wonder what could have become of Smoky Joe Wood if he could have avoided that fateful injury.

JACKIE ROBINSON: GAINING ACCEPTANCE AS AN ALL-STAR

July 12, 1949

Sometimes progress happens so slowly, it cannot be measured on a day-to-day basis. But July 12, 1949, was one of those days when progress happened right in front of everyone's eyes.

As the 1940s came to a close, the United States was still finding itself. The country was recovering after the end of World War II, and different norms were being established in every walk of life. In baseball, the 1940s are considered to be right in the middle of the "golden age" of the game. While the game saw growth and change in so many ways after the war, one of the biggest changes came with the breaking of the color barrier.

Much is written about the accomplishments of Jackie Robinson and the obstacles he faced when he became Major League Baseball's first black player on April 15, 1947. While Robinson, Larry Doby, and Monte Irvin were pioneers between 1947 and 1949, black ballplayers still struggled to gain acceptance by fans nationwide.

The rise of the black ballplayer in 1949 became an interesting subplot in a year dominated by the success of Hall of Famers like Ted Williams, Stan Musial, and Warren Spahn. As the season rolled on, four dominant teams separated themselves in Major League Baseball. In the AL, the Yankees and Red Sox were the top squads all year, while in the NL, Musial would lead the Cardinals in a fierce battle with the upstart Brooklyn Dodgers.

The Dodgers had a group of All-Stars led by Pee Wee Reese, Gil Hodges, and a young Duke Snider. What really bolstered their lineup were the black stars Branch Rickey had brought to the team. That group was led by Don Newcombe, Roy Campanella, and, of course, Robinson.

Robinson was already established as a star by 1949. He was the 1947 Rookie of the Year and received MVP votes in his first two seasons. Campanella debuted in 1948 and also garnered MVP recognition during his rookie year.

As the 1949 season went on, the one place where these stars hadn't made names for themselves was MLB's All-Star Game. Like today, the All-Star Game featured baseball's elite, but the game itself was played much differently then. Rosters were limited to 25 players from each league, and managers played the game to win, often leaving their starters in for most of the game. One similarity, however, was that the fans were able to vote in the starters. Despite the success of Robinson, Doby, and Campanella in '47 and '48, the fans did not see fit to vote them to start the All-Star Game. The leagues also kept the black ballplayers out when they filled out their rosters with subs.

That all changed in 1949. With the game scheduled to be played at Ebbets Field, the home of the Brooklyn Dodgers, Robinson was voted in by the fans as the starting second baseman for the National League All-Star squad. Doby, Campanella, and Newcombe were added when managers Lou Boudreau and Billy Southworth filled out the AL and NL rosters, respectively. It would be the first MLB All-Star Game to feature black baseball players.

The game was the 16th version of the Midsummer Classic, and the AL had won 11 of the first 15 games. The AL squad featured Williams, Yogi Berra, and Joe DiMaggio, who had actually missed much of the first half of the season with a heel injury. The NL would be led by Musial, Spahn, and Ralph Kiner.

The Dodgers sent seven representatives to the game, the most of any team in the majors. Robinson batted second, between Reese and Musial. The three Hall of Famers, in addition to Kiner, were the only NL players to play the entire game.

The AL jumped out to an early lead on Spahn in what would be one of the highest-scoring All-Star Games in history. With two outs in the first, DiMaggio singled to left to drive in George Kell, who had reached on an error by Johnny Mize. They tacked on three more runs, with the inning finally ending when Spahn struck out Mel Parnell, the AL's starting pitcher.

However, the NL answered in the bottom of the first. Reese led off the game with a comebacker that was handled by Parnell. Robinson promptly doubled to left in the first at-bat by a black player in an MLB All-Star Game. Musial followed with a homer to right to cut the deficit to 4–2.

In the top of the second, Spahn got Dom DiMaggio to foul out to first but allowed a single to Kell before walking Williams. Southworth would then make the first lineup change of the game when he called for Newcombe to face Joe DiMaggio. Newcombe got DiMaggio to fly to left and retired Eddie Joost on a popup to second to end the threat.

Newcombe was left in the game to bat in the bottom of the third with the bases loaded. A talented hitter who would go on to hit .271 with 15 career homers, Newcombe lined a shot down the left-field line. Williams ran down the liner for an out, but Willard Marshall came in to score on the sac fly to make it 4–3.

"Newk" pitched a scoreless top of the third, allowing the NL the opportunity to take the lead in the bottom of the frame. They tallied two runs to take a 5–4 advantage into the fourth.

Southworth inserted Campanella into the game, thus making for an all-Dodger and all-black battery. Both DiMaggio brothers were retired in the inning, but Newcombe still had to get through Joost to preserve the lead. The 13-year veteran playing in his first All-Star Game came through with a single to left to score Kell and Williams to give the AL a 5–4 lead. Newcombe retired Eddie Robinson as the book closed on his 2⅔-inning stint.

The AL never relinquished the lead in the game, as the closest the NL would come was when Kiner hit a two-run homer in the sixth to make the score 8–7. The AL added three runs in the seventh to take an 11–7 lead, and that was the way the game ended.

Robinson went 1-for-4 with three runs scored. Campanella went 0-for-2 with a walk, and although he pitched the NL out of early trouble, Newcombe picked up the loss. Doby entered the game as a pinch-runner for DiMaggio in the sixth and grounded out to first in his only at-bat.

The game itself may have lacked that true defining moment that All-Star Games are known for. There was no walk-off homer or dominant performances from Hall of Fame pitchers. There was no suspense in the outcome of the game, and the days of Mantle and Mays were still a couple of years away. The game was historic nevertheless.

Jackie Robinson had gained enough respect from the national baseball scene to become the first black baseball player voted to start the MLB All-Star Game. He was no longer a curiosity or a point of controversy in the grand scheme of things. Robinson was voted in by fans ahead of Hall of Famer Red Schoendienst, among other stars of the day.

Newcombe, Campanella, and Doby were handpicked as representatives for their teams as well. It was becoming evident that players were truly starting to be measured by their performance on the field by the fans and their peers, instead of being held back by the color of their skin.

BABE RUTH: TOPPING 50

September 24, 1920

Babe Ruth's called shot in the 1932 World Series against the Cubs has become one of the most iconic legends in his storied life. Thanks to a grainy image of Ruth gesturing with his arm extended toward center field, the only thing that's certain is that he pointed in someone's general direction. Ruth claimed that he pointed to center field and said he would hit the next pitch past the flagpole, which he did; however, Cubs catcher and Hall of Famer Gabby Hartnett claims he was just holding two fingers up to the Cubs dugout after taking a second strike, as if to say, "That's only strike two." Either way, the debate is likely to continue.

There is one Babe Ruth home run prediction that did come true and has a little more merit. According to the *Leominster Daily Enterprise*, Ruth claimed that during the 1920 season, his first with the Yankees, he would hit 50 home runs. That prophecy came true on September 24, 1920, when the slugger clouted number 50 off of the Washington Senators' José Acosta in the first game of a doubleheader.

To most, Ruth predicting he would hit 50 home runs while playing in the prime of his career wasn't a strange claim. He topped the 50 mark four times in his career and hit more than 45 homers five other times. But it was the timing of his prediction that made it so remarkable.

Ruth's beginnings as a Red Sox pitcher and his subsequent sale to the Yankees are a well-known tale. He made his debut as a 19-year-old lefty in 1914, and went 2–1 in limited action. During the next three seasons, he was one of the top pitchers in the game, as he accumulated a 65–33 record and topped the 20-win mark in 1916 and 1917. In his limited number of at-bats, Ruth showed he could also be a productive hitter, so in 1918, his games started as a pitcher were cut in half and he was given 75 games as an everyday player at first base and in the outfield. That season, Ruth hit .300 with a league-leading 11 home runs to lead the Red Sox to a 75–51 record and a win over the Cubs in the World Series.

Although Ruth batted just .200 in the World Series and performed well as a pitcher, winning two of the four games for the Sox, manager Ed Barrow gave him an even more extensive role as an everyday player in 1919. That year, Ruth broke the single-season home run record by knocking 29 homers, breaking Ned Williamson's mark, which had stood for 35 years.

The Red Sox' success on the field didn't continue, as they finished just 66–71, 20½ games out of first place in the American League. In the offseason, Ruth demanded a salary increase, and when owner Harry Frazee refused, he decided to force Frazee's hand by demanding a trade. Famously, Frazee accepted the Yankees' all-cash deal, and Ruth was sold to the Yanks for $100,000 and other cash considerations.

At the time, Frazee stated that he could use the extra money to buy more players to make the Red Sox a stronger team overall. The *New York Times*, citing the 258-foot right-field fence, claimed that Ruth could easily surpass the record he had set the previous year, when he belted 29 home runs. Ruth apparently set the bar even higher when he said that he would hit 50 home runs playing 77 games a year in the stadium. To that point, only Ruth and Williamson had ever hit even half that total in a season.

Ruth was converted into a full-time outfielder in 1920, and Miller Huggins wrote him in as the team's cleanup hitter immediately on Opening Day. Ruth slumped through the season's first two weeks and was batting just .226 with no home runs by May. His first homer as a Yankee came on May 1, against his former team, the Boston Red Sox. Ruth victimized the Sox the next day with another homer off Sad Sam Jones, and from that point onward, a slugfest ensued. That month, Ruth belted 12 home runs, while hitting .329.

In June and July, Ruth hit the ball at a torrid pace, batting .445 in 63 games and putting up power numbers in those two months that were unheard of in entire seasons. He belted 25 homers during that span and drove in an incredible 69 runs. On July 19, Ruth clubbed his 30th and 31st home runs in a game against the Chicago White Sox to become the first player to surpass the 30-homer mark in a season. With 60 games still remaining on the schedule, there was no telling how far he would extend his new record. Although the Yankees lost that game to the White Sox, who received a homer of their own from Shoeless Joe Jackson, they still remained in second place in the AL, just 1½ games behind Tris Speaker's Indians.

For Ruth to keep on pace for his 50–home run prediction, he would have to average one home run every three games, and he was on track. The Yankees' schedule had them start August with 14 straight road games, taking Ruth away from his short porch at the Polo Grounds. As the summer progressed, he slowed in August, hitting just seven homers, while hitting .292 for the month.

The schedule wasn't any kinder in September, as the Yanks would play just seven games at home that month. If Ruth was going to reach 50 homers, he was going to have to do it based on his pure hitting ability, not the advantage of his home field.

He got the month off to a good start, as he hit homers in each game of a doubleheader at Fenway Park on September 4, and then returned home for a three-game series against the A's. Ruth went homerless, however, and then set off on a 12-game road trip with his home run total standing at 45. In a pivotal series in Cleveland, Ruth hit two home runs as the Yankees took two of three from the Tribe to close to within a half game of first. On September 14, Ruth hit homer number 49 off pitcher Howard Ehmke as the Yankees topped Ty Cobb's Tigers 4–2 to take a half-game lead in the AL.

But the Yankees lost four of their next six to fall three games back in the race by September 24. With just seven games left, the Yanks not only would need to go on a hot streak, but the Indians and White Sox would also have to cool down if they wanted a shot at a World Series. Ruth hadn't homered in 10 days and went into a slump, hitting just .269 during that time.

On September 24, the Yankees were back home to take on Clark Griffith's Washington Senators in what amounted to a must-win situation for a Friday doubleheader. The Senators were mired in a dreadful season and were 27½ games out of first place. Walter Johnson was in the midst of his worst professional season, and outside of Sam Rice, the Senators had little on their roster.

The Senators jumped out to a 2–0 first-inning lead on Yankees starter Carl Mays, who was enjoying one of the best seasons of his career. Mays, who just five weeks prior had thrown the infamous pitch that killed Ray Chapman, would finish 26–11 for the Yankees in 1920. Down 2–0 already, the first two Yankees in the lineup, Aaron Ward and Wally Pipp, made quick outs in the first. Ruth came to the plate next and, with the bases empty, belted home run number 50 to cut the lead in half.

However, that would be Ruth's only hit of the game, as the Senators topped the Yanks 3–1 in the first contest. Acosta, the diminutive, Cuban-born righty, shut the Yankees down on four hits, allowing just two singles to Duffy Lewis and a single to Mays. It was Ruth's 50th home run that became news. Ruth topped the 50–home run mark three more times in the decade, including his 60-homer output in 1927. The next person to top 50 homers was Hack Wilson, in his historic 1930 season.

Ruth ended the 1920 season with 54 home runs, as he hit one more in the second game of the doubleheader on September 24, and then three more in a season-ending series against the A's. After splitting the doubleheader with the Senators, the Yankees went on to win four of the final five games, but it wouldn't be enough, as the Indians took the AL by 1½ games over the White Sox. The Yankees finished three games out, in third place.

Ruth's 54 home runs in 1920 was one of the most remarkable feats in baseball history. At the time, he outhomered every other major-league team, except the Phillies, who hit 64 home runs while playing in the Baker Bowl, which had a 280-foot right-field fence. George Sisler finished second to Ruth in homers in 1920, with a total of 19, still impressive for the era. In fact, Ruth's total of 54 home runs was more than the next three closest players' totals combined.

In his 1920 season, in which Ruth salivated at the chance to hit every day at the Polo Grounds, he ended up hitting 25 of his 54 homers on the road. Even in his historic 1927 season, during which he hit 60 home runs, Ruth actually hit more home runs on the road than at home (32–28). The numbers he put up in his era were so far ahead of everyone else's that his totals were unfathomable to fans. Finally given a full-time chance to develop as an every-day position player, Ruth crossed the incredible 50–home run milestone for the first time on September 24, 1920.

MICKEY MANTLE: CHANGING THE
GAME FROM BOTH SIDES OF THE PLATE

May 13, 1955

Throughout the history of baseball, there are players who have been categorized as stars, superstars, All-Stars, and legends. How do you quantify a player who seems to transcend even the greatest of accolades, players whose names evoke something beyond any kind of label? With players like Babe Ruth, Jackie Robinson, Hank Aaron, or Ty Cobb, it seems to do them barely enough justice to simply call them legends. These were the type of players who changed the game. Just their names conjure up a certain image and the thought that no matter how long the game goes on, they will always be immortals.

Players like Mickey Mantle have a special place in the game because they fundamentally changed a major aspect of a game that has been played for more than 150 years. Mantle, who was the embodiment of an American hero, essentially was the first true power-hitting switch-hitter. His power numbers as a switch-hitter were prominent through the steroid era and were so uncommon that there are still only a handful of players with power numbers that compare to Mantle's.

Mantle's power ability as a switch-hitter remained unmatched until Eddie Murray's career began, more than 25 years after Mantle's debut. As far as Mantle changing the game, it is clearly evidenced by the fact that there wasn't a single switch-hitter who played before Mantle to even draw a comparison to.

On May 13, 1955, Mantle accomplished a feat for the first time that became one of his staple records. On that date, he blasted home runs from both sides of the plate in the same game for the first time. While he wasn't the first to do it (it had been done five times before), the accomplishment seemed to be his trademark as his career advanced.

In 1955, Mantle homered from both sides of the plate twice. He was the first player to do it twice in the same year and the second to do it twice in his career. Prior to Mantle, the light-hitting Jim Russell homered from both sides of the plate in the same game in both 1948 and 1950. Russell, who played for the Pirates, Braves, and Dodgers, had just 67 homers in a 10-year career.

The first time Mantle accomplished the feat, the Yankees were playing against the Tigers. The Yankees were in the midst of their great run of play in the early '50s, and even as a player in his early 20s, Mantle found himself batting third in the powerful Yankees lineup.

The Yanks were coming off a season in 1954 in which they went 103–51, but finished in second place in the AL behind the Indians. Through the '54 season, Mantle had accumulated 84 homers before turning 24. Both the Yankees and Indians expected to be among the elite again in 1955. The Yanks were off to an inconsistent start in the first month of the season and were 14–10 on May 13. They had just come off a short two-game series at Yankee Stadium in which they were swept by the Indians. The Tigers were off to a good start in '54 and were 15–11 in the season's first month.

Whitey Ford, who was in just his third full season for the Yanks, was the starting pitcher that Friday in front of a crowd of just 7,177 at Yankee Stadium. Veteran Steve Gromek was on the mound for the Tigers. He was in his 15th year of a successful big-league career and had won 107. Because Gromek was a righty, naturally Mantle would be hitting lefty to start the game.

In the first inning, Ford retired the side in order, inducing a fly out from Hall of Famer Al Kaline to end the frame. Hank Bauer led off the game for the Yankees with a popup to first, and third baseman Andy Carey laid down a bunt single to bring up Mantle with one out. Mantle got the Yanks on the scoreboard first, as he belted a home run to right-center field as they took a 2–0 lead. Gromek got Yogi Berra on a foul out and Joe Collins on a fly to center, to escape any further damage.

With the score still 2–0 in the third, Bauer led off with a single and was bunted to second by Carey. Mantle then came through again, this time with a single to center to drive home Bauer, to extend the lead to 3–0. Meanwhile, Ford was pitching masterfully and, thanks to two double plays, had faced the minimum number of batters through the first four innings. He finally allowed his first hit, a single to center by Ray Boone, in the top of the fifth but didn't allow anything past that.

In the bottom of the fifth, Bauer and Carey made two quick outs to bring Mantle up with the bases empty. Gromek decided to go right at Mantle, and that turned out to be a mistake. The center fielder knocked his second homer of the game to extend the lead to 4–0. After an uneventful sixth inning, the Tigers finally broke through against Ford. Bill Tuttle led off the inning with a hit, but Ford got the next two outs and seemed like he could get out of the inning unscathed; however, Boone hit a two-run homer to cut the Yankees' lead in half.

Tigers manager Bucky Harris turned to 19-year-old reliever Bob Miller late in the game to try to keep the Yankees at bay. Miller's first task was facing Mantle as he was trying to keep Detroit within two runs. About the only good news facing the pitcher was that there was nobody on base as Mantle proceeded to crush an offering from Miller for his third homer of the game, this time batting right-handed. With the home run, Mantle became the first player to homer both righty and lefty in the same game since Russell had done so on July 26, 1950.

Miller retired the next three batters, but the Tigers couldn't mount anything against Yankees reliever Tom Morgan in the ninth, as the Yankees took home the 5–2 win. Mantle was the hitting star for the game, as he went 4-for-4, drove in all five Yankees runs, and scored three others. Ford and Morgan combined on a three-hitter in the Yankees' win.

Almost three months to the date, on August 15, Mantle equaled the feat again in the second game of a doubleheader against the Orioles. In the fourth inning, he homered batting lefty against starter Ray Moore and then hit one batting righty off Art Schallock in his next at-bat in the sixth.

Mantle went on to hit 37 home runs in 1955, which was seven more than Gus Zernial, as he won his first American League home run title. He finished fifth in the AL MVP voting that year, which was won by teammate Yogi Berra. Berra and Mantle led the Yankees to the AL pennant in 1955, as they finished three games ahead of the Indians in a great race that was close all year long. But the Yanks fell in the World Series, as the Dodgers finally broke through to win their only championship while playing in Brooklyn.

Mantle hit homers from both sides of the plate twice in 1956, becoming the first player to accomplish the feat at least three times. He began to make it look routine, as he switch-hit homers in the same game nine times between 1955 and 1962. During that span, not a single player was able to do it once. Finally, on May 30, 1962, Maury Wills of the Dodgers was able to homer from both sides of the plate. While Wills was the premier basestealer of his time, he wasn't known for his power, as he hit just 20 home runs in his 14-year career.

Mantle homered from both sides in the same game for the 10th and final time against the White Sox on August 12, 1964. Fellow Yankee Roy White developed a knack for switch-hitting home runs in the same game in the '70s, as he did it five times in the decade. It was not until the mid-'80s, more than 20 years after Mantle's first, that Eddie Murray proved he could threaten Mantle's record. Murray became the first player to switch-hit homers in back-to-back games on May 8 and 9 in 1987. Those were the seventh and eighth times the Orioles Hall of Famer did it, on his way to breaking Mantle's mark in 1994. Chili Davis, Nick Swisher, and Mark Teixeira eventually surpassed Mantle and Murray, and through 2015, Teixeira holds the career record of 14 games with home runs from both sides of the plate.

Mantle ended his career with 536 home runs, which at the time was more than 300 more than any switch-hitter in history. Reggie Smith ended his career with 314 home runs in 1982, and even though he was not close to Mantle's total, it was second all-time for switch-hitters. As of 2013, only Murray (504) and Chipper Jones (468) have approached Mantle's career mark.

Prior to Mantle, there were a few great switch-hitters. Max Carey pounded out 2,665 hits in a career that spanned from 1910 to 1929, and Frankie Frisch had a Hall of Fame career around the same time; however, the two combined for just 175 home runs while playing much of their career in the Deadball Era. Mantle was the player who came along and changed everything for switch-hitters. Lost in the legend of his tape-measure shots and superlative overall play is the fact that he was the first true power-hitting switch-hitter, a player who changed the game for generations to come.

· 8 ·

Baseball's Weird, Wild, and Colorful Characters

BOB UECKER: MR. BASEBALL VERSUS JUAN MARICHAL

April 19, 1962

Bob Uecker signed his first contract with the Milwaukee Braves in 1956, for $3,000. It was a lot of money for his father to pay the Braves to take him, but they put the money up anyway. That's the way the joke goes, and if you've heard it once from Uecker, you've heard it a hundred times. On April 19, 1962, Uecker got his first start as a major-league ballplayer when he was in the lineup for the Braves against the New York Giants, and so began one of the most colorful careers anyone can ask of a .200 career hitter.

Uecker became widely known in his postplaying days for his legendary sense of humor, which he displayed in numerous types of media. His steady job as an announcer with the Milwaukee Brewers kept him around the sport he loved, but other venues brought him into the national spotlight. Unofficially, he appeared on the *Tonight Show Starring Johnny Carson* more than 100 times, where he deadpanned about his failures in life and baseball. Despite the number of appearances he made on the show, Uecker was always hilarious.

Always introduced as "Mr. Baseball" and serenaded by Doc Severinsen with "Take Me Out to the Ball Game," Uecker was a crowd favorite. On one show, Carson asked Uecker if those were World Series rings he was wearing. Uecker responded, "Oh yeah, this is a World Series ring and this one is a National League championship ring . . . I stole them both."

In addition to his appearances on the late-night circuit, Uecker was in Miller Lite commercials, had a lead role in the sitcom *Mr. Belvedere*, and was announcer Harry Doyle in the *Major League* movie franchise. His accomplishments outside of baseball have made him a recognizable pop culture icon.

"The times I went out to dinner with him and the guys, he was just so well known in public," said Don August, who pitched for the Brewers from 1988 to 1991. "*Major League* had just come out when I first came up. We'd be at one place and within 10 minutes he'd be recognized, and before you knew it, he was mobbed and we'd have to leave."

As he said in his Hall of Fame induction speech after being named the Ford C. Frick Award winner in 2003, baseball was always first for Uecker. He may have embellished many of the stories from his career, like the time his manager, Gene Mauch, told him to "get up to bat and kill this rally," but when he talked about his woeful ability on the field, he was telling the truth.

Uecker hit exactly .200 for his career and may have been lucky to do that. In the final game in 1967, he got the start behind the plate as the Braves took on Bob Gibson and the Cardinals. Gibson struck out Uecker in his first at-bat and got him to hit a comebacker in his second. With his career average right at .200, Braves manager Ken Silvestri moved Joe Torre from first base to catcher and inserted Rico Carty at first, ending Uecker's career as an active player.

Five years earlier, Uecker got his start in the big leagues as the third-string catcher on the Milwaukee Braves. He didn't play much as a rookie behind All-Stars Torre and Del Crandall, but in the second game of the 1962 season, he got his first career big-league start.

The box score from that game shows a matchup of two teams rich with baseball legends. The Giants' 3–4–5 hitters were Willie Mays, Orlando Cepeda, and Felipe Alou. Their starting pitcher that day was the great Juan Marichal. They also had young stars like Willie McCovey and Gaylord Perry, who were just 24 and 23 years old, respectively. The Braves lineup was equally stacked, as they were led by Hank Aaron, Eddie Mathews, Torre, Joe Adcock, and a 41-year-old Warren Spahn. Mixed in with the Hall of Famers and All-Stars was Uecker, batting seventh and catching for the Braves.

Lew Burdette was on the hill for the Braves, and he got through the first inning unscathed, smartly pitching around Mays in the process. The Braves got on the board quickly against Marichal, who was 24 years old at the time. With one out, Mack Jones singled and Aaron walked to bring Mathews up to the plate with a chance to cash in early. At the end of the previous season, Mathews had just established a record that would stand for 40 years when he hit 370 home runs in the first 10 years of his career. He hit number 371 to give the Braves a quick 3–0 lead. Incidentally, that record wouldn't fall until Albert Pujols belted 408 homers in his first 10 seasons.

After the Mathews homer, Adcock fouled out, but Frank Bolling followed with a double. With a runner in scoring position, Uecker, the 27-year-old rookie, came to the plate for the second time in his career. Perhaps foreshadowing the next six seasons, Uecker struck out, ending the threat.

Burdette and Marichal settled into a pitchers' duel from there, as the game stayed 3–0 into the fifth. With these lineups, it wasn't bound to stay low-scoring for long.

In the fifth, Jim Davenport led off with a home run for the Giants, and Marichal followed with a walk. Harvey Kuenn, who would go on to become a legendary manager of the Milwaukee Brewers, singled and Chuck Hiller walked to load the bases for the dangerous heart of the Giants order.

With Mays up, Burdette threw a wild pitch and eventually walked the Hall of Famer to reload the bases. That would be all for Burdette, as he was replaced by Ron Piché, who looked like he might get out of the jam when he retired Cepeda and Alou; however, he walked Ed Bailey and gave up a two-run single to José Pagán as the Giants took a 5–3 lead.

Marichal got Aaron, Mathews, and Adcock in order in the fifth but walked Bolling to lead off the sixth. With the Braves about to mount a rally, up came Uecker for his third at-bat of the game. He promptly grounded into an around-the-horn double play, and Marichal would finish the sixth with a two-run lead.

With Tony Cloninger now pitching for the Braves, the Giants sent the heart of their order to the plate in the seventh, and Mays, Cepeda, and Alou extended the lead to 7–3. With Marichal pitching well, the game seemed to be out of reach at this point. But Adcock led off the bottom of the eighth with a solo home run to make it 7–4. Bolling flew out to right to bring Uecker up again. For the second time in the game, he struck out looking against Marichal, who would then also strikeout pinch-hitter Tommie Aaron for the third out of the inning.

The Braves had one more chance in the bottom of the ninth. They were down by three but had their big hitters up. With Marichal still in the game, the Braves began to rally. With one out, Jones singled, but Aaron followed with a strikeout. Mathews wouldn't let the game die easy, as he hit his second homer to bring the Braves within one; however, Marichal got Adcock to fly to right to end it.

While the game was high-scoring, two notable players did not take part in the slugfest, as Uecker and Aaron combined to go 0-for-8 with four strike-outs. Uecker went on to start 12 more games in 1962 and actually recorded the highest batting average of his career when he hit .250 (16-for-64). In his final game of the season, Uecker hit his only home run of the year. He saw the most playing time in any one season of his career for the Phillies in 1966. In 207 at–bats, he hit seven homers and drove in 30 runs. His average, however, was just .208.

Unlike the way Aaron is tied to the number 755 or the way DiMaggio is associated with 56, Uecker's legacy isn't about numbers. He's been involved with baseball for more than 50 years, and it would be impossible to count the number of fans who love him.

"I still live in Milwaukee," said August.

> When I'm driving I put the game on the radio and there's Uecker's voice calling the games, just the way it should be. People look back on the history of baseball and you hear Uecker's voice, Vin Scully's voice. I still can hear Bob Shepherd saying, "Number 19, Robin Yount" in Yankee Stadium. These voices really make it special.

During an appearance on the *Tonight Show*, Uecker expressed his mock aggravation to Johnny Carson about being passed up for the Hall of Fame once again. Uecker responded, "Now there's been a hint here and there that they want to put me in. Well now I'm not going."

Uecker did finally go, as the Ford C. Frick Award winner in 2003. At the time, he was only the second former player (along with Joe Garagiola) to be recognized as the Frick winner by the Hall of Fame. Predictably, Uecker's speech consisted of comedy that could rival any stand-up act of the time. Also as expected, Uecker finished with a sincere expression of gratitude to everyone who helped him along the way and made sure he told everyone listening that "it's been a great run, but number one has always been baseball for me."

REGGIE JACKSON AND BILLY MARTIN: BOILING OVER IN BOSTON

June 18, 1977

The notation in the box score on June 18, 1977, is simple enough. Paul Blair entered in right field for Reggie Jackson. But the events surrounding that substitution are the epitome of why the Yankees of the late '70s were called the "Bronx Zoo."

That day, the Yankees were taking on the Red Sox in a nationally televised Saturday afternoon game at Fenway Park. The Yanks and Red Sox were widely considered the top two teams in the American League and were facing off for the third time in the early season. The Sox entered the game in first place, just a half game ahead of the Yankees. The Yanks were coming off a loss the previous night to the Red Sox, in which Billy Martin pulled starting pitcher Catfish Hunter after just two outs in the first inning.

The Yankees–Red Sox rivalry was at its peak, and the hatred between the teams led to hotly contested games in an intense atmosphere. Fred Lynn was a central figure in the rivalry during his seven-year tenure in Boston and recalled what it was like playing against the Yankees: "I played football and baseball at USC, and we had those heated rivalries against UCLA and Stanford," said Lynn. "I was used to being involved in heated rivalries, and this was just as intense. We were the top two teams in the league at the time, so every game was like a World Series game."

"It was a civil war out there," continued Lynn.

> There were fights in the stands and fights on the field. It got so bad the Red Sox hired the Boston College football team to work as security guards. They gave them these blue coats, and when there was a fight in the stands, you'd just see this pack of blue coats descend from the stands. It was just as intense on the field too. [Carlton] Fisk and Bill Lee were always in the middle of things. They didn't like Billy Martin, Thurman Munson, and those guys. It was fun to be involved with.

Don Slaught, who played for Martin in New York in 1988, shared a story about Martin to give an idea of what it was like to play for him: "Billy and I got along great during the day, but during the games I was the one guy he yelled at," said Slaught.

> I think he liked yelling at me because I yelled back. When he yelled at me though, it was really directed at other players. The year I played for him it was the year umpires were emphasizing the balk. John Candelaria always worked really fast and had trouble with it, so Billy told me to remind him about it. One time he balked, and Billy just snapped at me. "I told you to remind him about the balks," screamed Martin. I said, "Billy, I just went out there the pitch before, what do you want me to do?" He screamed again, "Go out there every single pitch!"

With Martin always on edge, it created a virtual time bomb on any club he managed. Tensions always boiled high in the clubhouse on the Yankees in the late '70s, with characters like Lou Piniella, Goose Gossage, Thurman Munson, Sparky Lyle, Graig Nettles, and, of course, Reggie Jackson and Martin. Add owner George Steinbrenner, at what most consider the height of his insanity, into the equation and it became the recipe for volcanic eruptions.

However, the Yankees always contested that as crazy as their clubhouse situations got, it never affected them on the field. That idea was supported by their back-to-back World Series titles in 1977 and 1978, and general success during this era.

With the Yankees reeling from their 9–4 loss the previous night, they turned to veteran pitcher Mike Torrez, whom they had acquired in a trade earlier in the season. The Red Sox countered with Reggie Cleveland, a serviceable righty from Canada who was mostly a sub-.500 pitcher.

The Yankees seemed to shake off their troubles from the night before as they jumped out to a first-inning lead. Mickey Rivers led off the game with a single, and Willie Randolph followed with a double. Munson's groundout scored Rivers and Randolph on a wild pitch for a 2–0 lead.

In the bottom of the first, the Red Sox' potent offense answered back. Rick Burleson and Fred Lynn led off with singles, and Carl Yastrzemski belted a three-run homer to give the Red Sox a 3–2 lead.

Cleveland and Torrez would settle in, and the game stayed 3–2 until the bottom of the fourth inning. Bernie Carbo led off the inning with a home run, and Butch Hobson hit an infield single. Denny Doyle tripled down the left-field line to score Hobson, and Lynn's sacrifice fly gave the Sox a 6–2 lead.

In the top of the fifth, the Yanks got a run back when Carlos May scored on an error, but the Sox answered in the bottom of the frame on another solo homer by Carbo. With the score 7–3, the Yankees mounted a rally against Cleveland. With one out, Jackson singled and hustled from first to third on a single to center by Nettles. Roy White doubled home Jackson to make the score 7–4, knocking Cleveland from the game.

Bill Campbell, the Sox closer in '77, and one of the best in the game with 31 saves that year, was called in early by Boston manager Don Zimmer. The move worked, as he struck out May and got a bases-loaded groundout by Rivers after he walked Piniella.

In the bottom of the sixth, the Yankees, and Martin in particular, reached a boiling point. Burleson started the inning harmlessly with a groundout to short. Lynn then lined a single to right to bring Jim Rice up to the plate. The Hall of Fame right fielder hit a popup into short right that was tailing away from Jackson. As Rice ran down the first-base line, he noticed Jackson taking a nonchalant approach to the ball and decided to take a chance and stretch his hit into a double. He made it to second safely as Lynn crossed over from first to third.

After the play, Martin went out to the mound in what looked to be a routine pitching change. He pulled Torrez and called for Lyle to enter in relief. As Lyle was doing his warm-ups, Jackson leaned on the short right-field fence and was talking to some Yankees players in the bullpen. Martin returned to the dugout and decided to pull Jackson from the game due to his lack of hustle. He sent Blair into right field to call Jackson in. As Blair went, Jackson saw him and didn't seem to know what was going on at first. He pointed at his chest as if to say, "Who, me?" and asked Blair why he was approaching. Blair shrugged and told Jackson to ask Martin.

Jackson made his way off the field, and Martin waited for him at the entrance to the dugout. He dropped his glove and immediately questioned Martin on the move. It's embarrassing enough to be pulled from a game in the middle of an inning, but with Jackson's ego, the national TV audience, and the fact that the event happened in front of a raucous Fenway Park filled with more than 34,000 fans, Jackson was not going to let this go quietly.

Neither was Martin.

With NBC's cameras fixed on Jackson and Martin, the two got into a heated exchange. Jackson questioned the move first, and Martin, veins bulging from his neck, pointed and gestured vehemently as he screamed at the Hall of Famer. Yankees coach Elston Howard anticipated the escalation of the argument and was the first to step between the two. At first he just offered a buffer but then moved Martin toward the opposite end of the dugout. Jackson followed as they continued to jaw at one another. Yogi Berra, another coach at the time, stepped in to help Howard with the furious Martin, and Jimmy Wynn, a former All-Star playing out his final MLB season, stepped in to push Jackson away.

The whole thing lasted for just one minute, but due to the personalities involved and the extent of their anger, it was a minute that became one of the most enduring images of both of their stellar careers. It finally ended when Berra forcibly pulled Martin to the bench and Wynn coerced Jackson into the clubhouse.

"I had a front row seat for it on third base," said Lynn. "I watched [Reggie] come off the field and said, 'Oh, now this is gonna be fun.' When they started fighting I said to myself, 'We got these guys now.' I've just never seen anything like that in the game, except for maybe Little League."

At the time of the play, legendary Yankees announcer Phil Rizzuto immediately gave insight into what could have pushed Martin over the edge. Just 10 seconds after the argument started, Rizzuto said, "Reggie has done that on several balls hit to right field." Despite his colorful commentary and seemingly forgetful nature, Rizzuto was actually an astute observer of the game and always offered quick insight. After Rizzuto made that comment, fans assumed that this was something that had been brewing for a while.

As the game continued, Jackson showered quickly in the clubhouse and left the park before the end of the game, and Martin, frustrated by Jackson's antics and the Yankees' play during the past two nights, resumed his duties as manager.

When play continued, Lyle retired Yastrzemski and Carlton Fisk to end the threat. The Red Sox would score three more runs on homers by George Scott and Yastrzemski to top the Yankees 10–4 and move 1½ games ahead of the Yanks.

After the game, Martin defended his move when asked if he had gone too far in embarrassing his star on national TV. The aftermath turned into a short battle of "who said what" before both conceded that the team's success was what mattered most. For as many blowups as Jackson and Martin had, they often were quick to get back to business on the field.

The next day, Jackson was out in his customary position in right, still batting fifth in the Yankees lineup for the finale of the three-game set. The Red Sox beat the Yanks 11–1 behind the pitching of Ferguson Jenkins and homers from Yastrzemski, Carbo, Doyle, Rice, and Scott. Aside from two pitching changes, Martin did not make any other substitutions during the game.

The following weekend, however, the Yankees returned the favor as they swept a three-game series in the Bronx, despite the fact that a slumping Jackson went just 2-for-10. The Yankees and Red Sox fought closely for the AL East through June and July, and the Yankees finally took hold of the division when they beat the White Sox on August 23.

From then until the end of the season, which amounted to 37 games in five weeks of play, Jackson belted 10 home runs and drove in 34 runs, as the Yankees eventually won the AL East. They went on to top the Royals in the American League Championship Series and beat the Dodgers four games to two in the World Series. Jackson earned the World Series MVP after hitting .450 with five home runs, culminating in his historic three–home run performance in the sixth game.

"Reggie was a player who really got worked up," said Rudy May, a teammate of Jackson's with the Yankees and Orioles.

> One of my seasons in New York, Reggie hit a lot of homers in my starts. Reggie could get on your last nerve, but he was good with me. All of that "straw the stirs the drink" stuff didn't bother me; I took it with a grain of salt. One game I passed him in the dugout and said, "Come on Reggie, it's time for one!" He got all worked up, went up to bat, and just crushed one. While he was running down to first he smiled and pointed at me in the dugout.

On a team filled with some of the most intense players of the '70s, there were so many exciting events for the 1977 and 1978 Yankees. While the blowup between Martin and Jackson on June 18, 1977, might have been the most public, there were dozens of others behind the scenes.

Chemistry is said to play a large part in the success of the best teams; however, the Yankees of the late '70s proved that even if a team doesn't have the best clubhouse chemistry, as long as they can channel that hostility and use it against their opponents on the field, even a team full of miscreants and hotheads can reach the top of the sports world.

MARK FIDRYCH: "THE BIRD" CAPTIVATES THE SPORT

June 28, 1976

Every so often in a baseball season, a number of factors line up to create a story almost bigger than the game itself, captivating fans throughout the nation and whipping the baseball world into a frenzy. It may have started with Babe Ruth, when he became a national icon as the first big home run hitter. "Fernandomania" gripped the baseball world as the rotund 20-year-old Mexican burst onto the scene and debuted in a way few other pitchers have. Even Hideo Nomo became a national wonder at a time when players from the Far East were just making their way into Major League Baseball. During the 1976 season, the man who caused the biggest stir was Mark Fidrych. His coming-out party happened on June 28 of that year.

Fidrych was a decent prospect who made his way through the minors in just two seasons after the Tigers drafted him in the 10th round of the 1976 MLB Draft. His debut was about as inauspicious as could be, as he entered a tie game against the Oakland A's. He came in to face Don Baylor with one out and Claudell Washington on third base. Baylor promptly delivered a single to beat Fidrych and the Tigers 6–5. It got much better from there for Fidrych.

To understand the true significance of Fidrych, one must take a quick study on the depths of ineptitude that was the Tigers of the mid-'70s. In 1975, the Tigers finished 57–102 and had the worst record in baseball by far. It was the second year in a row they finished in last place, and it showed in their attendance. The Tigers, one of the proud franchises of the American League, drew fewer than 5,000 fans for weeknight games.

It looked like it was going to be more of the same in 1976. The team had a good mix of veterans like Bill Freehan and Willie Horton to go with such younger stars as Ron LeFlore and Rusty Staub, but they had no pitching to speak of. Besides Fidrych's unexpected year, their second-winningest pitcher in 1976 would be Dave Roberts, who went 16–17 with an ERA of 4.00.

The 1976 home opener for the Tigers drew 48,612 as they took on Hank Aaron and the Milwaukee Brewers. They played well but lost 1–0. They embarked on a five-game road trip right after, and when they returned home to Tiger Stadium in a week's time, the fans didn't show up. They played four games against the Rangers and A's, and only surpassed 10,000 fans in the first game of the homestand. The A's drubbed Detroit's mediocre pitching in a short two-game series by a total of 18–3, as Detroit had 11,000 in attendance combined at the two games.

As the middle of May rolled along, a crazy thing started to happen in Detroit. On May 15, manager Ralph Houk, who thought enough of Fidrych's talent to choose him for the big-league roster despite being a nonroster spring training invitee, decided it was finally time to give the 21-year-old a start. Fidrych outdid even the wildest of expectations, as he threw a two-hitter in a 2–1 win over the Indians. He allowed back-to-back singles to Buddy Bell and Rick Manning in the seventh and, aside from that inning, retired 24 of the other 25 batters he faced.

Fidrych was a gangly 6'3", 175-pound righty with a bright blond Afro. If that didn't make him stand out on the field, his antics on the mound sure did. At the start of each inning Fidrych crawled around the ground, manicuring the dirt to fit his liking. He also emphatically talked to the baseball and to himself, all the while gyrating his arms, legs, and neck as if overly nervous.

Based on that one start, the reaction of Tigers fans, and the dearth of pitching in Detroit, Houk had little choice but to put Fidrych in the rotation permanently. His next start came 10 days later, and he pitched well at Fenway Park but lost 2–0. By this time, in an era before ESPN, word of the crazy pitcher who was shutting down opponents had spread throughout the baseball world. His next two starts began to really put him over the top.

On May 31, 1976, people showed up to Tiger Stadium and saw one of the great pitching performances of the year. Fidrych pitched all 11 innings in a 5–4 extra-inning win over the Brewers. As if that wasn't enough, he pitched 11 innings in his next start in a 3–2 win over the Rangers.

By now, the hysteria was just starting to bubble. Fans in Boston and Texas had witnessed his antics and talent firsthand, and with a nickname like "The Bird," the pieces were starting to fall into place for one of those special runs in the time line of baseball.

Fidrych won his next four starts, including a return trip to Fenway and, through June 24, was 7–1 with a 2.18 ERA. Because the Tigers were on an 11-game road trip, fans were following their team and Fidrych from afar, waiting for another chance to come to the park. That finally happened on June 28.

The Tigers returned home after taking three of four games in Boston and were set to play a quick turnaround series with the Yankees. The Yankees had the best record in the AL at the time and had a team of stars like Thurman Munson, Graig Nettles, Chris Chambliss, and Roy White. Ken Holtzman was on the mound for the Yankees that night, but that didn't matter much. What did matter was that Fidrych was scheduled to start for Detroit, and ABC was in town to broadcast the game nationally on *Monday Night Baseball*. It would be the country's first true look at the sensation known as "The Bird."

Fidrych and the Tigers started out quick, as he worked a tidy first inning, allowing just a single to Carlos May. LeFlore led off the game by drawing a walk off of Holtzman, and one batter later, Staub hit a two-run homer to give the Tigers a quick 2–0 lead. The Yankees cut the lead in half, however, in the second, as Elrod Hendricks hit a two-out solo home run to make it 2–1. From that point onward, Fidrych and Holtzman settled in to a pitchers' duel and buzzed through one quick inning after another.

After the home run, Fidrych retired 15 of the next 18 batters he faced, all the while putting on a show for the crowd of 47,855 spectators. Fidrych worked incredibly fast when he settled into his groove and rarely even left the mound between pitches. If he did, it was to pop around on the balls of his feet after a great play, grab a return throw from catcher Bruce Kimm, or give himself a stern, animated pep talk. After he recorded the third out of an inning, Fidrych typically sprinted off the mound and directly into the dugout.

After Fidrych got through the seventh, the Tigers gave him an insurance run when Aurelio Rodriguez hit a solo homer to bring the score to 3–1. Fidrych made quick work of the Yanks again in the eighth, and in the bottom of the inning, Detroit finally put the game away. Staub drove LeFlore home with a groundout, and Alex Johnson doubled home Tom Veryzer as the Tigers opened a 5–1 lead.

As the game moved to the ninth, fans stood and cheered wildly as if it was Game 7 of the World Series. Fidrych struck out Chambliss to start the frame, and at the time, it seemed as if the fans were either going to pour onto the field or the stands were going to collapse. He got Nettles to ground out for out number two but allowed a single to Oscar Gamble to give the Yanks a glimmer of hope. With Hendricks up to the plate, Fidrych and the crowd fed off one another in an effort to end the game there.

As Fidrych took the ball from Kimm, "#20—Mark Fidrych 'The Bird'" flashed on the ABC broadcast. Fidrych was on the rubber, in the stretch, looking for a sign despite the fact that Hendricks was still making his way from the on-deck circle, home plate umpire Jim Maloney was bent over brushing dirt off the plate, and Kimm was standing by idly. At that moment, play-by-play man Bob Prince, not known for speaking in hyperbole, said, "He's giving me goose bumps, and I've seen over 8,000 ball games."

Fidrych fell behind Hendricks 2–0 quickly, and after he threw ball two, he quickly hopped off the mound toward home, even causing Kimm, who'd been catching him all along, to double clutch his throw back to his moving target. Fidrych was animated in telling himself to calm down and motioning with his pitching elbow to keep his arm tight to his body. He followed with ball three but stood his ground, got the ball back, and continued to work quickly. It took him all of eight seconds from the time he got the ball back from Kimm to deliver strike one to Hendricks, and that included time to remove his cap and adjust his curly blond locks.

Finally, on a 3–2 count, Fidrych induced another grounder, his 14th of the night, to put away the 5–1 win. The crowd was in a frenzy as second baseman Pedro García fielded and threw to first, and Fidrych didn't seem to know what to do with himself. He started toward first but stopped and sprinted toward Kimm to shake his hand and gave him a hug. His teammates took his cue and raced to him to offer congratulations on the effort. ABC announcer Warner Wolf said, "The Tigers and Fidrych are acting like it's the seventh game of the World Series!" and the fans were right there with them.

Fidrych scrambled around the field in chaos, at first going toward the dugout, but then turning back to shake anybody's hand he could find, including field security and one of the umpires. Even after he finally sprinted into the clubhouse, ABC refused to cut away from its telecast as the fans grew even louder, chanting for him to come back out for a curtain call. Police had to make their way to the top of the Tigers dugout to try to keep some order. One minute and 30 seconds later, with the crowd still screaming his name, Fidrych emerged from the dugout to tip his cap to the fans. Even Wolf, the seasoned broadcaster, cut himself off in midsentence to exclaim, "Here he comes! Here he comes!"

Fidrych emerged from the dugout, tipped his hat, and began shaking hands again. Even the police, who were supposed to keep the fans from mobbing him, turned around to shake his hand. Again, Prince laid on the accolades: "I've been in baseball 35 years, I have never in all my life seen anything equal this."

Sometime later, the third member of the broadcast team, Bob Uecker, had Fidrych return to the field to conduct a postgame interview for ABC. Even Uecker couldn't temper his excitement. He started the interview, "Mark, I've never seen anything like this in my entire life, and I know it's a very emotional time for you." In what would become his trademark charm, Fidrych, still visibly incredulous, simply replied, "Oh yeah, 48,000 people came out tonight . . . and we couldn't give them a better show."

Fidrych stood on the field and answered Uecker's questions for nearly five minutes without any shoes on. He bounced between being humble and incredulous. He credited his teammates, saying that they did two-thirds of the work and all he did was pitch.

Mark Fidrych's performance on June 28, 1976, was such a perfect combination of so many factors that it catapulted him to a meteoric rise as a national sensation. With a national TV audience watching, Fidrych made quick work of the vaunted Yankees in a game that lasted just 111 minutes. Because Fidrych was such a free spirit, his actions were seen as refreshing in a game that was at the precipice of becoming bogged down with free agency, legal battles, and poor labor relations.

In his next start, in front of an even bigger crowd, Fidrych outdueled Mike Cuellar, throwing a four-hit shutout against a Baltimore Orioles squad that featured Reggie Jackson, Brooks Robinson, and Lee May. Even though he lost a 1–0 decision in the start after that, Fidrych was tabbed to start the All-Star Game for the AL ahead of Catfish Hunter and Luis Tiant.

Fidrych won his first two starts after the All-Star Game but from that point on only went 8–7, and just as fast as he rose to superstardom he began his steep decline. He finished the year 19–9 and was the easy choice for the AL Rookie of the Year. He even finished second in the Cy Young voting to Jim Palmer and 11th in the MVP balloting.

In 1977, Fidrych got off to a good start, despite injuring his knee in spring training. After losing his first two starts of the year, Fidrych won his next six, throwing a complete game in each one; however, in a game at Baltimore on July 4, he felt his arm go numb after a pitch, and that would be the end of him. He never could regain his health, and it took a full eight years before doctors were finally able to determine that he suffered a torn rotator cuff. After the injury, he won just four games the rest of his career: two in 1978 and two in 1980. Fidrych attempted comebacks until 1983, but finally retired after going 2–5 with a 9.68 ERA for Pawtucket, the minor-league affiliate of his hometown Red Sox.

The story of Mark Fidrych is truly one of the incredible tales in baseball. Pitchers of that era were dominant and intimidating. The prototypical pitchers throughout the '70s were Tom Seaver, Bob Gibson, and Jim Palmer; ultra-competitive hurlers who would knock down their own mother if she was in the box. They maintained a stoic composure and snarled infinitely more than they smiled. If there was a player who was the complete opposite of that, it was Fidrych. He was a beloved free spirit who energized the city of Detroit and became a national phenomenon before his arm gave out too soon.

No matter how abrupt the ending was for Fidrych, the memorable run he put together will always live on in the hearts of Tigers fans. For one night, on June 28, 1976, the entire country got to share.

PASCUAL PEREZ: INCITING A RIOT

August 12, 1984

There's an old saying attributed to comedian Rodney Dangerfield that goes, "I went to a fight and a hockey game broke out!" Substitute "baseball" for "hockey" and you have what fans experienced on August 12, 1984.

Typical baseball fights seem to follow a common script. A player takes issue with something that happens on the field, tensions boil over, and the benches empty. From there, maybe one or two punches get thrown, but it usually ends up just being some jostling and maybe some angry shoves.

Sometimes, however, things get out of hand.

In 1965, Juan Marichal clubbed the Dodgers' John Roseboro on the head with a bat when the catcher buzzed a couple of throwbacks to the pitcher too close to Marichal's head. Another fight that stands out: Buddy Harrelson taking issue with a hard slide into second base by Pete Rose. The Yankees and Orioles had a memorable brawl in 1998 that spilled into the Baltimore dugout when Orioles closer Armando Benitez plunked Tino Martinez. While these fights surely stand out among baseball tussles, they don't measure up to the multiple brawls in the Padres–Braves game on August 12, 1984.

The game seemed to be an innocuous matchup between the Padres, who were the top team in the National League that year, and the Braves, who were in second place in the NL West at the time but 9½ games behind San Diego. The Padres won the first two games of the set, and Ed Whitson was on the mound for the Padres looking to top the eccentric Pascual Perez for the sweep.

Nobody ever quite knew what went on in the mind of Perez, as he had as long a list of crazy behavior as any pitcher in the '80s. The game took place on a Sunday afternoon in Atlanta, and as Perez walked out to take his warm-up pitches for the first inning, he allegedly told Padres leadoff hitter Alan Wiggins he was going to hit him. Sure enough, with the first pitch of the game, Perez drilled Wiggins in the back for seemingly no good reason.

Padres players exited the dugout onto the field but didn't charge at Perez. There was just a lot of finger pointing and threats. The next batter, Hall of Famer Tony Gwynn, hit into a double play, and despite the fact that Steve Garvey and Graig Nettles both also reached base, Perez escaped without allowing a run.

Word of Perez's intent to hit Wiggins and the subsequent beaning did not sit well with old-school Padres manager Dick Williams. While the Padres were intent on retaliating immediately against the Braves, the Hall of Fame skipper asked Whitson to wait until Perez came up to take care of business. At the time, Williams actually started planning not only for his and Whitson's inevitable ejections, but also for the ejections of their replacements, as he sensed this would be an ongoing issue.

Rafael Ramirez led off the third with a walk, and Bruce Benedict followed with a popout to bring Perez to the plate. Perez squared around to bunt on the first pitch, but it sailed behind him. Veteran umpire Steve Rippley did a good job of jumping out from behind the plate and putting himself between Perez and the mound. The pitcher took off his helmet and started wielding the bat threateningly as he ran around the home plate area, trying to get away from Rippley and around Padres catcher Terry Kennedy. Both benches emptied, but no punches were thrown.

Ramirez was able to advance on the pitch that went behind Perez's back, but once the at-bat continued, the pitcher struck out. Jerry Royster then singled home Ramirez to extend the Braves' lead to 3–0.

The game eventually moved to the bottom of the fourth, and with Perez due up second, everyone in the park already knew what was about to happen. Benedict grounded out, leading off the inning to bring Perez up to the plate again. Whitson threw the first pitch inside at Perez, but the lanky pitcher anticipated the move and backed out of the way before the ball was even released. Immediately, Whitson and his manager Williams were both ejected. Greg Booker replaced Whitson and subsequently walked Perez. A wild pitch allowed Perez to advance to second, and he came home on a single by Royster as the Braves opened up a 4–0 lead.

After getting the side in order in the top of the sixth, Perez again led off the seventh, and again the Padres came after him. With Perez anticipating being thrown at, the 6'2" pitcher whom Terry Kennedy called a "dancing toothpick" was difficult to plunk. Booker tried, however, and earned an ejection, along with replacement manager Ozzie Virgil.

Greg Harris replaced the ejected Booker and got Perez to ground out. He then struck out Royster and Hubbard to move the game along to the seventh. Nettles led off the seventh for the Padres and belted a homer to get San Diego on the board. The Padres went down in order after that, and the bottom of the seventh and top of the eighth went by without incident, bringing the game to the bottom of the eighth with Perez due up second. Despite the game pretty much being in hand, Joe Torre elected to leave Perez in to bat after Benedict led off with an out.

Craig Lefferts was in to pitch for the Padres, and again Perez anticipated being thrown at. On cue, Lefferts came inside at Perez, and the Padres' lefty finally was able to hit the elusive Perez with a pitch, despite the fact that by the time the ball got there, Perez had one foot out of the side of the batter's box.

The benches cleared again, and this time the fight turned nasty. As the players emptied onto the field, Perez went in the opposite direction and took cover in the Braves clubhouse. Both teams and the umpires ended up in a complete melee, with 300-pound umpire John McSherry on the ground in the middle trying to break it all up. Eventually, Padres outfielder Champ Summers, who wasn't even in the game, broke free of Bob Watson and took off toward the Braves dugout in search of Perez.

Summers was met by Braves All-Star Bob Horner, who was on the disabled list with a broken wrist at the time. Horner began the game in the press box, out of uniform as a fan, but had made his way to the clubhouse and put his uniform on in anticipation of the action. Horner intercepted Summers along the dugout railing. Braves pitcher Rick Camp crashed himself into Summers and Horner, knocking the group closer to the stands.

Meanwhile, a Braves fan had jumped onto the field and sprinted toward the fracas. He grabbed Summers from behind and tried to pull him off Horner. At the same time, another Braves fan stood atop the dugout and pelted Summers with a full beer, while another fan knocked Horner, Summers, and Camp to the ground. Seeing this, a large group of Braves sprinted toward their dugout to help. At one point, there were 15 Braves in that part of the fight against four Padres. Meanwhile, back toward home plate, Padres second baseman Tim Flannery got into a scuffle with Gerald Perry, who had gone after Lefferts.

The insanity finally died down, and the teams would eventually get back to playing ball. Goose Gossage replaced Lefferts, and Brad Komminsk mercifully came in to pinch-run for Perez. No runs were scored in the inning, and the teams would have to get through one more half inning, without incident, to call it a game.

Easier said than done. Donnie Moore was called in to finish the game for the Braves, and Torre would later say that he instructed his pitcher to just get the final three outs and get out of there. Torre also said that he took one look into Moore's eyes and knew that wasn't happening.

The Padres' leadoff batter was Nettles, who had homered in his previous at-bat. Moore drilled Nettles on the first pitch, and chaos ensued once again. Nettles charged Moore, and the pitcher got in a solid punch before Benedict and Chambliss tackled Nettles. The fight calmed down for a brief second, but Gossage got ahold of Moore, creating more havoc.

Perry, who was wrestled away from Lefferts by Flannery in the previous altercation, sought out the Padres' second baseman and sucker punched him in the face. Eventually, both teams went back to their respective dugouts, but as the Padres retreated to theirs, Braves fans pelted them with debris. This caused Kurt Bevacqua to jump onto the dugout roof and into the stands, after the fans. Bevacqua lost his footing, fell into the seats, and became fair game for the Braves fans until security arrived.

Padres players, including a shirtless, bat-wielding Whitson, gathered at the top of the dugout steps and continued to fight with the fans. A team of police and security guards were able to drag Bevacqua out of the stands and keep the Padres and Braves fans separated.

An incensed Whitson had to be restrained by Padres coaches Harry Dunlop and Norm Sherry. The umpires finally ordered both teams to their clubhouses for a 20-minute "cooling off" period while they decided whether to resume the game. They eventually decided to play out the final half inning. The Padres were able to plate two runs, but Gene Garber got the final out to preserve the 5–3 win.

The scene at Atlanta–Fulton County Stadium that day rivaled any kind of insanity ever seen on a baseball field. In total, there were 13 ejections, five fan arrests, and fines and suspensions levied on both managers.

Both teams featured some of the most intense players in the National League at the time, which certainly added to the excitement. Nettles and Gossage were no strangers to altercations from their days on the Yankees during the Bronx Zoo era. One year later, Whitson would famously brawl with his Yankees manager, Billy Martin, breaking Martin's arm and ribs. Even the mild-mannered Dale Murphy and Tony Gwynn ended up playing key roles in the fight.

The teams continued their battle after the game in the press. Torre, the usually reserved Braves manager, called Williams an "idiot," to which Williams offered to continue the fight personally, saying he was available "anytime, any place" and he "won't be intimidated."

The Padres claimed the fight unified them even more as a team and propelled them through the dog days of August and into the stretch run of the 1984 season. They ended up winning the NL West by 12 games, despite losing the final game of the season to the Braves and Perez in a return trip to Atlanta. Those games went off without incident.

San Diego took on the Cubs in the National League Championship Series and, despite falling behind 2–0 in the best-of-five series, came back to win three straight to claim their first NL pennant. They faced off against the powerful Detroit Tigers in the World Series, who, in 1984, fielded one of the top teams of the decade. The Tigers took home the World Series trophy by topping the Padres four games to one.

The 1984 Padres team is one of the most beloved teams in the franchise's history. The team was riddled with All-Stars like Steve Garvey, Nettles, Kennedy, and Gary Templeton, and featured three future Hall of Famers in Gwynn, Gossage, and their manager, Williams. For all of the accomplishments the great Padres team had that year, their most lasting image from the season might be their ongoing battle with the Atlanta Braves and their relentless pursuit to bean Pascual Perez, the gangly, bug-eyed, maniacal pitcher, and the complete insanity that followed.

GEORGE BRETT: THE PINE TAR GAME

July 24, 1983

The old baseball cliché is that you see something new at the ballpark every time you go to a game. It could be something as simple as a player recording his first major-league hit or achieving a team record; however, sometimes something so crazy will happen that it will be talked about in baseball circles for decades. On July 24, 1983, fans undoubtedly witnessed the latter.

The Yankees and Royals had one of the game's best rivalries in the late '70s and early '80s. The teams met in the postseason in the 1976, 1977, 1978, and 1980 ALCS, and the main cast of characters was similar in each series. The Royals were led by George Brett, Frank White, Hal McRae, and Willie Wilson, among others. The Yankees featured Graig Nettles, Reggie Jackson, Ron Guidry, and Goose Gossage during that time.

By 1983, the Yankees were starting to get old but still had some fight in them. The Orioles and Tigers were the up-and-coming teams and would finish ahead of the Yanks in the AL East standings. The Royals finished second that year but were never really in the race, ending the season 20 games out of first.

With Wilson, White, and McRae still in their prime, the Royals lineup was tough to negotiate for any pitcher. But Brett remained the focal point of the offense and was an incredibly difficult out for pitchers. "Brett was the toughest hitter I faced in my career," said Don August, a starter for the Brewers whom Brett went 5-for-11 against.

> I remember him standing way off the plate when I faced him, so I put a fastball on the outside corner. He hit it off the center-field wall. Next time up, I tried to come inside, and he turned on it and ripped it into the corner. How do you get Brett out? I guess throw it down the middle and hope he hits it at someone.

The Yankees had taken two of the first three games in this four-game set and faced off against the Royals in a Sunday afternoon game at Yankee Stadium on July 24. Bud Black and Shane Rawley were the starting pitchers for the Royals and Yankees, respectively, but they would be long gone by the time the events that made this game famous happened.

The first inning went by without incident, and the Royals were the first to get on the board when John Wathan scored on a groundout by White in the second. The Yankees quickly tied the game up when Dave Winfield homered off Black. The Royals regained the lead in the fourth when White again drove home Wathan, this time with an infield hit.

Black settled in after the Winfield homer, only allowing singles to Bert Campaneris and Roy Smalley as the game remained 2–1 through five. In the sixth, the Royals scored again on a triple to center by Don Slaught. The Yankees, however, would finally get to Black in the sixth.

Campaneris led off the frame with an infield hit, and Lou Piniella followed with a one-out single to center. Don Baylor tripled to center to tie the game, and Winfield singled to left to give the Yanks a 4–3 lead.

The game stayed that way until the top of the ninth. Despite having Gossage, the Hall of Fame closer, available in the bullpen, manager Billy Martin stuck with Dale Murray, who had retired all eight batters he faced to that point. Slaught grounded out to lead off the top of the ninth, and Pat Sheridan popped up to first for a second out.

However, U. L. Washington singled to center, and with Brett due up next, Martin opted to bring in Gossage. Brett launched a long home run to right off Gossage for what was apparently the go-ahead hit. He circled the bases, touched home, and took a seat in the Royals dugout next to Sheridan and McRae. What happened was iconic '80s baseball.

Earlier in his career, Nettles was involved in a play in which a similar illegal bat was used according to an archaic rule stating that no substance could be applied to a bat beyond 18 inches from the knob. The rule allegedly was put into place because players were applying pine tar toward the barrel of the bat and then using it to get a better grip. While the application of pine tar was not illegal, rules were changed to limit the application to 18 inches above the knob because too many batted balls were coming in contact with the pine tar and causing otherwise perfectly good baseballs to be thrown out of play because they were stained.

Nettles had approached Martin earlier in the year when he noticed that Brett's bat had pine tar that was obviously well past the 18-inch limit. The Yankees manager decided to wait until the right time to appeal Brett's bat to the umpire. The Yanks had played the Royals earlier that year, but Brett didn't have any big hits in the previous series, so Martin declined to call him on it. The home run he hit on July 24, 1983, was the perfect time.

Martin approached home plate umpire Tim McClelland with his concerns. The umpires convened, and third-base umpire Nick Bremigan suggested that crew chief Joe Brinkman measure the bat against home plate, which is 17 inches wide. It was estimated that the pine tar stretched more than 25 inches past the bat handle, clearly past the limit.

The problem that ensued was that there was no specific penalty listed for someone who had applied material past the 18-inch mark. Martin was ready for this and suggested the umpires invoke a rule stating that the umpires have the right to make any decision on any penalties not specifically listed in the rule book.

Slaught was sitting near Brett in the dugout during all of this: "I was sitting right near George, still in my equipment," said Slaught. "Someone said, 'Hey I think they're gonna call you out.' George said, 'If they call me out, I'll kill them.'"

At about the same time, McClelland took a few steps toward the Royals dugout, with Brett's bat in hand. McClelland raised his right hand, pointed at Brett with the bat, and called him out. After that, pure insanity erupted.

Brett jumped off the dugout bench and sprinted at McClelland, arms flailing and furiously screaming at the umpire, who stood 6'6". Brinkman grabbed Brett with a choke hold, and Brett began screaming and struggling to get loose as the entire Royals bench emptied onto the field. Almost as mad as Brett was Royals manager Dick Howser, who furiously protested the call.

In the fracas, Hall of Famer Gaylord Perry grabbed the bat from McClelland and handed it down in a relay to a Royals batboy, who went toward the clubhouse. Yankee Stadium security noticed this and, along with the umpires, sprinted down the runway after the illegal bat.

"It was wild," said Slaught. "Steve Renko and some of the guys were running around the hallways looking for the bat, and security was running right behind them through the halls."

Eventually, the bat was confiscated by the umpires and sent to American League president Lee MacPhail for investigation. The Royals filed a formal protest against the ruling and waited for a final decision to be made by MacPhail. MacPhail ruled in favor of the protest, citing the rule's archaic nature, the fact that the pine tar did nothing to enhance the ball's contact off the bat, and an incorrect penalty by the umpires. MacPhail stated that the way he read the rules, the umpires should've just removed the bat and continued play from there.

The bat was eventually returned to Brett. He removed the excess pine tar, drew a line with a red marker around the 18-inch mark, and continued to use it in games. But Perry advised Brett that the incident was so unique that his bat was a baseball artifact and he shouldn't risk breaking it. Brett agreed and eventually sold the bat for $25,000; however, Brett rethought the transaction and bought the bat back for the same amount. The bat is now on display at the Baseball Hall of Fame.

As for the game itself, MacPhail ruled that the remaining four outs would be played as part of a makeup on August 18. Martin and Yankees owner George Steinbrenner, always the competitors, were livid at the reversal.

On August 18, the Royals returned to Yankee Stadium to finish the game. Howser, Brett, Perry, and Royals coach Rocky Colavito were ejected from the original game due to their actions in the melee that ensued during the initial ruling.

"It may have been the most nervous I was for a game in my career, even including the postseason," said Slaught, who was in his second season in the bigs and went 3-for-4 in the game. "There were more reporters there than any post-season game that I played in. It was a weird, weird game. Gaylord Perry even had T-shirts made up for us and then tried to make us all buy them from him."

As the game was about to start, Martin appealed the fact that Brett actually touched every base. He contested that since it was an entirely different umpire crew, they would have no way of knowing that he indeed touched every base. But the umpires anticipated Martin might do this and had a sworn affidavit from the original crew stating that Brett did touch every base. Martin then informed the umpires that he was playing this game under his own protest.

When the action finally started, Martin made some lineup changes. Jerry Mumphrey, the original center fielder in the game, had been traded in the ensuing weeks and so was unavailable to continue. Martin decided to send his ace pitcher, Ron Guidry, out to center. He also inserted rookie Don Mattingly at second base. Mattingly, a lefty first baseman, became the first lefty to play a middle-infield position since Indians pitcher Sam McDowell in 1970. No lefty has played a middle-infield position since. Asked for his reasoning behind the moves, Martin said the resumption of the game was a mockery and he would play it like one.

With George Frazier pitching in relief for the Yanks, the game resumed. McRae, who was the on-deck batter when Brett homered, struck out to end the ninth. Royals closer Dan Quisenberry came on for the save and retired Mattingly, Smalley, and Oscar Gamble in order to finally give the Royals the 5–4 win in front of the 1,200 fans who showed up for the final four outs.

Brett flying out of the dugout is something that will live on in the annals of baseball history. Brett, Martin, Perry, and Nettles were some of the most colorful characters in baseball, making the incident even more memorable. The game itself brought the Royals to within one game of first place, but they went into a midseason slump, and that would be the closest they got to first place for the rest of the year. In the years after, all parties involved looked back on the incident with a sense of humor, accepting their place in baseball history and laughing about the events surrounding the end of the game.

Brett went on to have one of the greatest careers in baseball history. He finished the 1983 season with a .310 batting average and went on to record 3,154 hits in his career. He maintained his reputation as an intense player who was willing to do anything he could to play the game and play it well.

"Brett was just a regular guy, but incredibly talented," said Andy McGaffigan, who was Brett's teammate between 1990 and 1991. "He showed up and played hard and played hurt. He would DH, play third, play first, whatever it took to be in the lineup that day. He had no pride or ego, and that was contagious. It's what made him a great leader."

Another of Brett's teammates agreed with that assessment: "He was the best pure hitter I ever played with," said Jim Wohlford, who played with Brett the first four years of his major-league career. "You just knew the special talent was there, even as a 20-year-old kid."

Slaught also reflected on Brett's greatness: "George always seemed to hit what we needed," said Slaught. "It was unbelievable. If we needed a single or double, that's what he seemed to hit. Look at the pine tar game; we needed a homer and that's what he hit. He was the guy that did that the best of anyone I played with."

There are so many reasons George Brett is considered one of the greatest players in the history of the game. His clutch performance in the game and wild outburst after he was called out were two iconic moments in one of the most colorful and productive careers in baseball history.

· 9 ·

Historic Home Runs

HANK AARON: 715 WITH CLASS AND DIGNITY

April 4, 1974

In a sport where statistics are held sacred, there are a few numbers that stand alone. Joe DiMaggio's 56, Cy Young's 511, and Roger Maris's 61 are statistics in which the number itself has become so iconic, no explanation is needed. You just say "DiMaggio's 56" and even the most casual fan should know you're referring to his 56-game hitting streak in 1941. In games played through the end of the 1973 season, the number 714 might have been the most famous of all. Since 1935, 714 stood for the amount of career home runs of Babe Ruth. It was a record that many from the '40s through the '60s thought was unapproachable. On Opening Day of the 1974 season, Hank Aaron was on the doorstep, ready to stand alongside the Babe.

On September 29, 1973, Aaron blasted homer number 713 against the Houston Astros. It was the second-to-last day of the season, leaving Aaron one more game to tie or beat Ruth's mark. In front of 40,517 fans at Atlanta–Fulton County Stadium on the final day of the season, Aaron came up short in his attempt. He started the game 3-for-3 and came up in the eighth with one more shot at the record. He popped out to second, however, and ended the '73 season with 713 career homers.

Fans had to endure the six-month offseason waiting for Aaron to take another shot at 714. Anticipation grew as winter turned to spring and teams reported for spring training. The Braves were set to start the season in Cincinnati for a three-game series against the Reds. As the season approached, there was talk throughout the Braves organization that management was going to sit Aaron so he could chase the record at home. Eventually, Commissioner Bowie Kuhn stepped in and ordered that Aaron play at least two of the three games in the season-opening series.

Opening Day that year came on April 4, and the Braves readied for their matchup against the Big Red Machine. Jack Billingham was the starter for the Reds that day. He was fourth in the Cy Young Award voting the year before, when he won 19 games for the Reds. The 6'4" righty was at the peak of his 13-year career, and many felt he was finally turning into the top pitcher he was projected to be.

Aaron was batting fourth in the Braves lineup, so someone was going to have to reach base for him to get his shot in the first inning. Ralph Garr obliged when he led off the game with a walk. Mike Lum followed with a single as the Braves started a quick rally against Billingham. Darrell Evans flew out to left to bring Aaron to the plate. Cincinnati fans stood for Aaron, as they finally were going to see what Aaron could do after the six-month layoff. Aaron immediately blasted a homer to left-center on his first swing of the 1974 season to give the Braves a 3–0 lead and tie Babe Ruth's allegedly unbreakable record.

Not lost on the situation was the fact that it was a black athlete who tied Ruth at that sacred number 714. Ruth played in an era when integration was still decades away. But Ruth often teamed with Negro League stars on barnstorming trips and was an early proponent of integration. Now, the two people who stood side by side at number 714 were the legendary Ruth and a former Negro League player, Aaron.

After the celebration of Aaron's historic home run, there was still a full game to be played, and the fans had a new anticipation. The Reds went on to win the game 7–6, with Aaron failing to hit another home run in his subsequent at-bats.

The Braves rested Aaron the next day as they fell to the Reds 7–5, but because of the league mandate, they had to start him again in Cincinnati on April 7. Aaron struck out looking in his first two at-bats of the game and grounded weakly to third in his final at-bat, before being lifted for Rowland Office in the seventh. Some writers whispered whether Aaron didn't give his best effort so he could break the record at home.

This clearly did not sit well with Aaron, who opened his press conference addressing the issue: "I have never went on a ball field and not given my level best," he said, according to an article in the *Augusta Chronicle*. "I played in Cincinnati the two out of three games I was supposed to play. Contrary to some of the reports I have read that I was a disgrace to the ball club, I did my level best."

Braves fans were sure they'd get their wish to see Aaron break Babe's record at home as they returned for a 10-game homestand after beating the Reds 5–3.

Again, the prolific but reserved slugger would not make his fans wait long as they took on the Dodgers and Al Downing to start the homestand on April 8. In his second at-bat of the night, in front of 53,775 fans in Atlanta, Aaron blasted a 1–0 high fastball from Downing over the left-field fence for a two-run homer that set off a wild celebration, complete with fireworks and congratulations from teammates, family, politicians, and black baseball pioneer Monte Irvin at Atlanta–Fulton County Stadium.

Aaron had surpassed Babe on his way to putting up a sacred number himself: 755. While the ordeal was quite a spectacle, complete with a pre-game show and national TV audience, Aaron remained stoic and classy. Everyone got the sense that the celebration was more for the fans than it was for Aaron.

Tom House was a relief pitcher for the Braves in 1974, and ended up with the historic home run ball when it cleared the fence and landed in the Braves bullpen. He immediately ran toward home to present the ball to Aaron as he was mobbed by teammates and congratulated by his parents. Aaron held up the ball for pictures, presenting that dignified smile as fans cheered wildly.

A microphone was set up near the Braves dugout for Aaron to address the crowd. Unlike some of the in-game speeches and celebrations that have occurred in baseball previously, Aaron expressed more relief than celebration. He approached the mic and simply said, "I just thank God it's all over with. Thank you."

He addressed his teammates afterward in the locker room. Again, in true Aaron form, he offered an apology instead of heaping praise upon himself. He apologized to his teammates for the increased media presence, the sideshow nature the press created, and the added distraction. He thanked his teammates for understanding and being so patient with him. Of course, Aaron was probably the only one in the room who thought this chase at history was a distraction, and it's safe to say his teammates were happy and felt privileged to be along for the ride.

On April 4, 1974, Aaron figuratively stood shoulder-to-shoulder with Ruth as the two shared the most revered record in professional sports for four days. For a short time, Ruth's 714 became Ruth and Aaron's 714. Two legends, nearly 40 years apart, reached heights that no other Major League Baseball player had ever achieved. For those four days, 714 held more weight than it ever did. On April 8, Aaron took a step past Babe and continued his trek toward 755.

MIKE SCHMIDT: 500 FOR THE WIN

April 18, 1987

As the '60s turned into the '70s, the legends of the golden age of baseball began to fade. Mickey Mantle, Willie Mays, and Ernie Banks gave way to a new standard of superstars who would carry the game through the next generation. Hall of Famers like George Brett, Dave Winfield, and Carlton Fisk got their starts in the early '70s, and while they may not have been on the level of Mays or Mantle, they were adequate torchbearers for the new generation.

One player who may have been a step above those stars of the '80s was Mike Schmidt in Philadelphia. Playing a position that has a shortage of Hall of Fame representation, Schmidt was the total package and is considered by many as the greatest third baseman of all time: "Mike Schmidt played with me my first year in Puerto Rico," said Don DeMola, who pitched for the Expos in '74 and '75.

> He was touted as a big fastball home run hitter, one of the classiest guys I ever met, and we became pretty good friends. He always said to me, "I'm a fastball hitter." Well, every time we faced a guy with a decent heater, he had his troubles, so when I faced him I said, "Well he's going to have to hit mine."

After showing promise during part-time stints in the '72 and '73 seasons, Schmidt broke out in '74 and went on an offensive and defensive rampage that lasted 15 years. He was one of the premier power hitters of the era, as he led the National League in homers 8 times, slugging percentage 5 times, OPS 5 times, and RBIs 4 times. He won NL MVP Awards in '80, '81, and '86, and finished in the top 10 of the voting six other times.

In addition to his offensive prowess, Schmidt was the top defensive third baseman in the NL at the time as well. A converted middle infielder, he won his first Gold Glove in 1976, and went on to win the award 10 times in his storied career. Schmidt had sure hands, a powerful arm, and incredible range.

"When you played the Phillies during that time period, Schmidt was the guy you had to get out," said Matt Galante, who was a coach with the Astros and spent more than 40 years in the game. "He was a perennial Gold Glover and could beat you with his bat or in the field. You just didn't want him up with runners on base. You wanted him up there with two outs and the bases empty if you could get it."

Schmidt's talents led a resurgence of the Phillies, who had fallen on hard times for nearly a quarter century during the post–World War II era. Schmidt led the Phillies to three straight divisional titles from 1976 to 1978, each time falling in the National League Championship Series, however. Finally, in 1980, he and the Phillies broke through. He notched career highs in homers with 48 and RBIs with 121. He was the unanimous MVP and won the Gold Glove and Silver Slugger Awards. But the crowning achievement was finally leading the Phillies to their first NL pennant since the "Whiz Kids" team of 1950. In the World Series, Schmidt was spectacular, batting .381 to win the World Series MVP, while leading the Phillies to their first World Series title.

The Phillies team of 1980 consisted of veterans like Pete Rose, Steve Carlton, Tug McGraw, and Larry Bowa, in addition to Schmidt. After reaching the pinnacle, the Phillies' veterans began to break down and go their separate ways, sending Philadelphia back down in the standings as the '80s progressed. If there was one thing that kept the team going, it was the continued success of Schmidt. He continued his 30-homer seasons through the '80s and, it was evident that Schmidt was marching toward a surefire Hall of Fame career.

By staying highly productive through his mid-30s, Schmidt began to compile tremendous career statistics. Going into the '87 season, he needed just five homers to reach 500 for his career. At 37 years old and still productive, Schmidt got off to a good start and hit four homers in the team's first 10 games. His first chance at number 500 came on April 18, and he didn't disappoint the 19,361 in attendance.

Schmidt's Phillies were facing off against the Pirates for a Saturday game. They had beaten them in extra innings the day before with Schmidt connecting for career home run number 499 in the second inning. Bob Walk, Schmidt's former teammate from the 1980 World Series team, was the Pirates' starting pitcher that day, but he wouldn't be around long. Walk lasted just three innings and allowed five runs. But Schmidt didn't factor in producing any of the five runs, as he popped up and walked in his first two at-bats. The big hit came from All-Star catcher Lance Parrish, who belted a three-run homer in the third inning to give the Phillies a 5–0 lead.

The Pirates, however, chipped away at the deficit and eventually took a 6–5 lead. While closer Steve Bedrosian and the Phillies were upset at blowing a game they once led 5–0, the game set up perfectly for Schmidt, who was due up fifth in the top of the ninth. Milt Thompson tried to get the rally started with a one-out single, but Juan Samuel hit into a fielder's choice, leaving the Phillies down to their final out. Samuel stole second and advanced to third on a wild pitch. Von Hayes then worked out a walk to bring up Schmidt, who was 0-for-3 that day.

Don Robinson looked as if he was pitching around the dangerous Schmidt with Mike Easler waiting on deck. Easler was a solid hitter during his prime but was now 36 years old and playing in his final major-league

season. Robinson fell behind Schmidt 3–0 and probably would've been better off just walking the reigning NL MVP; however, Robinson grooved one
and Schmidt responded by blasting a long homer over the left-field fence for
number 500 and an 8–6 Phillies lead.

Schmidt's blast prompted a simple yet memorable call from Phillies
Hall of Fame broadcaster Harry Kalas. "Swing and a long drive! There it is!
Number 500 for Michael Jack Schmidt!" exclaimed the venerable broadcaster,
whose call accompanied a rare show of excitement from Schmidt. Always stoic
while on the field, this time Schmidt flipped his bat, clapped his hands, and
pumped his fists as he rounded the bases in a show of pure excitement at the
culmination of one of the great power careers in MLB history. At the time,
he became just the 14th player to reach 500 career home runs.

In interviews leading up to his historic home run, Schmidt had said he
hoped the shot would come at a time to help his team win a game. With that
in mind, it couldn't have come at a better time, as former Pirates fan favorite Kent Tekulve came in for the Phillies to close out Pittsburgh in order in
the ninth, retiring three lefty batters in Bobby Bonilla, Barry Bonds, and Sid
Bream to seal the 8–6 win.

Schmidt went on to have his last great season in 1987, nearly duplicating
his stats from his MVP year of '86. He hit 35 homers, drove in 113 runs, and
hit .293, which was three points higher than his previous season. But it was the
last time Schmidt played at that level. Schmidt suffered an injury to his rotator
cuff in 1988 and was limited to just 108 games. He hit just 12 home runs, and
his average dipped to .249. He attempted to come back in 1989, but after 42
unproductive games hitting just .203, Schmidt abruptly retired on May 29, a
day after going 0-for-3 in a game against the Giants, leaving a legacy as one
of the game's all-time greats.

"I felt like he was the most dynamic player in the National League," said
Barry Foote, Schmidt's teammate in Philadelphia in 1977 and 1978. "His offensive numbers speak for themselves, but he was also a great defensive player
and ran the bases well too. He was just a great, great overall player."

As Schmidt and his contemporaries were finishing their careers, a new
crop of young baseball players was emerging as the stars of a new generation.
Hall of Famers like Schmidt, George Brett, Steve Carlton, and Tom Seaver
were the old men of the game and would be calling it a career as the '80s
evolved into the '90s. The end of Schmidt's career overlapped the start of the
careers of Ken Griffey Jr., Greg Maddux, and Bonds, as those players would
usher in a new generation of milestones, championships, and their own legendary performances.

Like time, the game of baseball marches on. Fans grow up with players like Schmidt, who stay their entire careers with franchises, taking them

through the ups and downs of their favorite teams. But in baseball, time always pauses to honor their accomplishments. On April 18, 1987, it was Mike Schmidt's time in the sun as the baseball world took time to celebrate home run number 500, on his way to 548 career long balls and a final stop in the Baseball Hall of Fame.

MEL OTT: McGRAW'S BOY BELTS NUMBER 511

April 16, 1946

On April 16, 1946, Mel Ott dug into the batter's box and stared down Phillies pitcher Oscar Judd. As Judd raised his left arm in his delivery, Ott raised his right foot off the ground, hitched his hands down toward his waist, and deposited the pitch into the stands for the 511th time of his career. While the number 511 doesn't carry the weight of numbers 714 or 755, it is one of the most significant home run–related numbers in baseball history.

Ott's career spanned from 1926 to 1947, and during that time he was the preeminent slugger in the National League. Ott's career overlapped Babe Ruth's for a 10-year period and just about mirrored the career of Jimmie Foxx, another pioneer of the long ball. While Foxx and Ruth were hulking strongmen of the game, Ott's profile as a home run hitter was much less obvious. Standing just 5'9" and weighing 170 pounds, Ott used a quick swing and powerful wrists to generate power that was unique to his era. A dead-pull hitter, Ott took advantage of the inviting right-field seats at the Polo Grounds, which stood a mere 257 feet away.

As a high schooler growing up in Louisiana, Ott first received recognition as a power-hitting lefty catcher playing on a semipro team. He eventually landed on a semipro team in Patterson, Louisiana, where he continued to dominate as a 16-year-old. The team's owner arranged for a tryout for the New York Giants in front of Hall of Fame manager John McGraw. Another Hall of Famer, Giants second baseman Frankie Frisch, was at the tryout and recalled Ott smoking line drives and crushing long shots over the walls. Frisch claimed that McGraw pegged Ott as a future star right there and signed the youngster to a contract worth $400.

When Ott reported to the Giants in 1926, McGraw oversaw every aspect of his offensive and defensive development. Because he was worried that other instructors might not share the enthusiasm for the 17-year-old, who allegedly weighed about 150 pounds at the time, McGraw refused to send Ott to the minors and took him right to the big-league club. Ott was shifted to the outfield out of fear that his slight build could not take the everyday rigors of catching.

In 1926, Ott was brought along slowly in games while receiving on-the-job training from McGraw and other Giants veterans who took a liking to the quiet lefty. From Opening Day in 1926 until August 20, Ott only appeared in games as a pinch-hitter. He appeared in 25 games, and despite the fact that he didn't record an extra-base hit, Ott batted .375.

Finally, with the Giants in fifth place in the National League on August 21, 1926, McGraw gave Ott the first start of his career. Unfortunately, Ott was thrust right into the fire. McGraw wrote the 17-year-old into the lineup as the leadoff hitter as the Giants took on the first-place Cardinals, with 373-game winner Grover Cleveland Alexander on the mound. As might be expected, the three-time 30-game winner had his way with Ott as he went 0-for-4.

Not discouraged, McGraw put Ott back in the starting lineup the next day and kept him in left field, and in the leadoff spot, for the rest of the season. He started the final 10 games of the season and blossomed in his full-time role, hitting .389 in that span, with just two strikeouts in 37 plate appearances. Ott finished the 1926 season with a .383 average but no power to speak of. He tallied just two doubles out of his 23 hits and drove in just four runs on the year.

In 1927, McGraw increased Ott's role a little, but he still was not a full-time player. McGraw experimented with Ott in different spots in the order to find where he would be most comfortable. Ott started 27 games in 1927 and appeared in 55 others as a pinch-hitter. His batting average dropped to .282, and he ended the season with just one home run, a solo shot off of Hal Carlson, who was a journeyman for the Cubs.

McGraw believed in Ott, still just 18 years old and developing physically, as a future superstar and stuck with him in 1928. Ott homered in his first two starts of the season and earned himself a permanent place in the Giants lineup. In his first season as a starter, and still just 19 years old, Ott hit .322 and belted 18 home runs. While the home run total might not seem like a lot by today's standards, it led the ball club and was good for eighth overall in the NL.

As Ott finally reached his physical maturity, his power blossomed. Ott's 42 home runs in 1929 were just one behind Phillies Hall of Famer Chuck Klein for the NL lead and four behind Ruth's total of 46. Finally, after being brought along slowly, McGraw saw the culmination of his great plan, and Ott developed into a full-fledged superstar. In the next 10 seasons, Ott blasted 323 homers, while batting .315. He led the NL in homers five of those 10 years.

In 1932, McGraw retired as manager and turned the reins over to first baseman Bill Terry, who would serve as a player-manager. In 1933, Ott finally led the Giants to a World Series title, their first since 1922. In the series, Ott batted .389 with two home runs as the Giants topped the Washington Senators 4–1. Ott hit the series-winning homer in Game 5 off Jack Russell to deliver the championship to New York.

When Ott was dominating the NL, Foxx was putting up "Ruthian" numbers in the American League. From 1929 to 1938, when Ott hit 323 homers, Foxx belted 413, including two 50-homer seasons. The two sluggers filled the retirement void of Ruth and Lou Gehrig.

Ott's career was still going strong into the '40s when it would take two dramatic turns in one week. After a 1941 season in which the aging Giants struggled to a fifth-place finish for the third straight year, Ott was promoted to player-manager, replacing the retiring Terry; however, before Ott could plan for the upcoming season, Japan attacked Pearl Harbor and baseball took a backseat to U.S. involvement in World War II.

The Giants were hit hard with player enlistment in the military in the next few seasons, and Ott never had consistent success as a manager. Between 1942 and 1945, Ott's play remained stellar, as he hit 95 home runs, while still maintaining a .284 batting average. On August 1, 1945, Ott became the third member of the 500–home run club, alongside Ruth and Foxx. Foxx retired after the 1945 season after hitting just seven home runs to bring his career total to 534.

The 1946 season opened with Ott's Giants taking on the Philadelphia Phillies at the Polo Grounds. The Phillies were coming off a 1945 season in which they had the worst record in baseball, while the Giants were still an average team in the middle of the pack in the NL. The Phillies roster was devoid of any star players, while the Giants still had Ott and a supporting cast led by Johnny Mize, Ernie Lombardi, and a 22-year-old rookie named Bobby Thomson, who would go on to "Shot Heard 'Round the World" fame five years later.

Giants hurler Bill Voiselle got through the first inning quickly, leaving Judd to take the mound against the Giants. New York would do damage quickly, as Bill Rigney and Mickey Witek each reached base to bring up Ott for his first at-bat of the season. Ott proceeded to crack a homer into the right-field seats to give the Giants a quick 3–0 lead. It was homer number 511 of his legendary major-league career.

In the next game, Ott went 0-for-2 at the plate, but it was a play in the field that ended up impacting baseball history. On a fly ball to left field late in the game, Ott dove and injured his knee. He was replaced by Buster Maynard, who played in just seven games in '46. Ott appeared in 29 more games throughout the '46 season, but his injured knee robbed him of the torque he used to generate his power. In 70 at-bats in the remainder of the season, Ott batted a minuscule .065 with no home runs. He appeared in just four games as a pinch-hitter in 1947 but failed to get a hit. He retired from active play after 1947, and stayed on to manage halfway through 1948 before handing the reins over to Leo Durocher, a Brooklyn Dodger who was despised by Giants fans as a player, 76 games into the season.

Mel Ott's elite place in baseball history is something that cannot be overstated. At the time of his retirement, his 511 home runs placed him third all-time and were more than 200 more than the next closest National Leaguer. In an era in which home runs in the AL considerably outnumbered those hit in the NL, Ott's power transcended the game. The soft-spoken and beloved Ott was not only a hero to New Yorkers, but also a national celebrity. In a 1944 survey of war bond buyers, Ott was selected as the most popular athlete of all time, ahead of even Ruth, Foxx, Gehrig, and Joe Louis.

At the time of his retirement, Ott held the National League career record for RBIs, runs scored, and walks, in addition to home runs. Ott's NL home run record stood until Willie Mays hit his 512th on May 4, 1965.

In the landscape of baseball history, the true magic numbers need no explanation. Aaron's 755, Maris's 61, and DiMaggio's 56 are all above any explanation. For the better part of the twentieth century, Ott's 511 was just as significant. Not bad for a little lefty with a strange batting stance who was given a chance by a legendary manager as a 17-year-old kid in 1926.

· *10* ·

Hall of Famers' Last Hurrahs

CARL YASTRZEMSKI: FROM WILLIAMS TO YAZ

September 10, 1983

Replacing a legend is one of the toughest things to do in sports. Rarely are there times when one superstar retires gracefully and another just slides right in. Often, the replacements struggle with expectations and have difficulty carving out a niche of their own. Nobody remembers George Selkirk, but he played right field and batted third for the Yankees on Opening Day in 1935, replacing Babe Ruth. Names like Babe Dahlgren, Manny Alexander, and Ken Henderson don't ring immortal, but those were the players who stepped in for Lou Gehrig, Cal Ripken, and Willie Mays, respectively.

While that's often the case when a legend steps down, the Red Sox experienced the complete opposite in 1961. On the last day of the 1960 season, Ted Williams retired with a bang when he hit his 529th home run in his final at-bat. The fans at Fenway gave Williams a standing ovation, calling for one final curtain call that never came. The next year, the Sox had the daunting task of replacing the greatest hitter who ever lived and chose to thrust a 21-year-old rookie with no major-league at-bats into left field. Although that sounds like a recipe for disaster, it couldn't have worked out better. That rookie was Carl Yastrzemski.

Yastrzemski manned left field for the next two decades and went on to one of the great careers in major-league history. He experienced the ups and downs of playing with the Sox for the next 23 years, playing the game with class and success that rivaled that of the man he replaced. Yastrzemski was a highly touted rookie who batted .356 during his two-year minor-league stint and showed promise in 1961. He finished in the top three in most offensive categories on a bad Red Sox team but batted just .266 with 11 home runs.

After getting his feet wet in '61, by '63 he was an American League All-Star and Gold Glove winner. While Yastrzemski became a fixture in the All-Star Game and in the AL leaderboards, the Red Sox struggled through the early part of his career. Then came 1967, and Yastrzemski led Boston to heights they hadn't reached in 50 years.

The Sox were coming off a 1966 season in which they finished with the fourth-worst record in baseball and weren't expected to be in the '67 pennant race; however, Yastrzemski and Dick Williams, in his first year of a Hall of Fame managerial career, led an unlikely resurgence. Yastrzemski was phenomenal all year, channeling the all-around hitting expertise of the man he replaced, as he was near the top of all Triple Crown categories throughout the summer.

As the season progressed, the Red Sox stuck around and were firmly entrenched in a heated four-team pennant race as the season wound down. On September 13, the Sox were tied for first with the Twins, and the Tigers were just one game behind. From that point onward, Yastrzemski put the team on his back and turned in one of the best performances to end a season in big-league history. In the final 15 games, Yastrzemski hit .491 with five home runs and 18 RBIs. Of the 27 hits he recorded, 11 went for extra bases as he slugged .873.

On the final day of the season, the Red Sox and Twins were tied at the top of the standings and essentially played a one-game playoff for the AL pennant. With the Red Sox down 2–0 in the sixth, Yastrzemski stroked a bases-loaded single to tie the game and catapult the team to a five-run rally. The Red Sox went on to a 5–3 win to clinch the AL pennant behind a 4-for-4 performance by Yastrzemski. He ended the season with 44 homers, 121 RBIs, and a .326 batting average to capture the American League's Triple Crown. Although the Red Sox fell to the Cardinals 4–3 in the World Series, Yastrzemski had clinched his spot as one of the best players in the game.

"Yaz could really hit," said Fred Lynn, who was Yastrzemski's teammate in Boston for seven seasons.

> Sometimes you could get him out with breaking balls, but he just wouldn't miss a fastball. Even at the end of his career, I'd be on deck and they'd bring in a lefty to face him. They'd throw him a fastball, and he'd rip it. I'd be laughing and shaking my head in the on-deck circle wondering why in the world anyone threw him a fastball.

Yastrzemski sustained his excellence for years and stayed productive for the Sox throughout the '70s. As his career wound down, he began to compile some of the magic numbers that locked him in as a surefire Hall of Famer. In 1979, the 39-year-old Yastrzemski became the first American League player to hit 400 home runs and record 3,000 career hits, and he was also selected for his 15th consecutive All-Star Game.

As the '80s began, Yastrzemski finally started to show his age. Between 1980 and 1982, he batted .266 and played in just 327 games, as ankle injuries began to take their toll. He enjoyed a bit of resurgence in 1982, as he hit 16 homers and batted .275. Yastrzemski decided to return for the 1983 season, his 23rd in the bigs. He was now 43 years old and would spend much of the season as the team's DH. In a part-time role, Yastrzemski was able to turn back the clock and was hitting .323 at the All-Star break. He was rewarded for his first half performance with another selection to the MLB All-Star Game.

However, a midseason slump in which he batted .243 in the six weeks after the All-Star Game started rumors that this season could be the last for Yastrzemski. As September came, fans throughout the country figured they had one more month to watch Yastrzemski perform in the Red Sox lineup. He gave the fans one final glimpse of greatness on September 10, 1983.

The Red Sox were suffering through a poor season and stood at 68–74 on September 10, in sixth place in the AL East. They were playing the Cleveland Indians, the only team below them in the standings, in a Saturday afternoon game at Cleveland Stadium. The pitching matchup that day included two pitchers who had some good success in the '80s, Bruce Hurst and Rick Sutcliffe, but neither was on their game that day.

The Red Sox jumped on Sutcliffe for two runs in the first inning when Jerry Remy led off the game with a double and scored on a two-run homer by Jim Rice. Batting fourth in the lineup that day, Yastrzemski struck out in his first at-bat. The lead didn't last long, as Toby Harrah homered leading off for the Indians, and Gorman Thomas drove home Bake McBride with a sacrifice fly.

After a scoreless second, the top of the Red Sox lineup was due up in the third. Again, Remy got things started when he drew a leadoff walk. Wade Boggs, in his second full season as a 25-year-old third baseman, singled, advancing Remy to third base. Rice gave the Red Sox the lead back with a sacrifice fly, bringing up Yastrzemski with Boggs standing on second. With the Sox looking to extend the lead, Yastrzemski blasted the final home run of his legendary career to extend Boston's lead to 5–2.

Hurst, however, couldn't make the lead stand, as he gave up four runs in the bottom of the third. Pat Tabler hit a two-run homer and Harrah singled home two runs as the Indians took a 6–5 lead. Yastrzemski came through in the clutch again and laced a two-out double to right, to score Boggs to tie the game. But that would be the end of the Red Sox offense, and the Indians tacked on single runs in the sixth and eighth to win the game 8–6.

On the day, Yastrzemski gave fans one final glimpse of what it was like to watch him play as a young superstar of the '60s. Batting cleanup, he went

3-for-5 with a homer, a double, and three RBIs in the Red Sox loss. The home run was 10th of the season and his 452nd and final of his career. The game would also be the final multihit game of Yastrzemski's storied career.

In the next 16 games, Yastrzemski hit just .145 and didn't record an extra-base hit. His final 1983 stats were respectable, especially for his age. His final game came on October 2, in Fenway Park in front of 33,491 fans. He started the game just as he started his career 22 years earlier, batting fifth in the order and standing in front of the Green Monster as the Boston left fielder.

"I pitched against the Red Sox on Carl Yastrzemski Day," said Lary Sorensen, who was pitching for the Indians at the time.

> I had a tremendous amount of respect for Yaz and really wanted him to go out on a high note. I threw him fastballs all day; I didn't give in or take anything off, but nothing but fastballs. He came up as the last batter of the game [Yastrzemski's final big-league at-bat], and I was hoping he would get a nice single to right and give the fans one last chance to cheer him as a player. He ended up hitting a tapper back to me. I flipped it to first and got the ball right back. After the game I sent the ball to the clubhouse to have Yaz autograph it. He spelled my name wrong! But I kept the ball and still have it to this day. What a great, classy player.

In a game that doesn't lend itself well to players who replace legends, Yastrzemski far exceeded expectations for someone replacing Ted Williams. Aside from Williams's missed seasons while serving in the military, the Red Sox had just two regular left fielders for nearly 45 years.

"Yaz was really accurate with his arm and could play the wall like nobody else," said Lynn. "He was just the total package; he did everything. He could have stolen bases too if he wanted, but it just wasn't in the Red Sox style of play."

Yastrzemski led the Sox through the "Impossible Dream" season of 1967, suffered through the team's struggles in the early '70s, and led the resurgence in 1975 that earned them a World Series showdown against the Big Red Machine. He gave the Red Sox more than two decades of class, leadership, and incredible production on the field.

WILLIE McCOVEY: STRETCH'S FINAL HOME RUN

May 3, 1980

In every generation there are a few players who truly strike fear in the minds of the opposition. The intimidation factor comes into play when a player has prodigious, game-wrecking ability when he has the bat or ball in his hands. In the '60s, when Bob Gibson or Don Drysdale was on the hill, he barely had to do anything but glare at hitters to get them to doubt whether they chose the right profession. As far as hitters are concerned, there was probably no more intimidating presence on offense throughout the '60s and early '70s than Willie McCovey.

The Giants were a franchise in transition as the '50s came to a close. They reached a peak in 1954, when they won the World Series as the New York Giants; however, their reign didn't last long, and within three years, they had agreed to leave New York and head to San Francisco. After a poor season in 1957, their final year in New York, they rebounded and had a winning record in 1958. The franchise was led by Willie Mays and Orlando Cepeda, who were both in their prime. But the lineup tailed off after that, as no other players on the team batted higher than .260 or hit more than 17 homers in 1958.

In 1959, the Giants were experiencing more of the same. Cepeda and Mays were tearing up the National League, but the rest of their lineup lacked any other real threat. Even so, the Giants were 10 games over .500 by July 29, and were in second place in the National League, just a half game behind the Dodgers. Looking for a spark, the Giants called up McCovey, who had been skyrocketing through the Giants minor leagues as a youngster. In his first four and a half years in the minors, McCovey blasted 102 home runs. At the time of his call-up, he had 29 home runs and was hitting .372 through 95 games in the Pacific Coast League.

McCovey's highly anticipated debut came on July 30, 1959. He was thought of so highly that in his first game he supplanted Mays as the team's third hitter as manager Bill Rigney moved Mays up one spot, to number two. This gave the Giants the fearsome trio of Mays, McCovey, and Cepeda in the 2–3–4 spots in the lineup. As if taking Mays's spot in the order wasn't enough pressure, he had to face Phillies Hall of Famer Robin Roberts in his first game. He responded with a 4-for-4 game with 2 triples, 3 runs, and 2 RBIs to lead San Francisco to a 7–2 win. McCovey didn't stop hitting from that point onward.

McCovey played in just 52 games for the Giants that year and was so dominant that he was named the National League Rookie of the Year in a unanimous vote. He ended the season with 13 homers and a .354 batting average. In a 162-game schedule, that projected to about 40 home runs and 120 RBIs. McCovey suffered injuries in the next three seasons, but in 1963, he finally remained healthy for the entire season. That year, he led the league with 44 homers and 102 RBIs. He remained a prodigious home run hitter, even belting 36 homers and 105 RBIs in 1968, the year of the pitcher.

During this time, McCovey didn't just build a reputation for hitting home runs in quantities. What made him possibly the most feared hitter of the '60s was the distance he hit his home runs. The 6'4" McCovey, nicknamed "Stretch," never seemed to hit a cheap home run, and even in a pitchers' park like Candlestick, McCovey's homers cut through the swirling winds and traveled more than 400 feet regularly.

Don DeMola, who pitched for the Expos in '74 and '75, relayed a story about McCovey's might: "We were playing the Padres in San Diego, and the great Wallenda was going to walk his high-wire act over the stadium after the game. It extended from the left-field foul pole to the right-field one," started DeMola.

> Willie McCovey is up, I'm in the game, and he hits this towering fly ball that cleared the wire and just lands on the walkway. After the inning, I'm on the bench and here comes Duke Snider [who was a coach with the Expos at the time]. He saunters over to me and says, "Gee DeMola, good thing Wallenda wasn't on that wire."

McCovey was traded to San Diego after the 1973 season and spent two and a half subpar seasons there. After a brief stint with the A's, McCovey returned to the Giants in 1977, for the end of his career. At this point, he had 465 career homers, and despite being just 35 homers from 500, it was no cinch that he'd be able to accomplish the feat.

McCovey's injuries hampered him at his advanced age, and his production dropped considerably. In 1976, McCovey hit just .207 with seven home runs and seemed to be nearing the end; however, his return to San Francisco rejuvenated him, and he hit 28 homers while batting .280. It was his highest batting average since 1970. Now standing just seven homers from 500, McCovey returned in 1978. He finally reached 500 home runs on June 30.

Clearly at the end of his career and with no other personal milestones to accomplish, McCovey still returned for the 1979 season and did well, hitting 15 home runs in 117 games. As the '70s came to a close, McCovey brushed off retirement yet again and came back to the Giants as their first baseman in 1980. When he pinch-hit on Opening Day, he joined Tim McCarver and Jim Kaat as the only players to play in the '50s, '60s, '70s, and '80s. Minnie Miñoso would make an appearance later in the decade to become the fourth player to play in those four decades as well. To that point, only eight other players had appeared in four decades during the 1900s. On May 3, 1980, McCovey joined an even more elite club.

As a rookie in 1959, McCovey hit 13 home runs. In the '60s and '70s, he blasted 507 homers, many of them of the awe-inspiring variety. Even through his steep decline, McCovey always maintained the ability to leave the park.

On May 3, he connected one last time, for his 521st home run. The home run tied him with Ted Williams on the all-time list and was the final home run of his career. McCovey's home run came with more history, however, as he became just the second player to homer in four decades, joining a club that was so elite that the only other member at the time was Williams.

On May 3, the Giants were in Montreal for a Saturday game against the Expos. McCovey was set to lead off the top of the fourth inning. He hit into a first-inning double play in his first at-bat and was hitting just .193 when he came to the plate in the fourth. Even though he was ravaged by injuries and clearly at the end of his career, McCovey summoned his legendary power one last time and clouted one final home run. The solo shot gave the Giants a 1–0 lead and allowed McCovey to stand side by side with Williams at 521 homers and as a four-decade home run hitter.

The game remained 1–0 until the seventh, when the Giants tacked on another run against Sanderson. The lead was short-lived, as the Expos tied the game in the bottom of the inning on a sacrifice fly by Warren Cromartie and a double by Ron LeFlore. McCovey had a chance to further impact the game in the eighth when he came to the plate with runners on first and second and one out; however, he grounded out for the third time and the threat went by fruitless. The Giants won the game in the ninth on an RBI double by Milt May.

After the home run, McCovey went back into a power slump, and his batting average continued to hover around .200. While he played a majority of the time at first base during the first part of the season, manager Dave Bristol was turning to the younger Mike Ivie more frequently as McCovey continued to struggle. Eventually, on June 10, he was replaced as the everyday first baseman and used sparingly as a pinch-hitter. He appeared in just nine more games, starting one of them, before calling it a career on July 6.

"What a great hitter McCovey was," said Matt Galante, who played and managed for more than four decades professionally. "He had such great power to all fields. He hit some incredible shots into left-center field. You're talking about one of the all-time greats."

Willie McCovey's reputation among his peers is a combination of respect and awe. Playing in an era alongside sluggers like Reggie Jackson, Harmon Killebrew, Willie Stargell, and Frank Robinson, McCovey was considered the most fearsome slugger of the lot. He came up as a highly regarded rookie in 1959 and, during the next 22 years, peppered stadiums with his monstrous blasts. As of 2013, McCovey stood as one of 29 players to play in four decades and was joined in the four-decade home run club by Omar Vizquel and Rickey Henderson. He remains one of the most respected and beloved players in franchise history for the Giants and was the first true Giants star to begin his career in San Francisco.

GROVER CLEVELAND ALEXANDER:
THE UNDERRATED IMMORTAL

May 28, 1930

When one is asked about the dominant pitchers of baseball's Deadball Era, usually the names Cy Young, Christy Mathewson, and Walter Johnson come up. One pitcher who doesn't seem to hold the same lofty ranking in the annals of immortality, despite having accomplishments that rival those of the "Big 3," is Grover Cleveland Alexander.

Alexander, who pitched from 1911 to 1930 and had great success, is somehow overshadowed even though he had a truly legendary career in Major League Baseball. Alexander isn't just a forgotten name by modern fans, he was even underappreciated by his contemporaries. Mathewson and Johnson were easy selections in the Hall of Fame's historic first class of 1936, and Young's place as a baseball immortal has never been debated, but despite having similar statistics, Alexander received just 24 percent of the Hall of Fame vote in 1936, and had to wait three years before finally being elected.

Alexander compiled 373 wins, a mark that's still only tied with Mathewson as the most ever in the National League and third all-time behind Young and Johnson. He was a three-time 30-game winner and led the league in ERA four times. By comparison, Mathewson and Johnson led the league in ERA five times each, and Young did it twice. Johnson was a 30-game winner twice, Young topped 30 on five occasions, and Mathewson did it four times. Even in a modern statistical category like WAR, Alexander compares with the Big 3, as he, Young, and Mathewson each led the league in WAR for pitchers six times each, while Johnson led seven times.

The fact that Alexander doesn't have one huge accomplishment to hang his hat on may cause the average fan to overlook him as an immortal. Young's 511 wins and Johnson's 417 are respected equally as two of baseball's magic numbers. Johnson and Mathewson were mainstays of specific organizations (the Senators and Giants, respectively), while Alexander played for three different teams, costing him an association with any one franchise. Whatever the case, Alexander's accomplishments should not be overlooked.

Alexander caroused and dominated his way through 20 major-league seasons, appearing for the final time on May 28, 1930. He came up as a 24-year-old with the Phillies, where he had his greatest success. After eight years in Philadelphia, he was traded to the Cubs, where he spent the next nine seasons. He was picked up off waivers in 1926, by the Cardinals, and then traded back to the Phillies, where he pitched one final season at the age of 43.

Alexander had his best stretch between 1915 and 1917, with the Phillies. In that three-season stretch, he went 94–35 and pitched an ERA of 1.54. Young, Johnson, and Mathewson never had a three-year stretch with a win-loss record and ERA close to Alexander's. While Alexander remained a top pitcher after that, his sheer dominance waned after the 1917 season. A known partier and drinker, Alexander's production tailed off in his mid-30s, but he hung around the game until 1930, and had a winning record in every season until his final year, when he went 0–3 in nine games.

On May 28, 1930, Alexander's Phillies matched up against the Boston Braves at Braves Field. Neither team had high expectations, as they finished in the bottom of the National League in 1929, and each was off to a poor start in 1930. The Phillies had just one real star in their lineup: Chuck Klein. The power-hitting Hall of Fame right fielder was coming off a season in which he led the NL in homers, with 43, and was just coming into his own as a 25-year-old slugger. Boston featured Hall of Famers Rabbit Maranville and George Sisler, but both were at the tail end of their careers and well past their prime.

Phil Collins started the game on the mound for the Phillies and opposed the Braves' Socks Seibold. Neither pitcher had much of an impact on the sport, as they each spent eight nondescript seasons in the majors. Seibold held the Phillies scoreless in the first inning, and the Braves jumped on Collins for a run in the bottom of the first for a 1–0 lead on an RBI single by center fielder Randy Moore.

The Braves extended the lead to 2–0 in the second when Freddie Maguire scored on a single by Lance Richbourg, the Braves' leadoff batter. The Braves made it 3–0 in the bottom of the sixth on a solo homer by rookie Wally Berger. Berger would go on to be a four-time NL All-Star and was voted as the starting center fielder in the first-ever All-Star Game in 1933.

The Phillies finally got on the board in the top of the seventh when Fresco Thompson doubled and came in to score on a single by Harry McCurdy. With the Phillies back in the game, manager Burt Shotton, who would go on to skipper the Brooklyn Dodgers to two NL pennants, called on Alexander to keep the game close.

Alexander ran into trouble immediately, as he allowed singles to Richbourg and Maranville before Moore drove them both in to extend the Boston lead to 5–1. Seibold got through the Phillies in the top of the eighth, allowing Alexander to take the mound for the final inning of his career. He retired the Braves without allowing a run and left the mound for the last time in a major-league uniform. The Phillies didn't mount anything against Seibold in the ninth and lost by a final score of 5–1.

The outing for Alexander was his ninth appearance during the season, and he pitched ineffectively in each one. In 21⅔ innings, Alexander surrendered 40 hits and 24 earned runs for an ERA of 9.14. He was unable to win any games in 1930, keeping him tied with Mathewson for third place on the all-time wins list, with 373. The only pitcher to approach his total since he retired in 1965 was Warren Spahn, 10 wins shy of Alexander's total.

Grover Cleveland Alexander, nicknamed "Old Pete" and named after the president whose term in which he was born, had one of the truly remarkable careers of the early twentieth century. He had one of, if not the, greatest rookie seasons of any pitcher when he won 28 games in 1911, as a 24-year-old. His 28 wins are the most of any rookie pitcher, and the way the game is played today, it is unlikely that his total can ever be challenged.

Alexander dominated through the 1917 season, but after missing much of the 1918 season while serving during World War I, he was never quite the same pitcher. The best moment of the latter part of his career came in 1926, when he pitched two complete-game victories over the Yankees in the World Series and pitched out of a bases-loaded jam in relief by striking out Yankees slugger Tony Lazzeri to preserve the series-clinching win.

Alexander combined to go 37–19 in '27 and '28, at 41 years old, but finally fell off from there. He battled poor health, alcoholism, and the mental effects of his time in World War I for the remainder of his life. Despite his ill health and poverty, Alexander surfaced one final time at the 1950 World Series, when he attended a game to see the "Whiz Kids" firsthand. It was the first time the Phillies made the World Series since he had pitched them there in 1915. Less than a month later, Alexander died at age 63.

There are a number of factors that have caused Alexander's accomplishments to be underestimated by the casual fan. His teams never had a streak of dominance in the National League, and he isn't easily associated with just one team the way Mathewson and Johnson are; however, as the game progressed through the later part of the twentieth century, statistics and record-keeping became more advanced and baseball historians seemed to have preserved Alexander in his well-deserved place among baseball's immortals. He received the lofty ranking of number 12 in the *Sporting News* Top 100 Baseball Players of All Time, which was released in 1999. He was the third-highest-rated pitcher, behind Johnson and Mathewson, and ahead of Young. He was also nominated as a member of Major League Baseball's All-Century Team.

Despite those lofty accolades and his 1938 induction at Cooperstown, it took the Phillies until 2001 to honor him in their retired numbers gallery. Because Alexander played during an era before numbers were worn on jerseys, the Phillies hung a block letter "P" among their retired numbers in honor of Alexander. In a move that was way overdue, the franchise in which he was most dominant didn't recognize him until more than 70 years after he played his final game in the majors on May 28, 1930.

ROGERS HORNSBY: A LAST DISPLAY OF PURE POWER

April 24, 1931

The names of baseball legends from the early 1900s sound more like a roll call of royalty rather than a list of athletes. When someone says the names Babe Ruth, Lou Gehrig, Ty Cobb, or Cy Young, there's a special aura that accompanies these immortal players. Rogers Hornsby's name is cemented firmly in that group as well. The seven-time batting champion and .358 career hitter was the premier hitter in the National League during the '20s and is generally considered to be one of the top hitters in baseball history.

However, for someone who was such an immortal, Hornsby bounced around teams and played different roles throughout his career, something that was uncommon during his era. When April 24, 1931, rolled around, Hornsby found himself as a 35-year-old player-manager for the Chicago Cubs and on the downside of his career. His power numbers had dropped sharply during the past two seasons, but on this date he had the final power display of his legendary career.

Hornsby was so dominant throughout the '20s that he led the National League in all three Triple Crown categories for the decade, something only three other players have done in baseball history. But during the final four years of the decade, Hornsby played for four different teams. While his production was always outstanding, Hornsby's ornery disposition and gambling often angered teammates and owners, and he wore out his welcome quickly.

Hornsby's career bridged the Deadball and Liveball Eras, and one look at his career power numbers shows just where the line was drawn. In his first five years, Hornsby hit a total of 36 homers. Once the power boom of 1921 hit, Hornsby's home run total jumped to 144 during the next five years. While his power fluctuated, his average was consistently the best in baseball. He won six straight batting titles in the '20s and hit over .400 three times, including his incredible 1924 season, in which he hit .424.

Hornsby's 12-year stint in St. Louis ended after the 1926 season, when he was traded to the Giants for fellow Hall of Famer Frankie Frisch. He spent a single season each with the Giants and Boston Braves before being traded to the Cubs in 1928. Hornsby served as player-manager for partial seasons in each spot and was generally productive in both capacities. He was even at the helm of the 1926 Cardinals World Series championship team.

In 1931, Hornsby began to transition to more of a manager than a player as his role on the field diminished. He hit just two home runs in limited playing time in 1930, and batted just .308, his lowest number since 1918. In the first seven games of the 1931 season, Hornsby again showed a decline at the plate, hitting just .240 after the first week of the season.

On April 24, the Cubs went on their first road trip of the season and were set to take on the Pirates in a two-game series at Forbes Field. If there was one stadium that you would least expect a fading power hitter to have a renaissance, Forbes Field would be it. A cavernous stadium, Forbes Field's shortest dimension was 360 feet down the left-field line. Right field was 372 feet, and the center-field fence stood 442 feet from home plate.

The Cubs and Pirates were middle-of-the-pack teams in 1931, well behind the strong Cardinals teams but a safe bet to be significantly better than the Phillies, Reds, and Braves, who generally were near the bottom of the NL. The Cubs were set to face the Pirates and their young lefty, Larry French. Even though the Cubs and Pirates weren't elite teams in '31, each lineup had their share of early twentieth-century legends. In addition to Hornsby, the Cubs had Hack Wilson and Gabby Hartnett. The Pirates featured Lloyd and Paul Waner and had Pie Traynor in cleanup.

The 23-year-old French, who would go on to win 197 career games, got through the Cubs and Hornsby in the top of the first inning without allowing a run. The Pirates then scored two quick runs off of Cubs starter Sheriff Blake in the bottom of the inning to stake French to a 2–0 lead. The Cubs again went quietly in the second, and Pittsburgh added to their lead during their turn at bat. After putting up three runs in the bottom of the second, they opened a 5–0 lead.

However, French couldn't make the lead stand. Hornsby belted a three-run homer to left in the top of the third to get the Cubs back in the game. The game stayed 5–3 until Hornsby's next turn at bat, when he connected again off of French in the fifth. This time, Hornsby hit a mammoth opposite-field shot with two men on base to give the Cubs a 6–5 lead.

While Hornsby single-handedly turned a 5–0 deficit into a 6–5 advantage, Les Sweetland, who had come on to relieve Blake in the second, was keeping the Pirates at bay. Claude Willoughby came on to relieve French after Hornsby's homer in the fourth and pitched well his first time through the lineup.

However, in the fifth, he ran into Hornsby again. Hornsby was already 2–3 with six RBIs and came to the plate with Kiki Cuyler on second. Hornsby turned on another offering and planted it over the left-field fence for a two-run shot and his seventh and eighth RBIs of the game. By the end of the inning, the Cubs had opened a 9–5 lead.

The Pirates scored a harmless run in the bottom of the eighth that was answered by the Cubs with a solo run in the ninth, giving Pittsburgh a 10–6 win. For good measure, Hornsby added a single in his final at-bat. He ended the game 4-for-5 with eight RBIs and three runs.

Hornsby's power display was just a brief glimpse of the past, as he began to transition away from being an everyday player. He did have a productive season in 1931, even in the diminished role. He hit 16 home runs and batted .331, while leading the NL with a .429 on-base percentage.

The biggest contribution Hornsby made during the '31 season may have come with a managerial decision. He played the first 67 games of the season at second base, his customary position; however, on July 8, Hornsby took up residence at third base. This eventually cleared the way for a 21-year-old rookie Billy Herman, to join the club. Herman went on to play 15 years in the majors and was voted to the Hall of Fame in 1975.

Despite his shortcomings as a person and a teammate, Hornsby's place in baseball history puts him clearly among the game's immortals. His lifetime batting average is second only to Ty Cobb's, but unlike Cobb, Hornsby also had power. His combination of power and average was on a level that was equaled by few during that time. Hornsby led the NL in batting seven times, but he also led the league in slugging nine times, a record that still stood in 2015. Hornsby's power was also unique to the position he played. He hit 264 home runs as a second baseman, a total that stood for nearly 50 years, until it was surpassed by Joe Morgan in 1984.

Rogers Hornsby had a remarkable run from 1920 to 1929, before his power fell off. But for one game on April 24, 1931, he gave fans a final glimpse of the great power he once displayed as the Deadball Era ended with the power boom of the early '20s.

· *11* ·

The New Millennium

THE MONTREAL EXPOS: EXPANDING BASEBALL'S BORDERS

April 11, 2003

Since the turn of the twentieth century, baseball has evolved in just about every way possible. Babe Ruth, Lou Gehrig, Mel Ott, and Jimmie Foxx ushered the game out of the Deadball Era when they became the first players to club homers with consistency throughout the '20s and '30s. The '40s saw baseball fighting to stay alive during World War II, before Jackie Robinson and Larry Doby helped integrate the game. The '50s saw a tremendous rebirth as legends like Hank Aaron, Willie Mays, Mickey Mantle, and Stan Musial highlighted a golden era unlike any other.

Pitching dominated the '60s, and as the game moved into the '70s and '80s, national media coverage bolstered recognition throughout the United States and began to reach overseas markets. Finally, from the late '80s to today, baseball expanded into a true global sport, benefiting from the first real influx of Latin talent and subsequently reaching to the Far East for Asian players.

The globalization of Major League Baseball has led to unprecedented talent levels, as teams are truly reaching out to all corners of the world in search of great players. MLB made its first attempt to expand the sport beyond U.S. borders when expansion franchises were awarded to the Montreal Expos and Toronto Blue Jays in 1969 and 1977, respectively. Fan support in Canada had its ups and downs, but Montreal wasn't able to keep up with the sport's attendance and financial boom as the twentieth century came to a close.

"Montreal was not an easy place to play," said Andy McGaffigan, who pitched in 258 games for the Expos during two stints with the team in the

'80s. "It was not exactly in the mainstream of baseball, even though there was a small group of very loyal fans."

Don DeMola, who pitched for the Expos in '75 and '76, agreed: "Montreal, the greatest li'l city in the Northern Hemisphere," started DeMola. "Beautiful people, loyal fans. Even in the worst weather they sat in their seats, never a 'boo' for the home team."

Barry Bonnell played 457 games for the Blue Jays in the '80s and reflected on what it was like to play in Toronto: "Exhibition Stadium in Toronto was an afterthought. They wedged a tiny little grandstand into the corner of an old polo field," started Bonnell.

> I played in better stadiums in the minor leagues, and the Astroturf was as hard as concrete. The fans in those days acted like they were watching golf or tennis. It was quiet, and when something good happened, they used what we called a "golf clap" that seemed very polite and correct. I never understood that in light of their hockey crowds.

Bonnell continued,

> Anyway, there was no place like it. It was so cold at the beginning of the season that Rick Bosetti used ski gloves for batting gloves, and the rest of us would have done the same if we weren't so worried about how we looked at the plate. The wind blew off the lake and swirled around in left-center in a way that killed screaming line drives for outs by right-handers and carried popups for left-handers over the fence in right. By the time I was traded away, the crowds were way better, but I didn't miss the stadium at all.

In 2001, the Expos were purchased by MLB in what was believed to be the first step toward either contracting the franchise or moving it to a different location. Meanwhile, in Bud Selig's ongoing attempts to continue baseball's globalization, the commissioner announced that the 2001 season would open up in Puerto Rico for the first time at Hiram Bithorn Stadium in San Juan.

"Major League Baseball did everything they could to help the Expos succeed," said McGaffigan. "The city of Montreal just didn't support the team, so you can't blame Major League Baseball. The money just wasn't there. The taxes are incredibly high, and the economy in Montreal was struggling. They just couldn't draw."

It was a different story in Puerto Rico. Always a baseball-rich country, Puerto Ricans flocked to the stadium to see the Blue Jays take on the Rangers to start the season. In fact, thousands of fans had to be turned away from the stadium when it was determined that attendance would exceed the designated 18,000-person capacity.

With the decline of attendance in Montreal and the great reception MLB received in San Juan, eventually Selig decided to play a quarter of the Expos' home schedule at Hiram Bithorn Stadium in 2003 and 2004. "It was just a bizarre situation; the players really didn't have a home," said McGaffigan. "They didn't have a place to hang their hats those years. They were vagabonds. I know it was just a tough situation for the players."

On April 11, 2003, the Expos took the field for the first time in their new part-time home against the New York Mets. Despite turbulent times for the Expos franchise, the team was 5–4 in the early part of the season, coming off a surprising, if not shocking, second-place finish in the NL East in 2002. The 2003 team was led by Vladimir Guerrero, one of the top all-around players in the game, and a pitching staff that featured Javier Vazquez and Liván Hernández. The Expos also featured Puerto Rican–born All-Star José Vidro and Wil Cordero, instantly giving the fans multiple Latino players to root for.

The Mets, on the other hand, were coming off a last-place finish in 2002, and were bogged down by aging All-Stars Mike Piazza, Mo Vaughn, and Roberto Alomar. Alomar gave fans another player to root for, however, as the Puerto Rican superstar was seen as a favorite son of the country.

Hiram Bithorn Stadium, named for the righty pitcher who became the first Puerto Rican–born player in the majors in 1942, was a symmetrically built stadium that was expected to play like a hitter's paradise. The dimensions were 325 down each line, with relatively short power alleys set at 375. This potentially was not going to play well for Mets starting pitcher David Cone, who was attempting to make a comeback in 2003, after missing all of the previous season. Cone had a successful first start in his comeback attempt when he pitched five scoreless innings against the Expos in a 4–0 win just a week before, but April 11 would be different.

The first two innings went by scoreless, and the Mets went down in order in the top of the third against Expos starter Tomo Ohka. Cone was set to face the bottom of the Expos order in the bottom of the inning and immediately ran into trouble. He walked José Macías to lead off the frame and then gave up a homer to Brian Schneider as the Expos took a 2–0 lead. Cone retired Ohka on a groundout to 20-year-old rookie shortstop José Reyes but then allowed a single to Endy Chávez and a double to Vidro. Guerrero was intentionally walked to load the bases, but the strategy backfired, as Cordero singled home a run to make it 3–0. Left fielder Brad Wilkerson then blasted a grand slam on a 1–2 pitch to make the game 7–0.

Meanwhile, Ohka was making quick work of the Mets, who couldn't take advantage of the supposed hitter's ballpark. The game had one final dramatic turn left as Vidro came up to the plate in the eighth with Jamey

Carroll on first. Much to the delight of the crowd, Vidro blasted a first-pitch homer off of Graeme Lloyd to send the crowd into a frenzy. The fans chanted, "Vidro! Vidro! Vidro!" as he rounded the bases and touched home to make it 10–0.

Fittingly, Vidro was the star of the game, as the second baseman went 3-for-4 with three RBIs and two runs scored to lead the offense. The Expos lineup, which featured six Latino players, pounded out 11 hits in support of Ohka for the win.

The game atmosphere was frenetic the entire time, as fans banged drums, sang songs, and even did the wave on multiple occasions. It felt more like a World Cup soccer game than a regular-season Mets–Expos game, complete with a singing of "Take Me Out to the Ballgame" in Spanish and the obligatory dancing bear.

The Expos swept the Mets in the four-game series, and by the end of the weekend, fans were fully behind their new first-place team. They didn't care that the season was just two weeks old, all they knew was that the Expos were 9–4 and in first.

The Latin players enjoyed a tremendous series against the Mets, and Vidro quickly became their favorite player. The weight of playing in his home country was not lost on Vidro. In a *New York Times* article by Rafael Hermoso, Vidro said he was "more nervous today than in my first game in the big leagues." Vidro added that he felt like a rookie all over again.

The Expos' jaunt to Puerto Rico was a successful one, as the atmosphere remained consistent for all of the team's 22 games there. The fans had hoped all along that if they showed that kind of support for the Expos, Major League Baseball would consider moving them there permanently. When it came down to it, San Juan was a finalist among 10 cities that were considered for the relocation of the Montreal Expos. In addition to San Juan, MLB also considered Monterrey, Mexico. The league finally decided on Washington, DC, as the new home of the Expos and made the announcement on September 29, 2004, which was the same day they would play their final game in Montreal.

"The last game in Montreal was bittersweet," said Brendan Harris, the Expos' starting third baseman in their final game, who also became the last Expo to reach base safely when he drew a ninth-inning walk. "I don't think the city or fans were treated fairly. Major League Baseball had been discussing moving the team for a couple of years, and it really wasn't until the last week when an announcement was made."

"There were a lot of fans that were angry and disappointed," continued Harris.

> But the last weekend was sold out, and they came and supported what was left of the Expos. I also remember getting hit with a golf ball on the foot in

the field. I told an umpire, and he looked at me and rolled his eyes. Then the next inning [Marlins third baseman] Mike Lowell got hit with one, and they had to clear the field.

Ever since the Expos left, there have been many grassroots efforts to bring baseball back to the city, and they started to gain some serious traction in 2015. In early April of that year, the Blue Jays and Reds played two exhibition games at Olympic Stadium for the second straight year. The two games drew more than 96,000 fans, many of them carrying signs pleading for a second chance at an MLB franchise. Rob Manfred, who took over for Bud Selig as the game's commissioner in 2015, has expressed that he'd consider Montreal, among other cities, for future franchises. In May of that year, Manfred even met with Montreal mayor Denis Coderre to open the lines of communication.

Throughout the 2015 season the Blue Jays enjoyed a revival after two decades as an afterthought. With the Yankees and Red Sox each mired in seasons that failed to meet expectations and the Jays cranking home runs at a historic pace, the team traded for David Price and Troy Tulowitzki to capitalize on this rare opportunity. What followed throughout the remainder of the season until they met their demise at the hands of the eventual World Series champion Royals in the ALCS proved that Canada would support a successful baseball team. Over the season's first two months, the Jays had home attendance figures fewer than 25,000 in 17 of 26 dates. By comparison, over the team's final 20 home dates, attendance averaged more than 45,000 fans and throughout the playoffs, the Rogers Centre was perhaps the most hostile place to play.

As the era of MLB globalization continues, one can point to the Montreal Expos as pioneers in the field. They began international baseball play when they beat the Mets at Shea Stadium on April 8, 1969, and played their first game in Montreal on April 14, this time beating the Cardinals 8–7. The Expos did so well in their early stages that it encouraged MLB to award Toronto the Blue Jays in 1977. Even though the Expos didn't end up permanently in San Juan, fans there will forever celebrate the team that called Hiram Bithorn Stadium home for a few dozen games in 2003 and 2004, starting with a 10–0 win over the Mets on April 11, 2003.

TIM LINCECUM: TOPPING CHRISTY MATHEWSON

May 4, 2011

Anytime someone breaks a record set by Christy Mathewson, it's pretty impressive. When the record is one that took Mathewson 17 years to compile and is broken in just five seasons, it truly is incredible. That was the story of Tim Lincecum's early career in Major League Baseball. In his first four seasons, Lincecum won two Cy Young Awards, three National League strikeout titles, and a World Series title. He made his mark on the Giants' record books as well, which isn't an easy task for a franchise that has been around for more than 100 years.

"Tim Lincecum burst onto the scene and had more than a lot of success at a young age," said Shawn Estes, who is honored in the Giants Wall of Fame and is a postgame studio host for Giants games. "I really believe he was the best pitcher in baseball during that early stretch of dominance."

On May 4, 2011, in a game against the Mets, Lincecum struck out 12 hitters, his 29th game with double-digit strikeouts. The game broke Mathewson's franchise record for the most games with 10 or more strikeouts, which stood for 95 years.

Lincecum's immediate success in professional baseball did not come as a surprise to those who saw him dominate the college baseball world in 2006, when he won the Golden Spikes Award as the nation's top college baseball player. He was the 10th player taken in the MLB Draft, and because of his collegiate success, many figured he would be on the fast track to the bigs; however, Lincecum was not always seen as such a sure thing. He was drafted in 2003, by the Cubs, and, in 2005, by the Indians, but because those selections were both later than the 40th round, Lincecum never signed.

By the time he did get drafted high and sign, Lincecum was labeled as a pitching prodigy. He stood just 5'11" and weighed about 160 pounds but was freakishly athletic and flexible. His unique motion and slight frame caused many to worry about future arm problems, but that didn't deter the Giants from taking him. Lincecum went on to pitch 13 games in the minors between 2006 and 2007, and posted incredible numbers. He was 6–0 with a 1.01 ERA and struck out 104 batters in just 62 innings for a rate of 15 strikeouts per nine innings.

When Giants starter Russ Ortiz was injured in 2007, the Giants called on Lincecum, then 23 years old. In just his third major-league start, Lincecum faced off against Houston's Roy Oswalt. He showed he was up to the task, pitching seven innings, with 10 strikeouts, while allowing just two hits. It was the first double-digit strikeout game of his career. He finished his rookie season with a 7–4 record and a 4.00 ERA, and frequently showed flashes of dominance.

In 2008, Lincecum broke through as a legitimate superstar. It was his first full year in the Giants rotation, and he was penciled in as the number-three starter. By the end of the year, he was not only the top pitcher in the rotation, but also the best in the National League. He won the NL Cy

Young Award by a large margin over Brandon Webb and led the league in strikeouts. He had nine double-digit strikeout performances and allowed four hits or less in 10 games.

After a second dominating season in 2009, Lincecum fell off just a little in 2010. He went just 16–10 and, after winning two straight Cy Young Awards, finished 10th in the voting in 2010. But all of that was fine by him, since that was the year the Giants won their first World Series since 1954. He started five games in the postseason and went 4–1 with a 2.43 ERA, while averaging 10 strikeouts per nine innings. He won both of his World Series starts against the Rangers, including the fifth game, in which he pitched eight innings and allowed just three hits.

Lincecum came into the 2011 season needing three double-digit strikeout games to top Mathewson's mark of 28 games; however, it wasn't just Mathewson that Lincecum was surpassing. He was on his way to a career record with a franchise that also included Juan Marichal, Gaylord Perry, Sal Maglie, Carl Hubbell, and 1800s fireballer Amos Rusie.

Lincecum didn't take long to match Mathewson, as he struck out 13 and 10 batters in his second and fourth starts, respectively. After two starts with uncharacteristically low strikeout totals, Lincecum faced the Mets on May 4, in a matchup at Citi Field. The Giants were 15–15 after 30 games in the early part of the season, and the Mets had shown a knack in 2011 for fielding a team that was one of the top contact lineups in the National League.

The Giants were up against Chris Capuano, a reclamation project who missed the entire 2008 and 2009 seasons before returning in 2010 in a limited role. He set the Giants down without a hit in the first and gave his team the unenviable task of taking their turns against Lincecum. Daniel Murphy touched Lincecum for a one-out double, but the righty flashed his nasty stuff early and struck out David Wright and Ike Davis to escape without harm.

Capuano and Lincecum matched zeroes through the first five innings, as both pitchers were on their game. Through five innings, Lincecum struck out seven Mets and allowed just two hits. The Giants finally broke through against Capuano in the sixth when Aaron Rowand doubled and came in to score on a single by Mike Fontenot. Fontenot would then drive home Rowand to extend the team's lead in the seventh. Lincecum took his 2–0 lead to the mound in the bottom of the seventh and, despite pitching well, had already thrown more than 100 pitches.

This would likely be Lincecum's last inning, as he was due up fourth the next inning and manager Bruce Bochy didn't need to extend his pitcher this early in the season. If Lincecum wanted to top Mathewson's mark in this outing, he would have to strike out one batter. He struck out Scott Hairston, struck out José Reyes on three pitches, and fanned Murphy on a 3–2 count in a great nine-pitch at-bat. Four Giants pitchers, including Brian Wilson, faced the Mets in the final two innings without a threat, as the Giants won 2–0.

While the double-digit franchise strikeout record isn't one of the most prestigious, the feat is impressive nevertheless. The Giants franchise has been around since 1883, and has been the home of many Hall of Fame pitchers. The other impressive fact about the feat is that this is a record of pure dominance. Lincecum hasn't racked up double-digit strikeout games during a long period of time, compiling numbers as he stuck around past his prime. Mathewson had 28 double-digit strikeout games in 16 years. Marichal and Hubbell pitched 15 years each. Lincecum accomplished the feat in what amounted to about three and a half seasons.

It may have looked like Lincecum would go on to be one of the top pitchers in the game for his generation. From 2008 to 2011, Lincecum went 62–36 with a 2.81 ERA. He struck out 977 batters in those four seasons in 881 innings, and there were no signs of slowing down. But he hit a wall in 2012 and had two straight losing seasons, while pitching an ERA of 4.76. Despite showing improvements in 2014, Lincecum mysteriously still wasn't himself.

"The stuff is still there, but his velocity is down," said Estes. "The lack of velocity makes his other pitches less nasty. He's in the process of being able to learn how to pitch now though. He's reinventing himself; keeping the ball down and relying on movement."

On June 25, 2014, Lincecum again joined Mathewson in the record books when he became the second Giants pitcher to throw two no-hitters. He no-hit the Padres in both 2013 and 2014, to become the second pitcher to no-hit the same team twice. Addie Joss, a Hall of Famer who pitched for the Cleveland Naps, completed the feat in 1908 and 1910, when he no-hit the Chicago White Sox.

Despite these glimpses of dominance, Lincecum hasn't been nearly the same: "I don't think we'll see the dominant Lincecum we saw in the early part of his career," said Estes. "However, he's a smart kid. He improved his offseason work habits and can still be very effective. He definitely has the potential to be an All-Star again in his career. Maybe not consistently, but the potential is still there."

Lincecum's career path is easily tracked through the three World Series titles the Giants won in his first eight years with the team. In 2010, Lincecum was the ace of the staff, winning four postseason games, two of which were in the World Series. By 2012, Lincecum was still a valued member of the staff but started to give way to Madison Bumgarner as the team's true ace. He won just one postseason game in 2012, and his innings were cut in half.

By 2014, Lincecum was an afterthought in the postseason. After a 12–9 regular season in which he threw his second career no-hitter but pitched to a

4.74 ERA, Lincecum battled through a back injury and threw just 1⅔ innings in the postseason.

Unfortunately, Lincecum's health let him down in 2015, and he failed to appear in at least 30 games for the first time since his rookie year and finished with an ERA above 4.00 for the fourth straight year. With his contract expiring at the end of the 2015 season and Lincecum's health in question, his future with the Giants beyond 2015 was in doubt. Lincecum was a key part of three World Series championships in San Francisco and was wildly popular from the moment he arrived. It's unfortunate that he will be remembered more as a shooting star that burned out fast rather than an enduring dominant force.

Whether or not Lincecum is able to reinvent himself going forward, the accomplishments of the early part of his career are unmatched by anybody in Giants history. While Bumgarner has enjoyed a tremendous start to his career, including one of the great postseason pitching performances in MLB history, he never did have that "lightning in a bottle" start to a career that Lincecum enjoyed when he burst onto the scene as baseball's top young pitcher in the early 2000s.

ALBERT PUJOLS: A PACE MATCHED BY NO OTHER

August 22, 2007

From the start of his career, Albert Pujols has been an absolute beast of a baseball player. The numbers he's put up have been so incredible, he started accumulating career franchise records in less than a decade. On August 22, 2007, Pujols's dominance was quantified when he became the first player to hit at least 30 homers in each of his first seven seasons. He already was the first to do it in his first six seasons, so he was expanding his own record.

Pujols's first seven seasons were so dominant that he averaged 40 homers, 43 doubles, and 123 RBIs, while hitting an incredible .332. It was the most prolific offensive start to a career in Major League Baseball history.

The Cardinals were in a period in which they were enjoying great success in the National League. They won the NL pennant as underdogs in 2004, and the World Series in 2006. Pujols, who was considered the game's best player, was clearly their leader. In 2007, the Cards were in a pennant race as August was winding down. On the August 22, they found themselves three games out of first place in a tight NL Central race with the Cubs and Brewers.

Pujols was on a hot streak, as he was batting .338 with seven homers. He entered the game needing one home run to become the first player to hit 30 home runs in each of his first seven seasons and 19 RBIs to become the third player to drive in 100 runs in the same amount of time. It was a foregone conclusion that Pujols would reach those numbers, barring injury. Pujols came into the game having homered in each of his last four games as well, needing to homer that night to tie the Cardinals franchise record of five straight games with a home run.

The Cardinals faced off with the Florida Marlins, who were in last place in the NL East at the time. They had young, talented hitters like Dan Uggla, Hanley Ramirez, and Miguel Cabrera but had serious deficiencies in their pitching staff, eradicated by the sudden downfall of Dontrelle Willis's career.

Braden Looper started for the Cardinals that night as Tony La Russa experimented that year by moving the former closer into the rotation. He retired Ramirez, Uggla, and Cabrera in order, not allowing much time for fans to settle into their seats to see what Pujols would do.

David Eckstein led off the first for the Cards by flying out. Then So Taguchi lined a single to center on a 3–2 pitch from Scott Olsen to bring up Pujols. Not only was Pujols going for his 30th home run, he had also become one of those players whose at-bats became "must-see."

The big Wednesday night crowd of 42,147 anticipated the event, as Pujols was in one of those grooves where he seemed like he was going to hit a homer every time he came up to the plate. The fans didn't have to wait long, as Pujols crushed a long homer to left-center on a 1–2 count to surpass the 30–home run mark once again.

The Cardinals made easy work of the Marlins that night, winning 6–4. While the win helped them in the pennant race, the real story of the game was Pujols. He finished 2-for-4 with two RBIs to lead the Cardinals to their third straight win. While Pujols's 30th homer may have seemed like a foregone conclusion since there were still 40 games left in the season, it turned out not to be the case. Despite blowing by the 30–home run mark the previous four seasons, Pujols went into a power slump after his 30th and hit just two home runs in the remaining six weeks of the season to give him 32 on the year, his lowest output of his first 10 seasons.

Pujols would go on to hit 37, 47, and 42 homers in each of the next three seasons to extend his mark to 30 or more home runs in his first 10 years. He belted exactly 30 home runs in 2012, his first year with the Angels after signing a 10-year, $252 million contract. He failed to reach 30 home runs in 2013, when he played just 99 games while battling injuries.

Pujols topped the 100-RBI mark for the 10th straight in 2010. Only Jimmie Foxx and Alex Rodriguez have hit 30 or more homers with 100 RBIs for 10 straight years. Pujols went on to blast 408 home runs in his first 10 seasons, easily surpassing Eddie Mathews's record of 370. Mathews's record stood for 40 years before Pujols toppled it.

Pujols fell one RBI short of extending his streak to 11 straight 100-RBI seasons in 2011. Through 2015, he has played 15 seasons in the major leagues. During that period of time, Pujols has cracked more than 550 home runs. In 2015, he climbed past Ted Williams, Mickey Mantle, Mike Schmidt, and Jimmie Foxx to move himself into the top 15 on the all-time home run list. After a few years of declining production and health, Pujols enjoyed a revival in 2015, and made his first All-Star Game since 2010. He finished fifth in the American League with 40 home runs and ended the season 14th on the all-time home run list with 560. He is just 23 home runs short of reaching the top 10.

The list of records Pujols has broken is growing each season. He was unquestionably the player of the decade of the 2000s and has put up power and average numbers that are matched by nobody. His first-inning home run off of Scott Olsen on August 22, 2007, was historic because nobody had ever hit 30 home runs in each of his first seven seasons in the majors. In the grand scheme of Pujols's career, this will probably become lost in the shuffle; just another stepping-stone toward establishing one of the greatest offensive careers the game has seen.

ROGER CLEMENS: THE TURNCOAT ROCKET

July 31, 1999

In the current era of baseball, player movement is at an all-time high. Teams that are out of the race quickly drop veterans in hopes of acquiring prospects to boost their farm systems, and potential free agents are dumped so their team will at least get something in return. While there are All-Star players who have a tendency to bounce from team to team, there are others who become an institution with a certain franchise.

However, in most cases, there comes a time when players and franchises have to part ways, no matter how popular the player. That usually sets up an interesting dynamic in future seasons, when that player returns home to his original club. The way he departed usually dictates the reception that player will get. But if a player returns wearing the colors of a rival, the situation can get pretty sticky. Just ask Roger Clemens.

On July 31, 1999, Clemens returned to Fenway Park wearing the uniform of the hated New York Yankees. Clemens spent his first 13 seasons in Boston, where he was a true hero. In 1986, he went from a promising youngster to full-fledged superstar seemingly overnight when he went 24–4 and led Boston to the World Series. He won the MVP and Cy Young that year, and set a major-league record when he became the first pitcher to strike out 20 batters in a game. From that point onward, Clemens was the Boston Red Sox.

"Roger Clemens [and Andy Pettitte] were both great guys," said Dave Borkowski, who was on the Astros pitching staff with both players in 2006. "[They were] huge names in the game but were just one of the guys. They both worked their tails off to be who they were."

Stanley Jefferson, who was picked one spot behind Clemens in the first round of the 1983 Major League Baseball Draft, reflected on Clemens as well: "He threw the ball damn hard," said Jefferson, who hit a home run in his first at-bat against Clemens.

> He was extremely focused. Most Hall of Fame players I came across had routines they stuck by. Players like Tony Gwynn, Cal Ripken, Clemens. They were always the first to the ballpark and had routines to get their bodies and minds ready for the game. They got themselves better in order to make the team better.

From 1986 to 1992, Clemens averaged 258 innings per season, and in the next four seasons, it looked like that innings total was taking a toll on his surgically repaired right shoulder. During the next four seasons, Clemens's record was just 40–39, and his ERA was 3.77. After the '96 season, Clemens parted ways with the Red Sox under contentious circumstances.

According to general manager Dan Duquette in an article in the *Boston Herald* by Michael Silverman, the Red Sox offered Clemens "by far, the most money ever offered to a player in the history of the Red Sox." Duquette then declared that Red Sox fans got to see Clemens in his prime and "hoped to keep him in Boston during the twilight of his career."

Whether or not the allusion that Clemens was in the twilight of his career served as motivation for turnaround lies only with Clemens. What is well known, however, was that the turnaround came in a big way.

Clemens hooked up with the Toronto Blue Jays, who were transitioning into a team with younger talent after their success in the early part of the decade. His return to Boston was incredible, as he struck out 16 Red Sox in eight innings to gain a 3–2 win. The fans cheered Clemens at his every move. Clemens went 41–13 in two years with the Blue Jays, causing Duquette to look like he made one of the biggest talent evaluation mistakes in the history of baseball. Later, allegations began that Clemens's turnaround was attributed to steroids, but at the time, it just looked like he was simply back to his usual dominating self.

In the offseason of 1999, the Blue Jays made it known that they were open to trading Clemens. The righty was 35 years old, and the Jays figured he was at his peak value for trade. While he was dominating for the Jays and won the Cy Young Award both years, they still looked to capitalize while his value was at a premium.

The Astros, Rangers, and Yankees were in the mix for Clemens, and as far as Toronto was concerned, it was open bidding. The Yankees' offer intrigued the Blue Jays, but they insisted the Yanks include Alfonso Soriano, who was a highly regarded minor-league shortstop. In the past, George Steinbrenner was notorious for letting go of prospects in return for proven players, but he insisted on keeping Soriano this time. The Jays finally relented, and on February 18, 1999, Clemens was shipped to his third AL East team, the New York Yankees, for All-Star David Wells, promising youngster Homer Bush, and middle reliever Graeme Lloyd.

The ramifications of this trade were felt deeply. The season before, the Yanks set a major-league record by winning 114 regular-season games and 125 overall as they steamrolled to a World Series championship. They were returning most of the key pieces of that team and now were adding the two-time defending Cy Young Award winner to the mix.

The Red Sox, who were just starting their ascension back into baseball's elite, had a keen interest in these developments. With Clemens now pitching for the Yankees, he went from martyr to villain. Clemens had dominated the Red Sox since he left, so by the time he returned to Fenway wearing a Yankee uniform on July 31, 1999, the fans were ready to let him have it.

While the pitching matchup was Clemens versus rookie Brian Rose, the real matchup everyone awaited was Clemens versus the Red Sox fans. Clemens got a glimpse of what he would be getting as he appeared at the 1999 All-Star Game in Fenway Park. Standing on the field he owned in his early career, Clemens was roundly booed as he tipped his Yankees cap to the crowd.

This time, he got it worse. Fans booed him lustily every chance they had and serenaded him with exaggerated "Roger, Roger, Roger" chants. Red Sox nation also had their share of signs in the stands, each expressing their displeasure.

It took the Yankees two pitches to anger the Red Sox faithful even further, as Yankees second baseman Chuck Knoblauch launched an 0–1 pitch over the Green Monster to give New York a quick 1–0 lead. Just two batters later and eight pitches into the game, the Yankees took a 2–0 lead when Paul O'Neill belted one into the right-field seats to give Clemens an early lead to work with.

As he took the mound in the bottom of the first, the Fenway faithful let Clemens have it. He walked leadoff hitter José Offerman on four pitches, with the crowd growing louder on each pitch; however, nothing materialized, as Clemens retired the next three batters.

Rose did a good job pitching out of jams in the second and third innings, and the Sox came to bat in the bottom of the third, still down two. Highly touted rookie Trot Nixon, already a crowd favorite, greeted Clemens in the third with a home run to cut the lead in half. Offerman then drew his second walk of the day, stole second, and went to third on a wild pitch, as the usually unflappable Clemens began to rattle just a bit. John Valentin then lifted a fly ball to left, to score Offerman on a sac fly to tie the game at two.

The Yankees bounced back and built a 5–3 lead through five innings. After a quick bottom of the fifth, Nomar Garciaparra greeted Clemens in the sixth by grounding his first pitch of the inning through the hole between third and short for a single. Yankees manager Joe Torre had seen enough and pulled Clemens after 94 pitches. Needless to say, Boston fans were grateful, as it gave them one more chance to let the former favorite son hear it from the crowd.

The game was tied going into the ninth, and Offerman found himself in a key spot leading off the inning. He drilled the first pitch from Ramiro Mendoza over center fielder Chad Curtis's head for a triple, to bring the crowd of 33,179 to its feet. Mendoza got ahead of Valentin 0–1, but the veteran third baseman singled on the next pitch to give Boston a walk-off win.

The game didn't have much bearing on the standings, as the Red Sox spent the remainder of the summer a handful of games behind the Yankees. Boston went on to a 94–68 record that year and were the American League's wild-card team in the playoffs.

The Red Sox upset a powerful Indians team in the American League Division Series and found themselves going against the Yankees again in the American League Championship Series. Because the Yankees swept their divisional series against the Rangers and the Red Sox went five games, fans realized quickly that Clemens was due for a return trip to Fenway and would face off against their ace, Pedro Martinez. Martinez had won the '99 Cy Young Award and was in the midst of a seven-year run that many consider one of the greatest pitching stretches in the history of baseball. He was revered by fans and teammates.

"Pedro was a tremendous competitor and person," said Eric Valent, who played with Martinez during his stint with the Mets. "There's a reason guys like Pedro pitch for as long as they do. Great stuff, pitchability, tremendous work ethic, and great competitor. Every team needs a pitcher like Pedro."

Martinez won this battle with Clemens in a big way.

With the Yankees up 2–0, Red Sox fans were ready for Clemens. Their team responded by battering the righty for five runs in two innings on their way to a 13–1 win. But it would be their only win of the series, as the Yanks won in five and went on to sweep Atlanta for their second consecutive World Series win.

As the Yankees celebrated their World Series victory, Red Sox fans were on year 81 of their own World Series drought. No doubt Sox fans felt great animosity toward the Yanks as they paraded down Broadway on November 6, 1999, with their World Series trophy; however, if there was one thing in which they could take solace, it was the fact that when Clemens returned to Fenway, at least their beloved Sox did them the favor of battering him around on July 31, and again on October 6. For those days at least, it was okay to win the battle, but not the war.

• *12* •

Baseball Odds and Ends

PETE GRAY: A WINNER NEVER QUITS

April 17, 1945

One of the few things Pete Gray couldn't do on a baseball field is one of the most menial tasks people do in everyday life. Gray simply could not tie his own cleats without help. The inane task was more impossible for Gray to carry out than hitting major-league pitching, as the St. Louis Browns left fielder had just one arm. Gray, an accomplished semipro and minor-league player, finally got his chance to break through to the big leagues on April 17, 1945, when most able-bodied men in their prime were fighting in World War II.

Major League Baseball had to scramble to keep afloat during the World War II era. Many of the top players, including Ted Williams, Hank Greenberg, and Bob Feller, enlisted in the military as rosters became bereft of stars through the early '40s. The war turned baseball upside down, but its importance in the United States cannot be overstated. Baseball continued and gave Americans a sense of continuity. At a game, fans were taken away from the strife caused by war, and it served as entertainment as rations cut into everyday life.

The war also allowed for incredible opportunities in the game. With so many men in their prime forced into service, teams had to take on players who, for one reason or another, weren't involved in active military duty. In one extreme case, the Cincinnati Reds took 15-year-old Joe Nuxhall onto their roster. The club was scouting Nuxhall's father, and when he wasn't interested, they turned to his son.

World War II also threw off the competitive balance of the majors. The current Yankees dynasty was broken up when Joe DiMaggio and Yogi Berra enlisted, and the downtrodden St. Louis Browns broke through to win their only American League pennant in 1944.

Of the players who were given their opportunity during wartime baseball, none drew more recognition than Pete Gray. A farming accident when he was six years old took his right arm, but that didn't stop him from pursuing baseball. Gray grew up as an outfielder and had a routine of catching a ball and letting it roll down his wrist while he removed his glove. He then would pluck the ball with his bare hand and fire it back into the infield. By the time he reached the bigs, Gray was so adept at the technique that he had to repeat it in slow motion for teammates and reporters who wondered how he did it.

Gray batted lefty and throughout his time coming up through the minors had developed a reputation as an effective hitter and outstanding baserunner. He used a heavier bat than most and took a full swing despite his handicap. With excellent hand–eye coordination, Gray was able to slap the ball through holes in the infield and drop perfect drag bunts. Before the war, he was able to earn tryout appointments with both the Philadelphia Phillies and A's, but as soon as they saw Gray's handicap, they refused to let him go through with the tryout.

Gray finally got his chance with the St. Louis Browns in 1945. Coming off a loss in the '44 World Series to the Cardinals, the Browns acquired Gray from the minor-league Memphis Chicks. On Opening Day in 1945, a 30-year-old Gray found himself batting second and starting in left field, set to face Tigers Hall of Fame pitcher Hal Newhouser.

The Tigers finished second to the Browns in 1944, missing out on the AL pennant by just one game when the Browns swept a season-ending four-game series with the Yankees, while the Tigers split a four-game set with the Senators. Instead of crediting the Browns with winning their only AL pennant, most fans and reporters claimed that the war wreaked such havoc on Major League Baseball that it brought the rest of the league down to their level.

Newhouser was the league's MVP in 1944, after going 29–9, and is generally considered to be the most dominant pitcher of the World War II era. Newhouser beat the Browns four times in 1944, and was a tough pitcher for any team he faced. The starting pitcher for the Browns was another player given an opportunity because of the war. His name was Sig Jakucki, who had last pitched for the Browns in 1936. After going 0–3 in seven games, Jakucki was let go after the '36 season. To give an idea of just how deep teams had to look for capable players during wartime, the Browns found him pitching in an industrial league in Texas and signed him to their roster in 1944. He went 13–9 after being away from Major League Baseball for eight years.

Jakucki, now 34 years old, got through the Tigers without allowing a run in the first. After Newhouser retired Don Gutteridge, Gray was set to take his first at-bat as a big leaguer. Gray made an out in his first at-bat but was given an ovation by the 4,167 fans at Sportsman's Park. Mike Kreevich drew a two-out walk, and Vern Stephens, the Browns' top player, continued the inning with a hit. The rally led to two runs as the Browns took a 2–0 lead on Newhouser.

After a scoreless second, the Tigers broke through for a run against Jakucki in the third on a homer by Paul Richards. Richards was a part-time catcher with the New York Giants and Philadelphia A's, and was out of baseball by 1935. He got a second chance thanks to the war and caught on with the Tigers in 1943, even gaining MVP consideration in '44 and '45.

With the Browns up 2–1, Gray came to the plate for the second time against Newhouser and this time recorded his first career hit. While it may have seemed like the culmination of a tremendous journey to most, for Gray, getting his first big-league hit was just the start. Newhouser retired the side in the third without allowing a run and pitched effectively into the sixth. The Browns finally broke the game open as they scored three runs in the sixth and two more in the seventh to take a commanding 7–1 lead. Behind the solid pitching of Jakucki, the game ended with a 7–1 Opening Day win for the Browns.

The Browns enjoyed a successful campaign in 1945, finishing with a record of 81–70, but the team finished in third place behind the Tigers, who went on to win the World Series over the Cubs. The 1945 campaign would be the last winning season recorded by the Browns before the team moved to Baltimore in 1954, and became the Orioles.

Pete Gray's success story didn't end with his 1-for-4 debut against the Tigers. He went on to appear in 77 games for the Browns, starting 53 of them. He batted .218 on 51 hits and laced six doubles and two triples along the way. Perhaps Gray's best accomplishment was that he struck out just 11 times in his 253 at-bats in 1945.

At a time when attendance at the ballpark was low, the Browns drew well on the road as fans flocked to the park to catch a glimpse of Gray in action. He had periodic success, recording four three-hit games and a four-hit game against the Boston Red Sox. In what may have been Gray's top personal highlight, he went 3-for-5 against the Yankees at Yankee Stadium on September 15. Gray was an avid Yankees fan growing up and even claimed he was in the Wrigley Field stands for the 1932 World Series to witness Babe Ruth's "called shot."

After the 1945 season, with U.S. involvement in the war decreasing, players began to find their way back to major-league rosters. Just as the war had given so many opportunities to people like Gray, the return of those players took that chance away. After the '45 season ended, Gray was released by the Browns, putting an end to the one-year career of the only one-armed position player in major-league history.

Gray kept his career alive by playing in the minors and with independent teams through the end of the '40s. While his major-league career lasted just one season, he did leave a legacy on the game. Upon Gray's debut, the American League instituted a rule stating that if a ball was caught but subsequently dropped in the transfer from glove to hand, it would still be ruled a catch. While the rule underwent different levels of enforcement, it still stands today. Gray's other legacy came in his postwar efforts as an inspirational presence. His participation with the Browns drew national interest, and Gray was among the most well-known and respected players in 1945. He used that recognition to travel and speak with war veterans who had lost limbs fighting in World War II, drawing great reviews as an inspiration to those who were injured.

THE 1988 BALTIMORE ORIOLES: OVERCOMING FUTILITY

April 29, 1988

On April 29, 1988, the Baltimore Orioles finally won. The game had no ramifications on the standings and didn't boost the Orioles to any kind of winning streak, but they won, and that was all that mattered.

Despite the cutthroat competitive nature in American sports, one thing usually remains true: People root for the underdog. When the simple term *underdog* isn't sufficient to describe a poor team's on-field exploits, the moniker "lovable losers" is usually attached to the team. That name is reserved for the worst of the worst, like the 1962 Mets or the 1976–1977 Tampa Bay Buccaneers. The epic amount of losing done by the Orioles in 1988 created a groundswell of both ridicule and support throughout the country.

During a 15-year period, the Orioles had a run as one of the elite franchises in Major League Baseball. The names of Orioles superstars rivaled those of any franchise from 1968 to 1983. Players like Jim Palmer, Boog Powell, Brooks Robinson, Earl Weaver, Eddie Murray, and Cal Ripken would become Baltimore royalty as the O's won seven AL East crowns in that time.

Benny Ayala was a key role player on the Orioles then and revealed what made the Orioles organization special: "The Orioles treated everyone the same; there was no different treatment if you were a superstar," said Ayala. "This built everyone to play as a team, whether you were a superstar like Jim Palmer or anyone else. This came from people like Earl Weaver, Elrod Hendricks, Ray Miller, Frank Robinson, and Cal Ripken Sr. Earl Weaver respected me right from the start, and he did that with everyone."

However, 1988 was different. Aside from Ripken and Murray, the Orioles roster consisted of such veterans as Fred Lynn, Mike Boddicker, Terry Kennedy, and "prospects" who'd never pan out. "We had the hitting," said Lynn. "It just seemed like our pitching staff fell apart right from the beginning."

The team was led by manager Cal Ripken Sr., who took over as manager after Weaver retired in 1986. From 1983 to 1986, the Orioles' record declined each year, forcing Weaver out. He couldn't stop the slide as the O's record dropped to 67–95 in 1987, 31 games out of first place.

Ripken wouldn't get much of a chance in 1988. The team started 0–6, and he was fired, making it the quickest firing of a manager at the start of a season. In retrospect, the crusty baseball lifer may not have been the best fit to lead the young Orioles: "Cal Ripken Sr. was very tough on rookies," said Jeff Ballard, who was a rookie under Ripken.

> He was an old-school guy who felt like there should be a hierarchy in the clubhouse. You really had to prove your way, start on the outside and work your way in. Years after he was fired he came back as a coach, and I had proven myself as a big-league pitcher. At that point, I earned his respect, and he treated me well. He was a crusty guy but knew baseball very well.

The team chose Hall of Famer Frank Robinson to replace him. Robinson's reputation as a player was firmly cemented as impeccable, and he carried that same weight as a manager: "He's intimidating, but fun," said Jason Bergmann, who pitched for Robinson as a member of the Washington Nationals.

> He's a great person. The historic impact of having him as our manager weighed on us positively as a team. He's accomplished so much in the game, and we knew that. He was a better player than anyone in the dugout, so whatever he said, we always said to ourselves, "Hey man, we need to listen to him."

Despite Robinson's presence, the losses continued to mount. They were subsequently swept in two home series against the Indians and Royals, before heading out for a 12-game road trip. They lost their first nine games, swept again by the Brewers, Royals, and Twins, not exactly the cream of the crop in the AL in 1988. They hit Chicago for a weekend series against the White Sox with a 21-game losing streak, just two games from tying the MLB record for longest losing streak overall, set by the 1961 Phillies.

"It was just Murphy's law on the baseball field," said Lynn.

> We lost 12–0 on Opening Day, and it just went downhill from there. We just kept inventing ways to lose. One game was close and I came up with

the bases loaded, but everybody on base couldn't run. I hit a shot that hit just off the top of the wall. I took off around the bases, and as I passed first, I looked up and saw two guys on second base!

On the night of April 29, the Orioles took on the White Sox, a team that was also going nowhere fast in 1988. "When we landed in Chicago the press met us on the runway," said Lynn. "The national media got a hold of the story, and it really took off. It was just crazy."

The Sox had a marginal amount of talent on their team, with Harold Baines and a young Ozzie Guillén, who would go on to make his first All-Star Game that year. They also had Carlton Fisk on their team; he was still serviceable but clearly on the downside of his career. On this Friday night, Jack McDowell started for the Sox. He would go on to win the 1993 Cy Young Award but was a rookie in '88, making just his ninth career start.

For the Orioles, Mark Williamson took the mound. A young righty who would go on to an uneventful eight-year career, Williamson was making just his fourth career start that night.

During their 21-game losing streak, the Orioles managed to lose games in every way imaginable. They were blown out frequently, losing five games by six runs or more. They lost eight games by two runs or less, including an extra-inning 1–0 defeat at the hands of the Indians. "We tried everything," said Lynn. "One game we picked the lineup out of a hat. I was picked first and led off the game with a homer off Frank Viola. It didn't matter though, we ended up losing anyway."

One thing they rarely did was jump out to any kind of lead. The few times they did, their opponents came storming back and usually won the game going away. "During that streak I was happy to be in AAA," said Ballard, a lefty pitcher who made his debut the season before.

> I came up in 1987 and didn't pitch too well. If I was up in Baltimore during the streak, I would have been 0–5 like everybody else. If I had that 0–5 start to '88 after not pitching well in '87, it could have really set my career back. It worked out well for me that I was in AAA and came up later in the year.

On the night of April 29, the Orioles got off to a rare quick start. After McDowell got the first two outs, Ripken hit an infield single to third base. That brought up Murray, who was in the middle of his Hall of Fame career. The switch-hitter, batting lefty this night, belted a homer on a full count to give Baltimore a tenuous 2–0 lead.

Williamson and McDowell would then lock into a pitchers' duel into the fifth, with neither team really threatening. In the Orioles' fifth, Pete Stanicek singled, stole second, moved to third on a Billy Ripken sac fly, and scored on a wild pitch to make it 3–0.

With Williamson cruising, O's fans had to have a mix of anticipation and anxiety, waiting either for relief or for the other shoe to drop. Williamson retired six batters in a row to take the game into the seventh, where the Orioles broke the game open. They rallied for four runs to take a 7–0 lead into the eighth inning.

If there were any doubters as the game reached the final stages, they had to be convinced the streak would end when Cal Ripken hit a solo homer in the top of the ninth and Kennedy drove in Lynn with a single to right. With Williamson out of the game, veteran Dave Schmidt closed out the win when he got Baines to ground out to Stanicek at second.

There was no extensive celebration after the final out had been recorded; the O's simply came out of the dugout and shook one another's hands. There were some great sound bites after the game, however, as the streak and the O's had taken on a national following.

Robinson, whose O's were already 16 games out of first place, asked how the Indians did that night, mocking hope of shaving a game off their first-place lead.

Schmidt, who picked up the save in three innings of relief, probably echoed the feelings of Orioles fans with his postgame comments in an article by United Press International: "We couldn't relax until the last out, even with a nine-run lead," said the righty. "Strange things have been happening."

White Sox manager Jim Fregosi, a classy baseball lifer, was gracious in defeat: "It's Frank's [Robinson] night. I feel bad, but he needed a win."

The series before, Robinson had mentioned how the Twins fans were rooting for the Orioles "like it was a World Series game," and Kent Hrbek talked about the character they showed, putting up a good fight in the face of a streak that was about to reach 20 games.

One thing stood out among Baltimore fans during the streak. Despite the ineptitude, Orioles fans never booed their ball club. Fans grew to respect the fight the Orioles showed every night, and having class acts in the organization like Robinson and Ripken helped the cause.

However, once the streak was snapped, there was still more than five months of baseball left to be played. "Once the streak ended, reality set in," said Lynn. "It was still April, and we were already 20 games under .500. It was really tough on the families and something I wouldn't wish on anybody."

The Orioles went on to lose the next two games to the White Sox before returning home to Baltimore for a series against the Rangers. They had broken the streak but had been snapped back to reality after their two losses. While the players might have been too wrapped up in the games to really take in what the streak meant to everyone, they got a good preview of it when they arrived at the airport. Approximately 1,000 fans had gathered to cheer for their lovable losers in what was the biggest outpouring of support for any team that had a 1–23 record.

On May 2, the Orioles took on the Rangers in their first home game since breaking the streak. To everyone's surprise, more than 50,000 fans showed up at Exhibition Stadium to support the Orioles in what turned out to be a celebration of the infamously historic team. The O's responded by winning their second game of the year, 9–4.

As everyone knew on the night of April 29, the Orioles beating the White Sox wasn't going to spur them to a miracle run. By that time, most were already convinced the Orioles would end up with the worst record in baseball. Incredibly, however, Baltimore bounced back in 1989, and finished in second place, just two games behind the Blue Jays. With young talent like Brady Anderson, Steve Finley, Mickey Tettleton, Gregg Olson, and Curt Schilling, the bleak reminder of the 21-game losing streak was replaced by hope just one year later.

"That whole 1989 season was just incredible," said Ballard, who posted an 18–8 record that year.

> On Opening Day we beat Roger Clemens [an 11-inning, 5–4 win in front of 52,161], and that just sent us on the way. We were a bunch of no-names with not a lot of expectations, and we beat the best pitcher in the game. The momentum it gave a young team was tremendous. Even though we didn't win the AL East, we were right in the mix all year, and it was just an incredible turnaround season.

Stanley Jefferson was an outfielder on the 1989 Orioles team and looked back on that season fondly: "We were called the 'Why Not O's,'" said Jefferson, who played a large role down the stretch for the Orioles after coming over in a trade from the Yankees.

> It was the most fun I had playing during my career. After the trade I was in Rochester getting my swing down and they called me up pretty quick and put me right into the starting lineup. It was a little uncomfortable because they had great players like Steve Finley, Mike Devereaux, Joe Orsulak, and Phil Bradley already established, and all of a sudden my name was in there every day.

Jefferson, who played his first game for the Orioles on August 9 that year, continued,

I was pleased to be playing, but it was uncomfortable at the time because I felt like it was their team. They had put in the work to make this a great season, but I was happy to play well down the stretch and contribute. It was just so much fun, and Frank Robinson was like a father figure to me. He was really hands-on with me and helped me tremendously.

It would take a few more seasons before the Orioles became a consistent threat in the AL East. Exhibition Stadium would be torn down to give way to Camden Yards in 1992, injecting life again into the franchise and into Baltimore's Inner Harbor; however, for all the excitement of the beautiful new ballpark and for their long history of success from 1968 to 1983, Orioles fans will always hold a sympathetic place for their 1988 team and the night of April 29.

RON SANTO: A HALL OF FAMER AFTER ALL

September 21, 1971

One of the most polarizing debates in the world of baseball usually centers on induction to the Baseball Hall of Fame. Because the game changes so much, it creates an uneven evaluation process. People will fight for their favorite players' inductions as they try their best to quantify how to measure statistics between generations. The inclusion of borderline players like Bill Mazeroski and Phil Rizzuto, both undoubtedly beloved, usually calls for movements to defend other players not in the Hall.

One of the great Hall of Fame debates of the new millennium was whether Ron Santo deserved enshrinement. Santo played the majority of his career in the pitching-dominated '60s and appeared in just 15 seasons, as he faded fast in 1974. He was unable to hang on to reach certain career milestones that 18- to 20-year veterans often do, and that was probably the deciding factor that kept him out for so long.

However, Santo did reach the 300–home run plateau on September 21, 1971. That number doesn't stand out now, as the bloated statistics of the past three decades have rendered the 300–home run mark an afterthought. But at the time, Santo was just the second third baseman to accomplish the feat.

At the time of his retirement, only Braves Hall of Famer Eddie Mathews had hit 300 career homers while playing the hot corner, making Santo one of the top sluggers to play the position. Nonetheless, third base is an overlooked position when it comes to the Hall of Fame. At the time of his retirement in 1974, the only third basemen in the Hall of Fame were Home Run Baker,

Jimmy Collins, and Pie Traynor. Baker and Collins played their careers at the turn of the century, while Traynor started his in the '20s.

Santo was a fan favorite during his playing days and became even more beloved as the Cubs' affable announcer. While many fans today frown upon "homer" announcers, there was no way Santo could hide his unabashed love for his Cubbies.

Another factor that helped Santo's legend grow was that toward the end of his career, he went public with the fact that he battled a serious case of Type 1 diabetes throughout his adult life. Santo kept his condition secret while he played out of fear that he might be forced into early retirement, among other things.

Despite the physical toll the disease took on him during his playing days, Santo never let it affect his personality. As he got older and eventually lost his legs to the disease, he was always one of the nicest, most gregarious people. "I remember him being a really positive and pleasant man," said Shawn Estes, who played for the Cubs in 2003, and participated in the Cubs Caravan with Santo. "He was struggling with diabetes and really had trouble walking when I knew him, but he never complained."

From 1963 to 1969, Santo put together a great career peak, during which he was considered the top third baseman in the National League. He made six All-Star Games during that stretch, had three top-10 MVP finishes, and was awarded six Gold Gloves. He was also known as one of the game's top sluggers, as he finished in the top 10 in the NL in homers each year between 1963 and 1969.

As the 1971 season went on, Santo started accumulating impressive career numbers. Coming into the '71 season, he needed 21 home runs to reach 300 at a time when 300 still meant something. The last time he failed to reach 21 homers in a season was 1962, when he was a 22-year-old playing in his second full season. Santo started the 1971 season well and had 10 homers through the season's first six weeks. He slumped badly in July and August, hitting just .228 with three home runs in the two-month span.

Santo went into September needing just three home runs to reach 300 for his career. Homers in the fourth and 10th (both off Hall of Famer Steve Carlton) put him at 299 with 17 games left in the regular season. He went homerless for a week and a half but would reach the milestone on September 21, in a home game against the Mets.

The Cubs were already 12½ games out of first place, and the Mets were right behind them in the standings. The teams were two years away from staging one of the great pennant races in baseball history, but at this point in 1971, their seasons had been effectively done for a while.

The pitching matchup on that day was an interesting one, as the Mets started Hall of Famer Tom Seaver against rookie Burt Hooton. Hooton was making his third career start after being the second pick in the Major League Baseball Draft that June. He faced the Mets in his previous start as well and struck out 15 batters in a complete-game win.

The small crowd of a little more than 5,000 fans didn't have to wait long to see Santo's milestone home run, as the third baseman knocked an offering from Seaver out of the park in his first at-bat to give the Cubs a 2–0 lead. The Cubs tacked on a third run against Seaver in the third on a sac fly by Hall of Famer Billy Williams, and that would be all the help Hooton needed as he shut out the Mets on two hits for a 3–0 win.

Santo didn't hit a homer for the rest of the season, and his power numbers dipped slightly in '72 and '73, when he hit 17 and 20 homers, respectively. After the '73 season, Santo was dealt to the South Side of Chicago in a trade with the White Sox. Because the White Sox already had Bill Melton at third, they experimented with Santo as a second baseman. He didn't take well to the switch and hit just .221 with five homers on the year. At the end of the season, Santo decided to retire from baseball at 34 years old.

Upon his retirement, only Mathews had offensive statistics that rivaled Santo's among third basemen. Around the same time as Santo's retirement, third basemen Mike Schmidt and George Brett were breaking into the game and would put up offensive numbers that rivaled or surpassed those of Mathews and Santo. Their everyday numbers raised the standard of what would be expected of third basemen, as offensive numbers were on the rise throughout the league.

There were a number of factors that kept Santo out of the Hall of Fame. Santo himself cited the lack of national exposure, as his Cubs never played in a World Series during his time there. Some point out that playing alongside Hall of Famers Ernie Banks, Ferguson Jenkins, and Billy Williams actually hurt Santo. Some left him off based on the abrupt end of his career, but others argue that quick endings to careers were ignored in other cases. There was also a case against him that his numbers were inflated by playing in a hitter-friendly park like Wrigley Field; however, there are plenty of players in the Hall who have huge differences in their home and away splits. Also, one should take into account Santo's defense. Home-field advantage does not play into defensive prowess.

Santo finally earned the highest honor a Major League Baseball player can attain when he was elected to the Baseball Hall of Fame, 31 years after he received less than 4 percent of the vote in his first year on the ballot. Williams, his former teammate and good friend, made a fresh case for him to the 16-person Golden Era Committee, 15 of whom decided to vote Santo into the Hall.

Unfortunately, Santo was never able to enjoy his enshrinement, as he died from complications from his diabetes in December 2010, one year and eight days prior to his election.

In addition to his Hall of Fame induction, a statue of Santo was erected outside of Wrigley Field, joining Ernie Banks and Billy Williams as the only players to be so honored. Clearly, Santo remains one of the most revered figures in Cubs history. "He reminded me of my grandfather," said Estes. "They were both in wheelchairs and never once complained one day or said a single word about it. Just an awesome man, awesome spirit."

PETE REISER: LAST RITES

June 4, 1947

Major League Baseball in the '40s was filled with some of the greatest players to ever grace the diamond. Young legends like Stan Musial, Joe DiMaggio, and Ted Williams tore through the majors when they weren't serving our country in World War II. Mel Ott's career was in its twilight, while Johnny Mize was just entering the prime of his Hall of Fame career. Bill Dickey and Ernie Lombardi, both Hall of Famers as well, controlled the game from behind the plate, while pitchers like Carl Hubbell and Bob Feller were a nightmare for anyone in the batter's box.

Mixed in with those big names was a center fielder from the Brooklyn Dodgers who many considered on par with anyone in the game at the time, complete with all the tools and credentials others possessed; however, unlike those other legends, his final destination wasn't the Baseball Hall of Fame. His name was Pete Reiser, and he may have been the most injury-prone superstar in major-league history.

There is a long history of players who played the game "all out." The season is so much more a marathon than it is a sprint, so the number of players who took that type of performance to an extreme is a lot more select. The root of Reiser's injury-plagued career can be blamed firmly on the fact that he played with such reckless abandon. His competitive nature is what made him great, but also what robbed him of achieving higher levels of the sport. For fans who grew up watching in the '70s and '80s, Reiser's style could be compared to Fred Lynn, the Boston Red Sox Hall of Famer and one of the top all-around center fielders to play the sport.

Lynn became the first player to win the Rookie of the Year and Most Valuable Player Awards in the same season when he hit .331 and won a Gold Glove Award. Lynn seemed destined for greatness the same way Reiser was. By the age of 31, Lynn had made nine straight All-Star Games, won a batting title and four Gold Gloves, and averaged 28 homers and 100 RBIs per 162 games. But Lynn's playing style took a toll on his body. He failed to top 125 games played in his last six years and retired at the age of 38.

"Without a doubt [my style of play] took its toll, and I lost a lot of games over the years," said Lynn, who actually was asked to present Reiser with an award at the 1975 New York Sportswriters Dinner.

I played three sports in high school and baseball and football at USC. I was a wide receiver and defensive back, and the cumulative effect of those sports, as well as my baseball injuries, robbed me of a lot. I was 170 pounds too; I wasn't exactly built like Mike Trout as I was taking a pounding.

Reiser made a mark for himself before he even entered the majors. In 1938, Commissioner Kenesaw Mountain Landis ruled that Cardinals general manager Branch Rickey's minor-league farm system was a detriment to the integrity of the game. Before the advent of the draft, players were free to sign with any team they chose. Richer teams like the Cardinals were able to sign more players than small-market teams and then stash them in their extensive farm systems while they developed. Landis felt this was a significant unfair advantage, so he twice released dozens of players from their Cardinals minor-league contracts to keep a competitive balance.

At the time of one of Landis's rulings, Reiser was a stellar minor leaguer in the Cardinals system who, even at the age of 19, seemed destined to become a superstar. Fearful of losing Reiser to another club, Rickey worked out a deal with the Brooklyn Dodgers. Without Landis's knowledge, Rickey had an agreement in which the Dodgers would sign Reiser, keep him in the minors for a couple of seasons, and then trade him back to the Cardinals; however, once the Dodgers saw Reiser's talents and athleticism, they saw no way they could send him back to St. Louis, and by July of 1940, Reiser was on the Dodgers' major-league roster.

Reiser impressed as a part-time player in 1940, batting .293 in 58 games, while playing a flashy center field when given the chance. He also exhibited an unabashed passion for the game and operated at full speed on every play on offense and defense. Despite making a great first impression, Reiser seemingly faced a roadblock in trying to earn a starting spot in Brooklyn's outfield in 1941. The corner-outfield positions were manned by Hall of Famers Paul Waner and Joe Medwick, while All-Star Dixie Walker played center field and batted third. But after Waner batted just .171 through the first 11 games, the Dodgers released the 38-year-old legend, opening up a vacancy in the outfield that was quickly filled by Reiser.

Reiser took advantage of his opportunity immediately, as he hit .343 to become the first rookie to win the National League's batting title, outhitting his closest competitor by .024 points. He easily outdistanced Hall of Famers like Medwick, Mize, Enos Slaughter, and Arky Vaughan to instantly become the top young hitter in the NL. He also led the league in OPS, again with a significantly higher total than many Hall of Famers. As the team's new third hitter, Reiser led the Dodgers to a 100–54 record and the NL pennant. Reiser, however, hit just .200 in the World Series, as the Dodgers fell to a Yankees team that featured Red Ruffing and DiMaggio among a group of five future Hall of Famers.

In just his second full season, Reiser's reckless play began to wreak havoc on his body. He frequently crashed into outfield walls, dove for any ball that was near him, and ran the bases with abandon. While he didn't miss any significant stretches of time, he required frequent days off and missed 30 games throughout the season.

Lynn discussed the mentality a player such as himself or Reiser possesses when he plays the game that way: "When you're going back for a ball, you know you're going to hit the wall, so you might as well catch it," said Lynn.

> When you dive for a ball, you might as well catch it. Playing wide receiver at USC helped me develop that mentality. Going over the middle, I knew I was going to get hit hard one way or another, so I was able to develop tremendous focus on the ball. I knew the hit was coming, so I just focused on making the catch. The same went for baseball going back for a ball as well.

In 1940, Reiser was hitting .350 on August 1, but injuries hampered him the rest of the season, which lowered his final average to .310. His average was still good for fourth place in the NL, just .005 points lower than Musial, who was in his first full season.

Like many young players in the '40s, Reiser's career was interrupted by a stint serving his country in World War II. While playing baseball for the U.S. Army, Reiser maintained his style of play and incurred more injuries, most notably a separation of the shoulder on his throwing arm. Reiser, who was a switch-hitter during his time, taught himself to throw lefty to allow time for his shoulder to heal. Legend has it that he eventually developed his left throwing arm to the level of his right.

Reiser returned to the Dodgers in 1946, and continued the career arc that he had left behind when he left for the war in 1942. He continued to hit well in the early part of the season, but again injuries robbed him of 30 games and caused a late-season slump that dropped his average to .277. He led the majors with 34 stolen bases but again became more familiar with the unforgiving outfield wall in Ebbets Field than he would have liked.

As the Dodgers began their final decade in Brooklyn, the team began to develop the core that would lead them to their first World Series title in

1955. Duke Snider and Gil Hodges were young, part-time players, and Pee Wee Reese was just resuming his Hall of Fame career after his own military stint. Ralph Branca established himself as a young ace, and Jackie Robinson finally broke the color barrier and became an immediate star. Despite the star power on the roster, when Reiser was healthy, he was the team's top player.

On June 4, 1947, the Dodgers found themselves in a logjam at the top of the NL standings with the Giants, Cubs, and Braves. They were in the middle of an 11-game homestand and were set to take on the Pirates in the third game of a four-game series. Reiser had helped the Dodgers to a doubleheader sweep of the Pirates the day before by playing both games in center field and was back out there batting third and playing center the next day. The Dodgers had the 21-year-old Branca on the mound in a pitching mismatch against the Pirates' Elmer Singleton, who won just 11 games in his eight-year career.

While the Pirates lacked pitching and depth, they did have a pair of legends in the middle of their lineup in Ralph Kiner and Hank Greenberg, who was in his last major-league season. Kiner's first-inning homer gave the Pirates a quick 1–0 lead, but it didn't take long for the Dodgers to get to Singleton. They posted four runs in the bottom of the second to take a lead they would not relinquish. The Dodgers tacked on three more runs in the third to knock Singleton from the game and open up a 7–1 lead.

While the Dodgers seemed to be on their way to a laugher, the game took a somber tone in the late innings. Pirates center fielder Culley Rikard, who played just one full season in the majors, belted a long fly ball over Reiser's head in center field. Predictably, Reiser gave his full effort, corralled the drive, and crashed headfirst into the concrete outfield wall.

Reiser had already suffered numerous head injuries, but this incident was possibly the worst. Reiser amazingly held on to the ball for the out but lay motionless on the outfield grass. He was taken from the field on a stretcher and was barely conscious while doctors tended to him. The injury was so extensive that stadium doctors ordered that Reiser be read his last rites. Reiser spent the next week in the hospital with a fractured skull and in a literal fight for his life.

Lynn had a similarly dangerous situation in the sixth game of the 1975 World Series: "I went back for a ball off the bat of [Ken] Griffey and jumped as I got to the wall," said Lynn, who laid motionless in a heap as Griffey rounded the bases for a triple. "When I hit, I lost all feeling from the waist down. I thought I may have broken my back, but I didn't lose consciousness and I was aware. After a couple of minutes, I started to get a tingling sensation in my legs and the feeling started to come back. I didn't come out of the game though."

Reiser didn't have a choice whether he was going to come out. After the injury, he was replaced in center field by Snider, and the Dodgers went on to win the game 9–4. Reese was the offensive star for the Dodgers, going 2-for-3 with a home run and five RBIs in support of Branca's complete-game effort. Greenberg homered and drove in two runs for the Pirates, and Kiner ended the game 3-for-4 with two runs and an RBI.

Reiser ended up missing the next 35 games, returning to the field on July 12, as a defensive replacement. While it was incredible that he returned to play just a little more than a month after nearly dying on the field, Reiser never was the same player after the crash. He batted .332 with 10 stolen bases in 69 games after fracturing his skull on the outfield wall and helped the Dodgers to a 94–60 record and another National League pennant; however, Reiser struggled early with his defense and focus in the World Series against the Yankees and spent much of the series on the bench as the Dodgers fell to the Yankees in seven games.

In 1948, Reiser played an ancillary part in the fate of two Brooklyn Dodgers legends. Leo Durocher, Reiser's first major-league manager, returned to the helm of the Dodgers and decided that while Reiser could no longer play the outfield effectively, his bat and baserunning skills were too good to sit on the bench. Durocher decided to move second-year player Jackie Robinson from first base to second, to open a spot for Reiser in the infield.

While it was Durocher's intent to get Reiser in the lineup, the move ultimately gave Robinson the position in which he would gain his most success. But Reiser was a defensive liability and didn't hit up to his usual standards, so Durocher had no choice but to move him to the bench in favor of the 24-year-old Hodges, who would get his first significant playing time in the majors.

After the 1948 season, the popular Reiser was traded to the Boston Braves, where he enjoyed some success as a part-time player in the next two seasons. He played the 1951 season in Pittsburgh and the '52 season with the Indians in limited roles. After hitting just .136 in 34 games for the Indians in '52, the supremely gifted Reiser retired from the game at the age of 33, never realizing the true potential of the pure talent with which he was blessed.

To baseball people in the mid-twentieth century, Pete Reiser was the precursor to Mickey Mantle. He was the best athlete in the game and played center field with fervor unlike any other. The ball exploded off his bat, and when he ran the bases, his mighty legs were like pistons in the most powerful engine. He developed as a power-hitting righty but became a switch-hitter early on to take advantage of his great speed from the left side of the plate. The only thing that stood between Reiser and his place among the immortals of the game was his inability to play at anything but his top speed.

Reiser's legacy in the game is not just one of unrealized potential. He came to the Dodgers when Brooklyn was the joke of the National League. His amazing rookie season finally gave Dodgers fans something to cheer for, and he willed the franchise toward respectability and ultimately NL pennants. Reiser's career was the bridge between the downtrodden early years of the Brooklyn Dodgers and the glory days of Robinson, Hodges, Snider, and Branca. He was the man who batted third in the 1942 All-Star Game, ahead of Johnny Mize, Mel Ott, and Joe Medwick, and was the National League's answer to Joe DiMaggio.

By unofficial accounts, Reiser was carted off the field on a stretcher 11 times in his career, four times unconscious with a fractured skull. His style of play pushed forward the movement to add padding to the outfield walls and install warning tracks in outfields throughout the majors. In addition to his head injuries, Reiser suffered two broken ankles, a chronically dislocated shoulder, and multiple knee and leg injuries. Many refer to him as the most unlucky player in major-league history; however, the fact that he lived through the severe head injury suffered on June 4, 1947, after being given last rites, was nothing short of a miracle.

• *13* •

Extra Innings

The baseball season is like life. It's every day. It's a grind out there. You play hurt most of the time, but you play every day.—Jim Wohlford, 15-year MLB veteran

1977 will always be a highlight for me. The fans were terrific. I got several standing ovations one day in July that year when my batting average surpassed .400. It really touched me. The last game that year I also surpassed 100 RBI in a season for the only time. It was late in the game and I had 99 RBI. Sam Perlozzo got to second base and I was up. Gene Mauch called time out and went out to talk to Sam. The message, "If Rod gets a hit, whatever you do, don't stop at third." I got a hit, and Sam kept running until he scored.—Rod Carew, MLB Hall of Famer

The players make the impact in the game, the coaches are the instrument. What I've tried to do is help players become the best they could be. For example, Craig Biggio was a transformation project from catcher to second base. He didn't want to do it at first, but when he committed, he wasn't satisfied until he was a Gold Glove second baseman. He worked relentlessly on making the transition. He's the impact, I'm the instrument.—Astros coach Matt Galante, who helped Biggio and Jeff Bagwell transition to new positions and develop into perennial All-Stars

Hitting that grand slam in the All-Star Game [in 1983] was the accomplishment that stood out the most to me. The game had a lot of meaning. I had been an All-Star for each of the past eight years and we hadn't won once. The National League was just beating us like a drum. The game was played in my hometown [Chicago], and we were just tired of the NL's superiority. To add insult to injury, they walked Robin Yount to load the bases to get to me. I understood the move; Atlee Hammaker was a lefty. But I still didn't like it.—Fred Lynn, 1983 MLB All-Star Game MVP, on hitting the first grand slam in All-Star Game history to lead the AL to a 13–3 win. The win was just the second in 20 years for the American League.

You learn real quick that you are a marketable asset, a piece of meat. You're a widget that someone wants to buy.—Andy McGaffigan, who was involved in four trades and played for five teams during 11 years in the majors, discussing the business side of the game

The St. Louis Cardinals wanted to sign me when I was in high school, but there weren't very many opportunities for black ballplayers during those times. I asked them to guarantee that they'd pay for me to go to college for four years. They said they never heard of such a thing and wouldn't agree. I said no and went to Tennessee State to play football instead. It was the turning point of my life. I was an All-American quarterback, and when I was done I had three NFL teams and five major-league teams interested in me. The times weren't right for football though. They told me they didn't want to have a black quarterback and tried to switch me to defensive back. I chose baseball instead and signed with the Baltimore Orioles, who were very good to me.—Fred Valentine, outfielder for the Orioles and Washington Senators from 1959 to 1968, on the struggles he faced as a black athlete in the 1950s

My first career hit was against Jim Rooker, in Pittsburgh. Rookies are presented with the ball on the occasion of their first hit, and mine came back from center to Willie Stargell, one of the most famous players ever. He popped it up and down in his glove and flipped it to his open hand, then tossed it to me and said, "Here you go kid, only two thousand, nine hundred, ninety-nine more to go." My first home run came off Randy Moffitt, a grand slam and my only home run of the year. I played with Randy later on, in Toronto, and he teased me that my home run scraped the back of the fence on the way down. I told him it looked like a 500-footer in the paper.—Barry Bonnell, who had 833 hits and 56 home runs in his 10-year career, discussing his first career milestones

In 1989, I was starting a game for the Expos in the middle of the season against the Giants, who were the National League champs that year. I gave up a two-run homer to Will Clark in the seventh and finished the inning. The next day our general manager, Dave Dombrowski, called me in his office and told me I was traded for Mark Langston, who was one of the best. I said, "Come on, we had to include someone else, it couldn't have been just me." He said, "Ok, we included Randy Johnson too."—Brian Holman, on his trade to Seattle in 1989

When I played for the Cubs, a kid about eight years old came up to the dugout one game. He was a big Dave Kingman fan looking for an autograph. I grabbed the kid and put him in our dugout. He walked around and got some autographs. He didn't meet Kingman, but met a number of players before he had to get out of there. Years later I read about the story in some national publication because it turned out that kid was Jim Thome.—Barry Foote, on the good rapport he built with fans and kids during his playing career

My first major-league hit came in a really interesting game. In 2000, I was playing for the Rockies, and we went into extra innings against the Braves. We ran out of pitchers so Buddy Bell asked [catcher] Brent Mayne to pitch. He had been sitting out with a wrist injury and couldn't swing the bat but could throw. Eventually, I was asked to pinch-hit for Mayne, who had been pitching. I went on deck and could see Bobby Cox talking to his coaches, pointing at me in the on-deck circle. I ended up getting my first big-league hit for the walk-off win. After the game, our coach Toby Harrah said, "Thank God you got a hit, if you didn't you were going out there to pitch next inning." Good thing he didn't tell me that before my at-bat. I would have been even more nervous and probably went up there and laid an egg.—Adam Melhuse, on the unique surroundings of his first major-league hit

I was drafted and signed right out of UCLA, and my first spring training I was up in the big-league camp. They put me in a game to catch against the Reds, and Pete Rose came walking up to the plate. I was feeling my oats, and as he was walking up I said, "Hey Pete, how's it going!" He looked at me, put my hand on my shoulder, turned me around slowly, and said, "Fine, Slugg-it." I felt about an inch tall.—Don Slaught, who caught more than 1,300 major-league games, on his first camp as a big leaguer

Baseball isn't basketball. You can't put three stars out there and expect to win championships. There are so many different factors that come into play, like injuries, pitching performances, and trades, just to name a few. —Tim Leary, 1988 World Series champion

The things I remember the most in my career are winning the World Series in 1990, which was the final season of my career; Pete Rose's hits tying and breaking Ty Cobb's record; and Tom Browning's perfect game. Of course, my first hit and home run. All of my teammates, managers, coaches, and great fans in my years as a player in Cincinnati. Pete Rose coming back as a player-manager. Johnny Bench Day in Cincinnati, in which he hit a home run. Tony Perez Day in Cincinnati, to name a few. As far as my greatest accomplishments, they were getting to the big leagues, playing for 13 years, and getting a World Series ring.—Ron Oester, reflecting on a 13-year career as a second baseman for the Reds, which ended with an induction into the Reds Hall of Fame in 2014

I remember in '05, we were in a tight race with the Red Sox for the division. We thought we had to win the final two games of the season to win the East. During the second-to-last game of the year I went back into the clubhouse and Mike Mussina was there with his Stanford education looking at scores and breaking everything down. Well he figured out that if we won and one other game result went the right way, we would win the East. That ended up happening, and we were in the clubhouse celebrating. We went out on the field after the game and were telling the bullpen guys that we just won the East. They had no idea! It wasn't the way I'd dream up a celebration for winning the East over the hated Red Sox. —Aaron Small, who went 10–0 for the Yankees in 2005, to help the Yanks to the AL East title

If I was a pitcher today, these guys with all that armor they wear up to bat, I'd hit them every time!—Rod Gaspar, 1969 World Series champion outfielder

We played a 19-inning game against the White Sox in 1991. I had started a couple of days before and pitched into the seventh inning in a win. We ran out of pitching in the 15th inning, so I came in to pitch. I got hit in the face with a comebacker by Ozzie Guillén the first inning I pitched but still had to stay in. We had no other pitchers. I ended up pitching five innings and getting the win.—Brewers pitcher Don August, on one of his most memorable performances as a big leaguer

I went to high school with Robin Yount. He was a senior when I was a sophomore. Sometimes when I see him, I show him my 1982 World Series ring just to rub it in a little bit.—Kelly Paris, member of the 1982 Cardinals, who beat Yount and the Brewers in the 1982 World Series

I was in the dugout for the "Bartman Game" for the Cubs. I went back to the clubhouse at the start of the eighth inning and saw they had put plastic over the lockers and had the champagne ready to go. I came back into the dugout and told Kerry Wood, "I hope they didn't just jinx us by setting that all up." That ended up being the inning where everything fell apart. Everyone on the Cubs felt like with Wood pitching Game 7, we'd have a good chance to win anyway. I did a radio show that morning, and everybody was focused on the Bartman play though. We had chances to get out of the inning after that as well. For Game 7, there was definitely a different feeling in the park. It didn't have the same buzz; it was as if the fans were defeated already.—Shawn Estes, 13-year MLB pitcher who was on the 2003 Cubs pitching staff

The person who inspired me the most was my father. He was a very good amateur pitcher in Butler [Pennsylvania]; a legend even. I don't have many regrets in life, but one for sure is that he didn't get to see me pitch in the big leagues. He passed away during my junior year in college.—John Stuper, winning pitcher of Game 6 of the 1982 World Series for the champion Cardinals

One game stands out to me and that was in 2004, against the would-be World Series champs that year: the Boston Red Sox. I went toe-to-toe with Curt Schilling, threw seven scoreless, and got the "W." Stephen King wrote a book about that season, and I was in it. That was pretty cool too.—Dave Borkowski, who pitched in 181 games for the Tigers, Orioles, and Astros in the early 2000s

Tom Glavine is a great person and a great pitcher. When I have the ability to hire people in a baseball department, he's the one guy I would love to have as a consultant on the pitching side. He has the background and has a great way about him.—Eric Valent, Glavine's teammate with the Mets in 2004 and 2005

Hitting home runs in seven straight games was a memorable feat; so was hitting three consecutive home runs in three straight innings. The game before I started my home run streak I hit a ball off the top of the wall, so I came that close to tying the record. I was just going about my business, having fun with it. I had the chance to talk to Don Mattingly [who shares the MLB record of eight home runs in eight games] about it. He did his over an All-Star break, so he had those days in between. Mine was done all on one homestand as well. The consecutive-inning feat is really something unique though. I didn't even know I was one of the only people to do it until about five years later, when a Latin radio host told me about it. They're cool places in history.—Kevin Mench, on being the only right-handed hitter in MLB history to homer in seven straight games and one of two players to homer in three consecutive innings

Playing in a Game 7 was better for me than watching it. I was a nervous wreck as a spectator. Once I went in to catch, I calmed right down. Hitting is always tough, but my World Series at-bat in Game 7 was the only bunt in my 16-year career that I didn't get down and one of just two times in 16 years I failed to advance the runner. I don't look back upon it favorably, but we ultimately won the game and the series, which is the important thing.—Gregg Zaun, 16-year MLB catcher who was the Marlins' catcher for their Game 7 win to clinch the 1997 World Series

The Mets were one of the first teams to really scout Puerto Rico. They were also the first team to have a program to teach English to Latin American players. Whitey Herzog signed me from a tryout in Puerto Rico based on my throwing arm. I was ready to leave Puerto Rico [at age 19] to go start my career. I got to the plane and didn't want to go. I didn't want to miss home and miss my family. But I took advice from my family. They told me to get on the plane and go make a future in the United States.—Benny Ayala, 10-year MLB veteran and member of the 1979 and 1983 Orioles World Series teams

I was standing in the locker room when I first came up in 1979. Looking around I saw Nolan Ryan, Frank Tanana, Rod Carew, Don Baylor . . . all guys like that. I get a tap on my shoulder, turn around, and it's Gene Autry [then Angels owner and original singing cowboy]. He said [in his distinctive voice], "You know, Jim Kaat's got more years in the majors than you have years." He then gave me a belt buckle with a picture of himself with a guitar and a horse on it and said, "Welcome to the big leagues kid, good luck."—Dave Schuler, member of the 1979 AL West champion Angels

In spring training of my second year, Andre Dawson hit a towering home run off of me in an intrasquad game over the center-field wall, which was 30 feet high. My fastball, his swing . . . he crushed it! Afterwards, I'm sitting on the bench, and here comes Duke Snider. He sits down next to me and says, "You know, DeMola, I had to jump in my car and rush back to the hotel so I could open my window before that ball Dawson hit broke it." Priceless! The Duke was probably one of the most awesome human beings I have ever met; I miss him to this day. By the way, that spring I was 4–1, and the next time up I K'ed Dawson looking. Nobody ever got me twice.—Don DeMola, Montreal Expos pitcher who now is active with www.pastpros.com, a site that helps fans interact with former big leaguers online

During David Cone's perfect game there was a rain delay after three innings. I joked in the umpires' room that we have to get back out there because of the perfect game. I looked up in the ninth and knew he faced the minimum but wasn't positive it was a perfect game until afterwards. With Matt Cain, I knew it was a perfect game all along. He just had dominating stuff. Just to sit back and say, "Wow, I was part of that." Calling two perfect games and being the third-base umpire for a third is pretty amazing. It's definitely great to be a part of baseball history.—Veteran umpire Ted Barrett, who is one of only a handful of people who have been in uniform for three perfect games and the only umpire to have a home plate assignment for two perfect games

I grew up in Oklahoma, so players from that state were most of my favorites. Johnny Bench and Mickey Mantle the most. I also liked the Yankees, so Yogi and Whitey Ford were a couple of favorites. Nolan Ryan will always be my favorite.—Ted Power, veteran pitcher who pitched in 564 games between 1981 and 1993, discussing his favorite players growing up

One of my favorite players was Earl Battey. He lived in my neighborhood growing up, and he's the one who got me to Bethune-Cookman College, which led me to the majors. If it wasn't for him, I wouldn't have had the chances I did. In the summer, he got me a job with him, working with the Con Ed Kids program with the Yankees. We'd teach them baseball and also educate them as well. For example, we came up with lesson plans that would teach the kids arithmetic through figuring out batting averages. He was just a great guy who did so much for me and gave so much back to kids.—Stanley Jefferson, former MLB outfielder, on the impact made by All-Star catcher Earl Battey

I was playing video games with my son in our basement one day, and his school principal called me up. He said, "I'm watching one of your games on these classic reruns they show. It's the 11th inning; how long do I have to watch before you do something?" I said, "Just keep watching." I flipped the game on myself, and in the 12th inning, I hit one over the center fielder's head to win it. My little son looked at me and said, "Wow daddy, they really like you there!"—Don Slaught, discussing sharing his memories with his family

Playing against the Yankees, they're always the hated "Evil Empire," but once you get there, you realize they're just great guys. When they signed me, I asked Scott Brosius what it was like over there. He said that there were more solid guys in that organization than any other. He was right. There were just so many good Christian men there in that clubhouse.—Aaron Small, on joining the Yankees after pitching in the majors for seven seasons

I had so many rewarding moments as a manager in the minors. Two guys who really stood out to me who I felt like I made a nice impact on their careers when they were young were Matt Joyce and Evan Gattis. They had so much potential, and I feel like I was able to pass along a lot of my experience on how to carry yourself as a big leaguer. I tried to teach them how to control their controllables, and they seemed to take it to heart. Not that there was anything negative before, but just stepping up their game, dressing right on the road, things like that. It was very rewarding to see them get called up and do so well.—Matt Walbeck, former catcher and minor-league manager on the impact he was able to make as a mentor

Jim Rice was extremely successful against me. He not only had a high average, but did a lot of damage with RBIs and runs scored. When I was broadcasting in Detroit after I retired, I came across Rice at a game. He said, "Lary, I'm happy to see you're still in the game with Detroit. Now I know where to send the limo when we have a home run hitting contest."—Lary Sorensen, former All-Star pitcher, on Hall of Famer Jim Rice, whom he considered perhaps the toughest hitter he faced in the game

Deep down it was awesome to be a major leaguer; it was the culmination of a long-term dream. But in the moment it was more nerves than anything. Having been a player with little self-confidence, it was hard to believe I deserved being one, so I never was very comfortable at that level for a few reasons I figured out since. I've come to appreciate the accomplishment so much more in the last few years.—Jack Perconte, seven-year MLB veteran who retired with the highest all-time stolen base success rate (86 percent) for any player with at least 80 career stolen base attempts

I had a game one night against the Twins where I struck out 16 batters. I had electrifying stuff that night. Physically and psychologically, I don't even know how it happened. That's being in a zone. It happens sometimes, and you can't explain it. Once against the Indians I threw a shutout and had 15 strikeouts. Thurman [Munson] looked at me after the last pitch and said, "You didn't even realize the game was over, did you?" He was right, I was so in that zone that I didn't realize I was done.—Rudy May, 156-game winner in 16 major-league seasons

I still look at Dan Quisenberry as the epitome of closers in Kansas City. I was lucky to surpass some of the records he established, but I still see him as the best.—Jeff Montgomery, Royals all-time saves leader and member of the Royals Hall of Fame

One of my great memories was hitting a home run in the clinching game of the 2001 NLDS. It's one of those things where I'll always remember the pitch, the count, the swing. It's really special. The home run put us ahead, and we cruised from there. It's something that will always stick out for me personally from my time in the majors.—Paul Bako, 12-year major-league veteran and catcher for the 2000 and 2001 NL East champion Atlanta Braves

The postseason was great. Much different atmosphere, felt like the purest form of the game. Everyone is so focused on each pitch, each at-bat, really pulling for one another. It also was very draining and just a battle. Every little thing is magnified, and each at-bat and each inning seems like it takes a lot more energy and effort to get through. The atmosphere in New York was just electric as well.—Brendan Harris, eight-year major-league veteran who was the starting third baseman and DH for the Twins in the 2009 NLDS versus the Yankees

George [Brett] was my first major-league strikeout. As a rookie the umpires won't give you the call on a close pitch, especially against a Hall of Famer like Brett. I had two strikes on him, and I threw one right down the middle, belt high. I mean it was right there, and Brett took it. The umpire [Terry Cooney] looked at Brett and gave him a look like, "George, you know I have to call this," almost apologizing, and punched him out. I don't know why he didn't swing, but I was lucky he didn't because he would have hit it a mile.—Jeff Ballard, Baltimore Orioles lefty starter who went 18–8 and finished sixth in the AL Cy Young Award voting in 1989

I had a good relationship with George Steinbrenner. He asked me to stay on as a special assignment scout once my career was cut short due to a back injury. I answered directly to George with the job. He was just a bigger-than-life personality. He did a lot of great things that didn't make the papers. He had his shortcomings, like everyone else. But what he did for people far surpassed his shortcomings. He did so much for the city and kids of Tampa, and worked a lot with the New York police and fire departments, especially for families who lost loved ones on the job.—Barry Foote, on his relationship with George Steinbrenner during his time as a Yankee

I was very fortunate to come up when I did. I played against many terrific players from different generations. In 1967, my first All-Star Game alone, I played against I believe 21 Hall of Famers, from Willie Mays and Mickey Mantle to Hank Aaron and Roberto Clemente. In 1984, my last All-Star Game, the names had changed to Tony Gwynn, Cal Ripken, and Rickey Henderson. All told, these players' careers spanned more than 50 years of baseball. It was incredible to be a part of it.—Rod Carew, MLB Hall of Famer

Bibliography

"Babe Ruth Makes 50th Home Run." *Leominster Daily Enterprise*, September 24, 1920.

"Baseball Almanac." *Baseball Almanac*, www.baseball-almanac.com. Accessed November 4, 2015.

"Beaned by a Pitch, Ray Chapman Dies." *New York Times*, August 17, 1920.

Belfiore, Michael. "Nolan Ryan." *Encyclopedia.com*, 2004, www.encyclopedia.com/topic/Nolan_Ryan.aspx. Accessed October 14, 2012.

Bishop, Morin. *Sports Illustrated*, August 24, 1987, 26–28.

Bryant, Howard. *The Last Hero: A Life of Henry Aaron*. New York: Pantheon, 2010.

Chass, Murray. "The Pine Tar Home Run." *New York Times*, July 24, 1983, NY sec.

"Clemente, Pirates' Star, Dies in Crash of Plane Carrying Aid to Nicaragua." *New York Times*, January 2, 1973.

Coffey, Wayne. "25 Years Later, Thurman Munson's Last Words Remain a Symbol of His Life." *Daily News*, August 1, 2004.

Collier, Phil. "Braves, Padres Brawl Will Lead to NL Action." *Washington Post*, August 14, 1984.

Cook, William. *Jim Thorpe: A Biography*. Jefferson, NC: McFarland, 2011.

Crehan, Herbert F. *Red Sox Heroes of Yesteryear*. Cambridge, MA: Rounder, 2005.

Crowe, Jerry. "A Bitter J. R. Richard Is Busy at Nothing." *Washington Post*, June 30, 1987.

"Detroit Tigers vs. New York Yankees." *Monday Night Baseball*, June 28, 1976.

Edwards, Lauren. "Pumpsie Green Changed the Face of the Game for the Better." *NESN.com*, August 4, 2009, http://nesn.com/2009/08/pumpsie-greens-legend-live-on-50-years-later. Accessed May 21, 2012.

Finkel, Jan. "Pete Alexander." *Society for American Baseball Research*, http://sabr.org/node/13564. Accessed October 11, 2011.

"Gehrig, Iron Man of Baseball, Dies." *New York Times*, June 3, 1941.

Ginnitti, Toni. "Death of Pitcher Stuns Ballplayers, Fans. Body of Cardinals' Kile, 33, Found in Hotel Room; Baseball Game Canceled." *Chicago Sun-Times*, June 23, 2002.

Goldstein, Richard. "Pete Gray, Major Leaguer with One Arm, Dies at 87." *New York Times*, July 2, 2002.

Hermoso, Rafael. "Fences Too Close to Give Any Comfort." *New York Times*, April 12, 2003.

Hill, Vernon. "Twilight Reunion: Dan Duquette, Roger Clemens on Comeback Trail?" *Mass Live*, November 6, 2011, www.masslive.com/redsox/index.ssf/2011/11/twilight_reunion_dan_duquette.html. Accessed December 29, 2011.

Hinckley, David. "Damages: Pete Reiser." *Daily News*, September 16, 2003.

"Home." *Baseball Hall of Fame*, http://baseballhall.org. Accessed November 11, 2011.

Horne, John. "The Babe's Called Shot." *Baseball Hall of Fame*, 2008, http://baseballhall.org/archive-collection/called-shot. Accessed September 15, 2011.

"J. R. Richard Struggles with Homelessness." *New York Times*, January 22, 1995.

Livingstone, Seth. "Jeter Makes History as Yankees Rookie Shortstop." *USA Today*, 1996.

Madden, Bill. "The True Story of the Midnight Massacre: How Tom Seaver Was Run Out of Town 30 Years Ago." *Daily News*, June 17, 2007.

"Major League Baseball's First All-Star Game Is Held." *History.com*, July 6, 2010, www.history.com/this-day-in-history/major-league-baseballs-first-all-star-game-is-held. Accessed October 12, 2012.

Martin, Jorge. "25 Years after Fernandomania." *Dodger Magazine*, August 18, 2006.

McCallum, Jack. "Faith, Hope, and Tony C." *Sports Illustrated*, July 5, 1982.

"MLB.com." *MLB.com*, http://mlb.mlb.com/home. Accessed May 12, 2012.

Newnham, Blaine. "Mariners Drop 3–2 Decision to A's on Opening Day." *Seattle Times*, April 4, 1989.

O'Connor, Ian. "Torre Has No Idea What He's Getting Into." *Daily News*, November 3, 1995.

Olney, Buster. "Pettitte Would Go, but Clemens Deal Is Unlikely." *New York Times*, December 9, 1998, www.nytimes.com/1998/12/10/sports/baseball-pettitte-would-go-but-clemens-deal-is-unlikely.html. Accessed March 11, 2012.

"Orioles Finally End 21-Game Losing Streak." *Deseret News*, April 30, 1998.

Putterman, Alex. "Montreal Mayor to Meet with Rob Manfred about MLB Return to City." *Sports Illustrated*, May 28, 2015.

Rothe, Emil. "The War of 1812: The Wood–Johnson Duel." *Society for American Baseball Research*, http://research.sabr.org/journals/war-of-1912. Accessed September 21, 2011.

Rotstein, Gary. "Ruth Ball Fetches $805,000 at Auction." *Pittsburgh Post-Gazette*, July 11, 2006, www.post-gazette.com/breaking/2006/07/11/Ruth-ball-fetches-805-000-at-auction/stories/200607110165. Accessed December 17, 2011.

Snelling, Dennis. *Johnny Evers: A Baseball Life*. Jefferson, NC: McFarland, 2014.

Spatz, Lyle, and Steve Steinberg. *1921: The Yankees, the Giants, and the Battle for Baseball Supremacy in New York*. Lincoln: University of Nebraska Press, 2010.

Stein, Fred. "Mel Ott." *Society for American Baseball Research*, http://sabr.org/bioproj/person/3974a220. Accessed February 11, 2012.

"This Week in Baseball." *This Week in Baseball*, Mel Allen. June 21, 1977.

Webb, Melville. "Joe Wood Beats Walter Johnson in Fenway Classic." *Boston Globe*, September 12, 1912.

Wulf, Steve. "Darryl Kile." *Sports Illustrated*, September 20, 1993.

"Yankees Buy Babe Ruth and Home Run Bat for Over $100,000." *New York Times*, January 5, 1920.

Young, Dick. "715! Hank Aaron Breaks Babe Ruth's Home Run Record." *Daily News*, April 9, 1974.

Index

About the Author

Rocco Constantino is a lifelong baseball fan who has worked as a writer in many capacities. Most recently, Constantino has worked as a baseball columnist and had a stint as a feature columnist for Bleacher Report. His writing on Bleacher Report drew more than 500,000 reads and numerous awards in his first year writing for the popular website. Constantino was also an NCAA softball and women's soccer coach in addition to working as a journalism teacher. When Constantino moved on from coaching, he left his institution as the winningest coach in both sports during the Division II era. He is one of just three softball coaches in Central Atlantic Collegiate Conference history to have won more than 200 games on the Division II level. He is currently the director of athletics at New Providence (NJ) High School, which was recently rated as one of the top 50 public high school sports programs in the nation.

Constantino is a lifelong Mets fan with a great passion for baseball history. He attributes his baseball fanaticism to the influence of his family members, especially his father Rocco and uncle Canio. The Constantino family's baseball links go back generations as his uncle Charlie was navy buddies with Phil Rizzuto and his aunt Lucille turned down an invitation to play in the All-American Girls Professional Baseball League, made famous by the movie *A League of Their Own*. In a newspaper article at the time, she cited the league rules banning drinking, smoking, and wearing pants as her reason for passing on the tryout.

Constantino attributes his path into sportswriting to former *New York Daily News* journalist and noted author Bruce Chadwick, who not only helped him hone his writing style, but also encouraged him to seek publication.